MACWORLD

Read Me First Book

Macintosh experts
on
Macintosh products and technology

Edited by Jerry Borrell
Editor-in-Chief, *Macworld*

Foreword by Jean-Louis Gassée
Chairman/CEO, Be Labs Inc.
Former President, Apple Products Division

IDG Books Worldwide, Inc.
An International Data Group Company
San Mateo, California 94402

Macworld Read Me First Book

Published by
IDG Books Worldwide, Inc.
An International Data Group company
155 Bovet Road, Suite 610
San Mateo, CA 94402
(415) 358-1250

Library of Congress Catalog Card No.: 91-75702

ISBN 1-878058-19-3

Printed in the United States of America

10 9 8 7 6 5 4 3 2 1

Distributed in the United States by IDG Books Worldwide, Inc.
Distributed in Canada by Macmillan of Canada, a Division of Canada Publishing Corporation; by Woodslane Pty. Ltd. in Australia/New Zealand; and by Computer Bookshops in the U.K. and Ireland.

For information on translations and availability in other countries, contact Marc Jeffrey Mikulich, Foreign Rights Manager, at IDG Books Worldwide.
Fax: (415) 358-1260.

For sales inquiries and special prices for bulk quantities, write to the address above or call IDG Books Worldwide at (415) 358-1250.

Publisher and CEO
John J. Kilcullen

Project Editor
Jeremy Judson

Editor-in-Chief
Michael E. McCarthy

Copy Editor
Felicity O'Meara

Production Manager
Lana J. Olson

Text Preparation and Proofreading
Sue Grant-Marsh
Shirley E. Coe

Indexer
Ty Koontz

Editorial Department Assistant
Dana Sadoff

Book Design and Production
Peppy White
Francette Ytsma
University Graphics, Palo Alto, California

Information Graphics
Arne Hurty

Chapter-Opening Art
Peppy White
Mimi Fujii

Contents at a Glance

Table of Contents

Chapter 4: Macintosh Databases
by Charles Seiter 81

Chapter 5: Managing Your Personal Finances on the Mac
by Alan Slay 103

x

Chapter 6: Picking a Printer
by Jim Heid **119**

Chapter 7: Hard Disks and Other Storage Devices
by Cheryl England **137**

8

Chapter 8: Video and the Macintosh: A Developing Relationship
by Franklin Tessler, M.D., and Peter Marx 155

9

Chapter 9: Choosing a Monitor for Your Mac
by Robert C. Eckhardt 171

Chapter 10: Understanding System Software
by Lon Poole 189

Chapter 11: Utilities for the Macintosh
by David Pogue 211

12 **Chapter 12: HyperCard**
by Liza Weiman **239**

13 Chapter 13: Backup — Defending Your Data
by Tom Negrino 261

Acknowledgements

Thanks go to Felicity O'Meara for the top-notch job she did as line editor and copy editor; and to Susan Grant-Marsh, who coordinated the project from the start with diplomacy and skill, acting as liaison between authors, editor, and publisher throughout the manuscript preparation stages. Without their contributions this book would not exist.

(The publisher would like to thank Bill Murphy and Jonathan Sacks, without whom this book would not have been possible.)

About IDG Books Worldwide

Welcome to the world of IDG Books Worldwide.

International Data Group (IDG) is the world's leading publisher of computer periodicals, with more than 150 weekly and monthly newspapers and magazines reaching 25 million readers in 50 countries. If you use personal computers, IDG Books is committed to publishing quality books that meet your needs. We rely on our extensive network of publications — including such leading periodicals as *Macworld, Computerworld, InfoWorld, PC World, Lotus, Portable Office, Publish, Network World, Computer Buying World,* and *SunWorld* — to help us make informed and timely decisions in creating useful computer books that meet your needs.

Every IDG book strives to bring extra value and skill-building instruction to the reader. Our books are written by experts, with the backing of IDG periodicals, and with careful thought devoted to issues such as audience, interior design, use of icons, and illustrations. Our editorial staff is a careful mix of high-tech journalists and experienced book people. Our close contact with the makers of computer products helps ensure accuracy and thorough coverage. Our heavy use of personal computers at every step in production means we can deliver books in the most timely manner.

We are delivering books of high quality at competitive prices on topics customers want. At IDG, we believe in quality and we have been delivering quality for 25 years. You'll find no better book on a subject than an IDG book.

John Kilcullen
President
IDG Books Worldwide, Inc.

International Data Group's publications include: **ARGENTINA'S** Computerworld Argentina; **ASIA'S** Computerworld Hong Kong, Computerworld Southeast Asia, Computerworld Malaysia, Computerworld Singapore, InfoWorld Hong Kong, InfoWorld SE Asia; **AUSTRALIA'S** Computerworld Australia, PC World, Macworld, Lotus, IBM World, Digital World, Government Computer News, Communications World, Profit; **AUSTRIA'S** Computerwelt Oesterreich; **BRAZIL'S** DataNews, PC Mundo, Automacao & Industria; **BULGARIA'S** Computer Magazine Bulgaria, Computerworld Bulgaria; **CANADA'S** ComputerData, Direct Access, Graduate CW, Macworld; **CHILE'S** Informatica, Computacion Personal; **COLUMBIA'S** Computerworld Columbia; **CZECHOSLOVAKIA'S** Computerworld Czechoslovakia, PC World; **DENMARK'S** CAD/CAM WORLD, Computerworld Danmark, PC World, Macworld, Unix World, PC/LAN World, Communications World; **FINLAND'S** Mikro PC, Tietoviikko; **FRANCE'S** Le Mond Informatique, Distributique, InfoPC, Telecoms International; **GERMANY'S** Computerwoche, Information Management, PC Woche, PC Welt, Unix Welt, Macwelt; **GREECE'S** Computerworld, PC World, Macworld; **HUNGARY'S** Computerworld SZT, Mikrovilag; **INDIA'S** Computers & Communications; **ISRAEL'S** People & Computers Weekly and Monthly, Macintosh; **ITALY'S** Computerworld Italia, PC World Italia; **JAPAN'S** Computerworld Japan, Macworld, NextWorld; **KOREA'S** Computerworld Korea, PC World; **MEXICO'S** Computerworld Mexico, PC Journal; **THE NETHERLAND'S** Computerworld Netherlands, PC World Benlux, AmigaWorld; **NEW ZEALAND'S** Computerworld New Zealand, PC World New Zealand; **NIGERIA'S** PC World Africa; **NORWAY'S** Conputerworld Norge, PC World Norge CAD/CAM, Macworld Norge; **PEOPLE'S REPUBLIC OF CHINA'S** China Computerworld, China Computerworld Monthly, PC World China; **PHILLIPPINE'S** Computerworld Phillippines, PC Digest/PC World; **POLAND'S** Komputers Magazine, Computerworld Poland; **ROMANIA'S** InfoClub; **SPAIN'S** CIM World, Communicaciones World, Computerworld Espana, PC World Espana, AmigaWorld; **SWEDEN'S** ComputerSweden, PC/Nyhetherna, Mikrodatorn, Svenska PC World, Macworld; **SWITZERLAND'S** Computerworld Schweiz, Macworld Schweiz; **TAIWAN'S** Computerworld Taiwan, PC World, Publish; **THAILAND'S** Computerworld; **TURKEY'S** Computerworld Monitor, PC World/Turkiye; **UNITED KINGDOM'S** Graduate Computerworld, PC Business World, ICL Today, Lotus UK, Macworld UK; **UNITED STATES** AmigaWorld, CIO, Computerworld, Digital News, Federal Computer Week, InfoWorld, International Computer Update, Lotus Magazine, Macworld, Network World, NextWorld, PC Games, PC World, Portable Office, PC Letter, Publish, Run, SunWorld; **USSR'S** MIR PC, Computerworld, Computer Express, Network, Manager Magazine; **VENEZUELA'S** Computerworld Venezuela, Micro-Computerworld; **YUGOSLAVIA'S** Moj Mikro.

 The text in this book is printed on recycled paper.

Foreword

Two factors make *Macworld Read Me First Book* more opportune than ever: the arrival of System 7, and the accelerated development of new media hardware and software products for the Macintosh.

When I moved from Apple France in 1985 to run Product Development in Cupertino, California, many were questioning the future of the Macintosh, citing shortcomings in the product and lack of support from the third-party community. To this day, I remember how much it meant to all of us at Apple to see the enthusiasm and creativity of the developers of software and hardware at the Boston Macworld Exposition. Their commitment meant they too saw the potential contained in the first incarnations of the platform and they had faith in our ability to turn it into a reality.

Today, through the work of these early enthusiasts and the ones they in turn inspired, the Macintosh is now the center of a universe of products for work and fun, for creative and productive endeavors.

It's a wonderful world if you can find your way in it. Confusion can become the price of success, and now we have System 7 which is spawning new products, versions, and questions. Add to that all the multimedia boards, peripherals, and software, and you have even more reason to use this book as your guide both now and in the future. Use *Macworld Read Me First Book* to discover all the wonderful uses of your computer you didn't even dream of when you started — to discover the artist within the accountant, or to run the books of the graphic designer.

This is your user's guide to the Macintosh galaxy.

Enjoy the trip.

> Jean-Louis Gassée
> Chairman, CEO Be Labs Inc.
> Former President, Apple Products Division

Conventions used in this book

This book also contains Shopping Tips, Author Picks, and Background information to keep in mind as you read and are indicated by icons in the margins. Here is what to look for:

 Shopping Tips explain what to look for when buying a product or give you its retail price.

 Author Picks provide the author's product of choice in each of the categories in a chapter.

 Background helps explain a technical concept or just provides interesting information to supplement what you might already know.

Other titles to enhance your Mac knowledge

When you're through reading this book and you want to know more about Macs and what they can do, reach for the *Macworld Complete Mac Handbook* — the ultimate Mac reference that includes hardware and software from soup to nuts and powerful tips and shortcuts.

The author, Jim Heid, is the "Getting Started" columnist for *Macworld* where his column is the most widely read in the magazine.

You've got all the hardware and software you need and now you want to know how to manipulate them in the Mac's new operating system — you need *Macworld Guide to System 7*. Let Macworld columnist Lon Poole show you the ins and outs of System 7 in this heavily-illustrated, national bestseller. You'll find valuable undocumented tips and secrets throughout the book.

For those interested in making music with the Macintosh, there's Christopher Yavelow's *Macworld Music & Sound Bible* — the only comprehensive and authoritative guide to using music, sound, digital audio, and multimedia on the Mac. Yavelow is a Macworld contributing writer and Hollywood guru in the music field — his clients and colleagues include David Copperfield, Jan Hammer, Quincy Jones, Herbie Hancock, Julian Lennon, Bob Moog, Steve Wozniak, and Frank Zappa.

Introduction

Looking for information that will help you decide what monitor or word processor to buy? Not really certain what all of the terms mean? Want to cut through all of the computer jargon? Concerned in this throw-away society that your investment will become antiquated before you really understand how to use it? Or worse, that you'll invest a lot of money only to find that you bought the wrong product?

You need the *Macworld Read Me First Book*.

Whom this book is for

From the beginning of my discussions with the founders of the *Macworld* series of books, we envisioned one volume that would help users of Macintosh technology find their way through the morass of products and technology. *Read Me First* is that volume — the book to which you can turn when you are trying to make a decision about what type of product to buy, or what product will most appropriately fit your needs — organized by major areas of products or technology.

From the inception I have also thought of this book as an ongoing work — something to be updated at least yearly — that will reflect the latest in hardware and software technology. In most instances books, particularly books about personal computer products, are out of date before they are printed. But because all of the authors in *Read Me First* write frequently on the subjects you'll find here, I believe that this material will retain its currency more than most books of this sort.

On the subject of authors, the contributors to *Read Me First* represent the most knowledgeable writers in the Macintosh community today. Some of them (Lon Poole, Jim Heid) have written other books in this series, many of them are contributing editors to *Macworld* (Lon Poole, Erfert Fenton, Jim Heid, Robert Eckhardt, David Pogue, Steve Roth, Tom Negrino, Franklin Tessler, Charles Seiter), and two are editors at *Macworld* (Cheryl England, Liza Weiman). I chose these individuals to write chapters because they have been working with Macintosh hardware and software for several years. They know the products about which they write, have tested them several times, and have watched the development of the technologies or products over the last eight years of the Macintosh. They have written more extensively on the Macintosh as a group than any other group of writers (outside of Apple and Addison-Wesley) in the world.

Best of all dear reader, these writers will save you time and money. Take their advice — they have made all of the mistakes that you want to avoid.

The "Where to buy" listings in the back of each chapter will help you track down the products you'll find recommended here, but as the book ages and between editions of *Read Me First,* pick up a copy of *Macworld* and look for a more current article on the subject.

And if you'll fill out the card in the back, we'll send you a notice when the second edition of the book is out together with information on how and where to buy your next copy.

Summary

Please write and let me know your thoughts about the book — help us make *Macworld Read Me First Book* the book you need.

Jerry Borrell, Editor-in-Chief, *Macworld*
501 Second Street, Suite 500, San Francisco, California 94115

How this book is organized

Macworld Read Me First Book is divided into 13 chapters by software, hardware, and then the more esoteric topics like HyperCard. At the end of each chapter you'll find a "Where to buy" section that will allow you to easily find that product you've got to have.

Chapter 1: Choosing the Right Word Processor details the top-selling word processors including what they can and cannot do, and compares them to one another. This chapter will help you determine which program is right for your needs.

Chapter 2: Deciding on a Page-Makeup Program divides page-makeup programs into categories — design-intensive, long-document, inexpensive, multifunctional — and clearly points out the advantages and disadvantages of each.

Chapter 3: Fonts introduces you to basic font terminology and explains how to install and organize your fonts. It also covers dozens of utilities that let you do everything from reorder a font menu to add special effects to type.

Chapter 4: Macintosh Databases covers every level of database software — from table-like flat-file databases to programming-intensive relational databases. Also included is an introductory discussion on Structured Query Language (SQL).

Chapter 5: Managing Your Personal Finances on the Mac explains the various personal finance management programs available for check writing, tax planning, determining insurance needs, and teaches you how to track your investments and make a will.

Chapter 6: Picking a Printer looks at the four types of printers — dot matrix, ink jet, laser, and color — available for the Mac, with special focus on laser printers.

Chapter 7: Hard Disks and Other Storage Devices spells out the secrets of storage and demystifies the confusing options available. Hard drives, removable-cartridge drives, and erasable optical drives are featured, along with a summary of the kind of service and support you can expect for each product.

Chapter 8: Video and the Macintosh: A Developing Relationship defines what and where Mac video technology is today as well as what the future holds. Discover how to import still video images into your Mac, display and edit video, and combine Mac graphics with video.

Chapter 9: Choosing a Monitor for Your Mac focuses on what to look for when buying a black-and-white, gray-scale, or color monitor. Tips on finding the monitor that's right for you abound.

Chapter 10: Understanding System Software begins with a background discussion on what system software is and does, and then compares System 7 to older system versions.

Chapter 11: Utilities for the Macintosh teaches you what utilities are and what they can do for you. Full of recommendations for every utility category.

Chapter 12: HyperCard introduces you to HyperCard's basic structure and tools. You'll learn how to organize information, teach difficult concepts to others, and solve problems at work with HyperCard. Also included is a resource guide for finding out more about the program.

Chapter 13: Backup — Defending Your Data assesses your backup options and explains why backup should be important to you. Sample backup regimens and practical backup tips round out the chapter.

Chapter 1
Choosing the Right Word Processor

by Robert C. Eckhardt

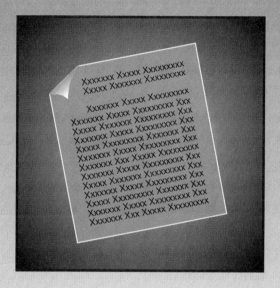

In this chapter...

- Inexpensive word processors best suited for low-cost, short-on-memory Mac systems.

- Mail merge: what it is and the programs that make it least painful.

- Handling graphics in word processors: the good, the bad, and the ugly.

- The one word processor that makes tables and forms a snap.

- Which programs best handle complex page layouts and very long documents.

- Built-in productivity enhancements — glossaries, outliners, style sheets, macros — and how they can make writing easier.

L ike most longtime Macintosh owners, I've used the same word processor for about as long as I can remember. But like most people entering their midlife crisis, I often wonder if it isn't time for a change. If I could start all over again, buy all new software and a new wardrobe of loud Hawaiian shirts and baggy shorts, which word processor would I pick today? What if my midlife crisis leads to a new job as well as a new wardrobe, what word processor would I choose then? And what about all those people buying Macintoshes for the first time, what should they buy?

Such decisions depend, of course, on the kind of work you do and the types of documents that your work entails. Most documents can be categorized as one of seven basic types: correspondence (letters and memos); reports; form letters; academic papers; fill-in-the-blank forms; structured documents (brochures and newsletters); and long documents (manuals and books).

In the pages that follow, I consider which word processors are best suited for each of these major document types. The word processors under consideration include all those currently available: old familiars like Microsoft Word 4.0 (Microsoft, $395); WriteNow 2.2 (T/Maker, $199); MacWrite II v1.1 (Claris, $249); old unfamiliar WordMaker 1.01 (New Horizons, $124.95); recent revisions FullWrite 1.5s (Ashton-Tate, $349); WordPerfect 2.0 (WordPerfect, $495); Nisus 3.06 (Paragon Concepts, $395); Taste 1.01 (DeltaPoint, $149); and odd man out Microsoft Works 2.00 (Microsoft, $295), an integrated application whose word processing module is the only part that concerns us here.

Personal and business correspondence

All Macintosh word processors have in common a skeletal set of features (multiple windows, on-screen rulers, basic find and replace commands) and formats (fonts, font sizes, paragraph justification and indents, etc.). For letters and memos, the simplest of documents, only a few additional attributes are required: a program design that's straightforward and spare with a simple menu structure, uncluttered windows, and an easily navigated set of options; a spelling checker; easy to use on-line help; stationery files (such as ready-made letterhead) which can be created once and used again and again; and a clear and concise manual. (Regrettably, no word processor provides easy or convenient envelope printing. You can print envelopes, however, with an envelope printing desk accessory such as KiwiEnvelopes 3 [Kiwi Software, $49.95].) If letters and memos are all you write, you'll probably also want a word processor that's inexpensive and runs well on a low-cost hardware setup (1MB of RAM and, in a pinch, floppy drives only). Most high-end word processors, including WordPerfect, Nisus, Taste, and FullWrite, are clearly overqualified for letter-writing jobs. They have prices and hardware requirements (2MB of RAM are suggested for both Taste and FullWrite, for example) that are hard to justify if they're used only for simple documents. In addition, their overabundance of high-end features is just so much extra baggage — Taste's cluttered window borders get in the way of a quick scroll, for example, and at 1,290 pages, WordPerfect's manuals are about as compact as a steamer trunk.

WordMaker was created specifically for simple tasks like memos and letters, but despite its rock-bottom price and streamlined design, I can't recommend it either. The problem is that WordMaker's designers, in an attempt to make the program as simple as possible, threw the baby out with the bath water. Gone, for example, are page margin controls and a fully WYSIWYG (what-you-see-is-what-you-get) page view. As a result, page formatting is harder, not easier, and WordMaker really isn't a good choice for any kind of document, simple or otherwise.

The word processors that best fit the criteria for letter- and memo-writers are WriteNow, MacWrite II, Word (with the Short Menus option turned on), and Works. Word offers something the other three can only dream about: it can be upgraded to a high-end word processor merely by turning off the Short Menus option. But Word also costs $100 to $200 more than the others and its manual is, of necessity, filled with all kinds of high-end details. Works brings a lot to the party as well: its database and spreadsheet modules dovetail nicely with the word processing module and it sports drawing tools the other three lack. Word is a good choice if your other writing chores require high-end functions, and Works certainly makes sense if you also need basic spreadsheet and database programs.

But it's MacWrite II and WriteNow that really shine at basic writing tasks. WriteNow costs a little less, feels faster under the fingers, and makes the most modest demands on RAM and disk space. MacWrite II, on the other hand, is one of those rare programs that are obvious and easy the first time you use them; its spell checker is better designed, and its manual is better written. Although MacWrite II is my favorite, either one should keep a correspondent quite happy (see Figure 1-1).

Impersonal correspondence

Mail merge — creating form letters by merging a generic letter with coded instructions and a data document containing such information as names and

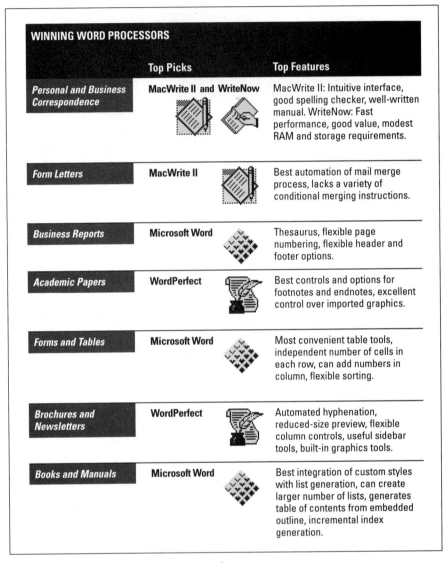

Figure 1-1: The top word processing programs by category.

addresses — is used by businesses for everything from overdue bill notices to direct-mail solicitation. If form letters are on your agenda, your word processor should automate merge-code entry as much as possible, readily accept data from databases and spreadsheet programs, and offer conditional instructions (if a client's income is astronomical, then insert a sentence asking for even more money, for example) and special instructions (such as inserting the contents of another file).

Mail merge is available in all Mac word processors. Many merge facilities are fairly basic; others (such as those in Taste and WordPerfect) try harder but nonetheless fall short. Altogether, the best mail merge facilities are found in Word, WriteNow, Nisus, and MacWrite II. In all four programs, you can easily use the raw data exported from almost any information storage program. WriteNow, Word, and Nisus, all of which have nearly identical merge facilities, offer the widest variety of conditional and special instructions, but entering merge codes is a tedious, manual affair in all of them. MacWrite II automates merge coding better than any program I know of, but lacks the variety of merge instructions found in the other three. If your merge needs are simple and you don't want the hassle of manual coding, go for MacWrite II; if you need all the bells and whistles, grit your teeth and try either Word, Nisus, or WriteNow (see Figure 1-1).

Business reports

Reports to the manager, the board, the stockholders, or just about anyone and everyone, are an essential part of many business people's lives. Because they're long and, one would hope, more logically structured, business reports require document elements that letters and the like do not. For example, your word processor should be able to generate page numbers automatically in any of several styles (letters, Roman or Arabic numerals) and allow you to reset the numbering sequence or style anywhere within the document (reset the page number to one after the introductory material, say, and change from Roman to Arabic numerals).

Your word processor should also be able to display headers and footers (repeated text or graphics that appear at the top or bottom of each page) — different ones for right- and left-hand pages (such as the report title on the left and the quarterly period on the right), different ones for different sections within the report (such as document subdivision titles), and a special one (or, as is common, none at all) on the first page. It is also helpful to have an on-line thesaurus (so you can find a euphemism for "declining profits") and a collection of comprehensive editing tools that you can use to quickly accommodate all the boss's changes.

Overall, WordMaker, MacWrite II, Works, and Taste prove to be disappointments when it comes to reports. Of course, the lack of a thesaurus in some of these programs can be rectified easily with the purchase of a thesaurus desk accessory such as WordFinder (Microlytics, $59.95) or Big Thesaurus (Deneba, $99.95). And the absence of a suite of editing shortcuts could be considered just an inconvenience. But inflexibility in page numbering and headers and footers can't be ignored. In all of these programs, a document must be numbered from beginning to end in a single sequence, and it must also use the same single or right/left pair of headers or footers throughout. And some of these programs can't prevent the header, footer, or page number from appearing on the first page.

WriteNow and Nisus are somewhat more appropriate for reports (especially Nisus, with its many editing shortcuts, including a 10-compartment clipboard and multiple undos), but are also hobbled by inflexible page numbering. The best choices for report writing are Word, FullWrite, and WordPerfect. All three offer thesauruses; more important, all three have highly flexible page numbering and header and footer options. If I had to pick a favorite, it would be Word because of its many editing shortcuts and mid-level price. My least favorite of the three is WordPerfect; it's the most expensive, it has a poorly designed thesaurus, its selection shortcuts (if shortcut is, in fact, the right term) are unnecessarily awkward, and it still doesn't automatically eliminate the extra space when you double-click on a word and press the Delete key (see Figure 1-1).

Academic papers

Whether you're writing a paper for a class, an advanced degree, or the *New England Journal of Medicine,* your document will most likely require the kind of special touches only an academic could love. Foremost among these are every writer's vision of hell: footnotes and end notes. Most word processors these days offer both footnote and end note automation: they position them automatically, renumber them when notes are added or deleted, and permit symbol references (such as asterisks) as well as reference numbers. Some programs can restart footnote numbering with each new page or section; draw a line between footnotes and main text; add a notice when a footnote is continued on the next page; offer reference-number format options; and automatically format every footnote with a custom footnote style (see below for more about custom styles).

Displaying and manipulating graphics

Also important in academic papers is the ability to display imported graphs, charts, and illustrations. All Macintosh word processors allow you to add graphics to a document; where they differ is in the variety of graphic formats they accept and how the graphics can be manipulated and positioned on the page. The most important differences are in positioning (in Taste and WordPerfect, you need only drag the image to the desired location; in MacWrite and WriteNow, you must specify the location numerically or adjust the amount of text above the image) and how text wraps around the graphic. To speed up scrolling through the text, it's also helpful to be able to "hide" graphics temporarily.

Counting words in a document

Because many academic journals charge their authors a fee based on the length of the article, a word count utility is useful. Most word processors can count words (only Nisus cannot); some can count lines and paragraphs as well. Very few programs, however, provide help for two other common academic albatrosses: citations and mathematical formulae. Only FullWrite offers a bibliography reference function, but it's too inflexible for most purposes. And only Word has built-in tools for creating mathematical formulae, although they're limited in scope and difficult to use. Thus, no matter what word processor you use, if your papers are loaded with citations, you'll want a stand-alone bibliographic utility such as EndNote (Niles & Associates, $149) or Pro-Cite (Personal Bibliographic Software, $395). And for mathematical articles, an equation editor such as Expressionist (Prescience Corp, $129.95) is essential.

Citations and equations aside, WordMaker, Works, and WriteNow can be ruled out for academic papers, since the first two don't support footnotes or endnotes of any kind, and WriteNow doesn't support end notes. MacWrite II and Taste offer only basic footnote and end-note automation, although Taste gets extra points for its custom footnote and end-note styles and graphics capabilities. The programs that top the dean's list are FullWrite, Word, WordPerfect, and, to a lesser degree, Nisus. All but Nisus have word counters. Word and WordPerfect provide the best options and controls for footnotes and end notes. WordPerfect and FullWrite offer the best combination of simplicity and power when it comes to imported graphics. Overall, WordPerfect is probably the best — and, alas, the most expensive — choice for academic pursuits (see Figure 1-1).

Forms and tables

Forms and tables are often used by both ivory-tower and real-world inhabitants. Academics frequently display data in tabular form and create application forms of various sorts; business people generate a myriad of product and price tables; and bureaucrats are undisputed masters of forms of all kinds. Although the family resemblance is sometimes hard to see, forms and tables are actually close relatives. Crudely put, a form is really just a partially empty table dressed up with black borders. Thus, for both tables and forms, the editing and formatting tools that are required are essentially the same. And more than any other word processor, Word offers the best tools for tables and forms.

FullWrite is bundled with Tycho Table Maker, a stand-alone application specifically designed for table creation. But Tycho Table Maker is not especially convenient: the selection of tables you can create is quite limited; you must convert a table into a graphic and then copy it into your FullWrite document; and to edit a table once it's in FullWrite, you usually need to copy it back to Tycho Table Maker.

In contrast, Word's table tools are more convenient and far more adaptable. For example, the number of columns (cells) in each row is independent of the number of columns in the rows above and below; data, titles, and column and row headings can thus be organized in almost any fashion. Tables can be symmetrical or asymmetrical in design, and rectangular, triangular, or polygonal in shape. In addition, because you can turn borders on and off for each side of each cell in a table and can format the text in each cell separately, you can create almost any kind of ruled, bordered, or boxed-entry form with a Word table.

In programs that lack table tools, you can always generate lists or simple tables with the judicious use of the Tab key, of course. Many word processors (MacWrite II, Works, Taste, and WriteNow are the exceptions) can sort the items in a list or table — in ascending or descending order — according to the characters at the start of each row. A few, such as Word and WordPerfect, can also sort the rows by the contents of any column within the table (such as the zip code at the end of each address row). Word can also add a column of figures for you, even if it's buried within a multicolumn table. (In Works, you can do all this if you move the table into the database or spreadsheet module.)

Brochures and newsletters

Although there's nothing like PageMaker, QuarkXPress, or FrameMaker when it comes to complex layouts or book-length manuscripts, it is possible to put together many kinds of brochures, newsletters, even entire books with a word processor alone. For brochures and newsletters, the problems your word processor must overcome pertain mainly to layout and design. Primary among them is multiple columns. Almost all word processors can divide a page into equal-width, equally spaced columns. Few, however, can create columns that are irregularly spaced and/ or of unequal width. Rare, too, is the ability to change from one column format to another in the middle of the page. In newsletters and other publications intended for public consumption, right-justified text is commonplace. That and the narrow line-width dictated by multiple columns makes automated hyphenation essential. Sidebars containing pull quotes (boxed, large-type excerpts) and supporting text are also common elements in newsletters and brochures; the ability to create and manipulate sidebars is a definite advantage. Built-in graphics tools and kerning can also be useful; the former makes it easy to add minor graphics elements, and the latter enables you to adjust letter spacing — essential in headlines. Finally, with complex layouts, it's helpful to be able to see a full page (or two complete side-by-side pages) on the screen without scrolling. Unless you have a full-page or two-page monitor, this means your word processor must be able to display a reduced-size preview of the document.

> **It is possible to put together many kinds of brochures, newsletters, even entire books with a word processor alone.**

For complex layouts with multiple columns, sidebars, and graphics, it's a difficult choice between FullWrite, WordPerfect, and Word. Taste is also a strong contender here; it has flexible column controls, hyphenation, kerning, a variety of enlarged and reduced views, and built-in graphics tools, and for all that it's surprisingly inexpensive. But it comes up short in some of the important document elements discussed

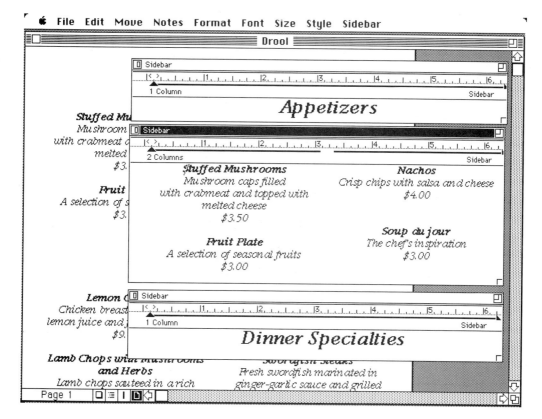

Figure 1-2: To mix various column widths on the same page with FullWrite, you must create multiple sidebars. While this technique can be cumbersome, it can allow you to perform formatting feats impossible on other programs.

earlier, including headers, footers, and page numbers, and thus doesn't quite make the cutoff.

FullWrite, WordPerfect, and Word all offer hyphenation, reduced-size full-page views, and kerning (kerning in Word is much more difficult than in the other two, but it can be done). FullWrite has a good selection of built-in graphics tools and an excellent sidebar feature, but its column controls are relatively weak (see Figure 1-2). Word has no graphics tools and costs more, but for the extra money you get flexible and powerful column controls and sidebars (although these require a great deal more effort than in FullWrite). WordPerfect, however, exceeds the other two in both price and performance; its column controls surpass those in Word and its sidebar and graphics tools are equal to or better than those in FullWrite and it costs $100 more than the next more expensive word processor.

Manuals and books

With long documents such as manuals and books, the layout is usually fairly straightforward and, in most instances, the least of your worries. Far more troublesome are the lists that appear at the beginning of many long publications — tables of contents, lists of figures, tables of authorities (often found in legal documents), and lists of graphs and tables — and the index at the end. Unless you really relish compiling lists and indexes by hand, your word processor should let you indicate the items you want listed, and then automatically compile the list (eliminate duplicates and alphabetize it, too, if it's an index) and add the page numbers. Ideally, your word processor should be able to keep track of several different lists within a single document, so you can have a table of contents and a list of figures, for example, and should automatically format entries in list or index custom styles for easy formatting later on.

Marking entries for lists or an index is always tedious, but the amount of effort it requires varies significantly. In some programs you must manually enter codes; in others you simply select the desired options from a dialog box. The form of the finished list or index also varies from program to program. Some word processors can generate multilevel lists and indexes with subentries beneath main entries (and sometimes subentries beneath subentries), while others make no provision for subentries at all.

In most word processors, cross-references to specific pages must be entered and updated by hand. A few, however, can update cross-references automatically, eliminating the need to check and cross-check right up until the moment you print. A few can also number one or more groups of items, such as tables or figures. As items are added or deleted, the program automatically updates the item numbers in the text (such as the figure caption numbers); if the program is really smart, it can keep the item numbers in cross-references and lists of figures or tables properly updated as well.

For sophisticated tasks such as these, the top contenders are Word, WordPerfect, Nisus, and FullWrite. Nisus automatically updates cross-references, is the only program that can create several different indexes for one document (product and vendor indexes, for example) and, of the four, most easily generates standard index format. I put it last of the four, however, because it generates only single-level lists and indexes, list generation is more complex than it needs to be, lists must be stored in separate documents in order not to alter existing page numbering, and compiled lists and indexes do not take advantage of Nisus' custom styles.

FullWrite ranks third. On the positive side, it creates multilevel indexes and tables of contents, automatically applies the appropriate custom style to index and list entries, and craftily combines automatic item-numbering with its cross-reference and list-generation facilities. On the negative side, FullWrite can create only one list per document, places compiled lists and indexes in special sections which are off limits to standard editing and formatting techniques, and can generate only modest-size indexes.

The remaining two, Word and WordPerfect, share top honors for long documents. WordPerfect automatically updates cross-references, provides a much easier system for marking list and index items, and can generate an index from a concordance (a separate list of words). Word, on the other hand, does a better job of integrating custom styles, can create a larger number of different lists, can generate a table of contents from an embedded document outline, permits a greater number of levels in both lists and indexes, can generate an index in chunks if it is too large to compile in one pass, and compiles each list separately (in WordPerfect, all lists and the index are compiled all at once, erasing all previous lists and any changes you might have made). In short, WordPerfect attempts to make these tasks as effortless as possible, while Word is more concerned with covering all the bases. I prefer Word's flexibility; if you don't need all the options, you may prefer WordPerfect's ease of use.

Productivity enhancements

Whether you're writing a brochure or a book, a number of word processing extras can make your job more enjoyable and save you a lot of time and effort. Take glossaries, for example. A glossary stores often-used graphics or text (from a few words to many paragraphs); you type one or two keystrokes or invoke a simple command and the corresponding glossary entry is instantly inserted in the document. Type wwf, for example, and a glossary will replace it with World Wildlife Fund. Nisus, Word, and FullWrite have glossary functions that differ in the details but are all more or less equally capable.

Outlining your options

Although some people have a distinct aversion to outlining, others find an outliner helps them organize their thoughts and makes their writing more effective. Word, WordPerfect, and FullWrite all have built-in outliners; all take a little getting used to, and none is perfect. Overall, Word's is the best because of the ease with which outlines can be edited and the way the outliner is integrated with the rest of the program, especially with Word's styles and table-of-contents facilities.

Selecting your style

A custom style defines a combination of formats frequently called upon for a specific purpose (such as 12-point Helvetica bold for section heads). A simple style command is all it takes to apply a style, and if you change a style's definition, text

> 66 *If you trade files with colleagues who use other word processors, it's important that your word processor be able to read your colleagues' documents and that they be able to read yours.* 99

already formatted in that style changes as well. FullWrite, WordPerfect, Taste, Word, and Nisus all support custom styles. In Word and WordPerfect, styles always apply to one or more full paragraphs; FullWrite, Taste, and Nisus are more flexible in that styles can be either paragraph-based or character-based. In all but WordPerfect, custom styles are stored in individual documents. In WordPerfect, custom styles can be stored in a common style library available to all documents, even all users on a network. Although this makes sharing custom styles a snap, having to wade through a long list of styles just to find the few of interest to you can be a drawback. Overall, although they may be less than perfect, the custom style functions in FullWrite and especially Word are the best designed, easiest to use, and most thoughtfully integrated with the rest of the program.

Locating and replacing text

The ability to find words or formats and replace them with something else is always handy. All word processors have at least a simple find/change function which can locate and replace text. Only FullWrite, MacWrite II, Nisus, Taste, and WordPerfect can find and change formatting, too. The find/change functions in MacWrite II and Taste are both highly versatile and easy to use; those in WordPerfect and FullWrite are also versatile, but not so easy to use. The find/change function in Nisus far outstrips all the others; unfortunately, however, it requires considerable effort to understand and use.

Reading files from other word processors

If you trade files with colleagues who use other word processors, it's important that your word processor be able to read your colleagues' documents and that they be able to read yours. Text-only documents can be created and read by all word processors, but, as the name implies, they contain no formatting whatsoever. Beyond reading text-only files, the abilities of word processors vary widely. At one end of the spectrum are Nisus and WordMaker, which can read very few document formats other than their own and text-only. At the opposite end are Word, WordPerfect, and MacWriteII; not only can they read documents in a number of different Macintosh formats, but they can also read some types of word processing documents created on a PC.

Play it again, Sam

Finally, macros replay one or more previously recorded actions (text entry, menu commands, or a combination of the two). Macros come in handy when you want to automate repetitive tasks, and they can substitute for a glossary when one is not available. Nisus, WordPerfect, and Works have built-in macro facilities, and Word is bundled with AutoMac III, a separate macro program. Any word processor, however, can be outfitted with a commercial macro utility, such as QuicKeys (CE Software, $149.95); unlike built-in macro facilities, commercial utilities can save you time and effort in all your applications.

Something to write home about

Although an understanding of the types of tasks any given word processor can best perform and a knowledge of the productivity enhancements each program includes are both important, they don't tell the whole story. They don't tell you that you still have to deal with arcane embedded codes in some parts of WordPerfect (a legacy of the program's origins in the PC world), or that Word still identifies fonts by ID number (instead of by name), creating more printing problems than necessary. They don't tell you that FullWrite can add sound notes to your documents, that WordPerfect's menus include a suite of file-management commands, that Taste has a built-in address book, that Nisus can make sure all your parentheses are properly paired, or that Word can send your e-mail for you. In short, they don't tell you about all the little beauty spots and blemishes that writers come to love (or hate) as they become more intimate with a word processor. But they do tell you whether or not you can get a particular writing job done, and get it done quickly and efficiently, and in the end, that's probably what matters most of all.

Summary

✔ When buying a word processor, base your decision on which program is best suited for the types of documents you intend to create. Don't buy a program just because it has glitzy new features, features you may never need to use.

✔ For simple, straightforward documents and Macs with minimal amounts of RAM, stick to simple, straightforward word processors, such as WriteNow and MacWrite II.

✔ For business reports, academic papers, brochures, newsletters, and book-length documents, your best bets are Word, WordPerfect, FullWrite, and to a lesser degree, Nisus.

✔ For multicolumn tables and fill-in-the-blank forms, Word has no peer.

✔ If writing is a major part of your work, a well-integrated style sheet, a well-designed glossary, and/or a comprehensive Find-and-Change function can save you time and effort.

Where to buy

Big Thesaurus, $99.95
Deneba Software
3305 NW 74th Ave.
Miami, FL 33122
305-594-6965
800-622-6827

EndNote, $149
Niles & Associates
2000 Hearst St., Ste. 200
Berkeley, CA 94709
415-649-8176

Expressionist, $129.95
Prescience Corp.
939 Howard St.
San Francisco, CA 94103
415-543-2252

FullWrite Professional 1.5s, $395
Ashton-Tate
20101 Hamilton Ave.
Torrance, CA 90509
213-329-9989

KiwiEnvelopes 3, $49.95
Kiwi Software
6546 Pardall Road
Santa Barbara, CA 93117
805-685-4031

MacWrite II 1.1, $249
Claris Corp.
P.O. Box 526
Santa Clara, CA 95052
408-727-8227
800-544-8554
408-655-6099 (FAX)

Microsoft Word 4.0, $395
Microsoft Corp.
One Microsoft Way
Redmond, WA 98052-6399
206-882-8080
800-426-9400

Microsoft Works 2.00, $295
Microsoft Corp.
One Microsoft Way
Redmond, WA 98052-6399
206-882-8080
800-426-9400

Nisus 3.06, $395
Paragon Concepts
990 Highland, #312
Solana Beach, CA 92075
619-481-1477

Pro-Cite, $395
Personal Bibliographic Software
P.O. Box 4250 Ann Arbor, MI
48106
313-996-1580

QuicKeys, $149.95
CE Software
1801 Industrial Circle
West Des Moines, IA 50265
515-224-1995

Taste 1.01, $149
DeltaPoint, Inc.
2 Harris Ct., Ste. B-1
Monterey, CA 93940
408-648-4000

WordFinder, $59.95
Microlytics
2 Tobey Village Office Park
Pittsford, NY 14534
716-248-9150
800-828-6293

WordMaker 1.01, $124.95
New Horizons Software
206 Wild Basin Road, Ste. 109
Austin, TX 78746
512-328-6650

WordPerfect 2.0, $495
WordPerfect Corp.
155 N. Technology Way
Orem, UT 84057
801-225-5000

WriteNow 2.2, $199
T/Maker Co.
1390 Villa St.
Mountain View, CA 94041
415-962-0195

Chapter 2
Deciding on a Page-Makeup Program

by Steve Roth

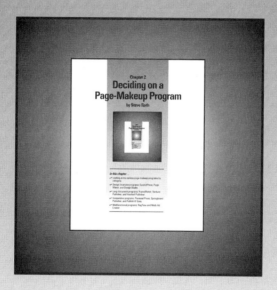

In this chapter...

- Looking at the various page-makeup programs by category.

- Design-intensive programs: QuarkXPress, Page-Maker, and Design Studio.

- Long-document programs: FrameMaker, Ventura Publisher, and Interleaf Publisher.

- Inexpensive programs: Personal Press, Springboard Publisher, and Publish It! Easy.

- Multifunctional programs: RagTime and Multi-Ad Creator.

Life used to be so easy. In the old days (three years ago), choosing a page-makeup program for the Mac meant deciding between three or maybe four programs. The field has always been fast-moving, but back then you could keep up.

These days it's a maelstrom. Choosing a page-makeup program for the Mac isn't as bad as choosing a spreadsheet or word processor for the IBM PC, but in the past two years the field has burgeoned. There are a dozen programs to choose from now — some fresh off the design table, others recently updated, and a couple that are pretty static. And they're all pretty good in their own ways (though some are definitely better than others). It's just a matter of deciding if their ways are your ways.

To try to make some sense of this diversity, I'm dividing the available page-makeup programs into four categories. (Any category system, of course, is somewhat artificial. Programs in one category often share attributes from another.)

Design-intensive programs

QuarkXPress, PageMaker, and Design Studio (*née* ReadySetGo) are all designed for laying out documents in which each page is different. They're strong on color features, object placement, and image control for bitmapped images.

Long-document programs

FrameMaker, Ventura Publisher, and Interleaf Publisher aren't so strong when it comes to positioning and manipulating individual elements, and they're weak in the color department. But they're exceptional when it comes to automatic numbering, cross references, footnotes, indexes, and tables of contents. And they're popular with technical publishers because they also excel at creating equations and tables.

About the author

Steve Roth operates Open House in Seattle, writing, editing, and producing books about computers and desktop publishing. He is the coauthor of *Real World PageMaker 4* (Bantam, 1990) and editor of *The QuarkXPress Book* (Peachpit Press, 1991).

Inexpensive programs

Personal Press, Springboard Publisher, and Publish It! Easy are all vying for the attention of occasional page makers — those who want an easy-to-use program and who don't need all the professional features that a full-time designer or production person does. These programs' main feature is low price, though they offer some features that you won't find even in the high-end programs; in skilled hands, they can produce top-notch documents, albeit with a bit more work.

No category

There are two programs left, neither of which fits in a category with any other program. RagTime, which offers page-layout, spreadsheet, database, graphics, and word processing, all right on the page, is more a competitor with Microsoft Works than with any of the page-layout programs. And Multi-Ad Creator, a single-page layout program that lets you create multiple renditions of a given design within one file, is more comparable to FreeHand or Illustrator (it's missing the fancy drawing tools, but it's designed for the same kind of user).

PageMaker — the most popular of all

Even with all the new contenders, a roundup of Mac page-makeup programs has to start with PageMaker. It's the most widely used, boasts an interface that users have come to love and competitors have been hard-pressed to equal, and with version 4.0, addresses many of the objections that professional users have leveled against it.

Several features combine to make PageMaker's interface a favorite with the reach-out-and-touch-it crowd — those who want to play around with designs on screen. You can see text and graphics as you're dragging and scaling them, rather than just the bounding box displayed by most other programs. You can scroll with a grabber hand. You just place or create the page elements without first creating frames to contain them. You can drag objects off a page onto an underlying "pasteboard," where they're accessible from any page in the publication. You create irregular text wraps by clicking and dragging the wrap boundaries, rather than specifying a numerical text-repel distance for the wrap.

These features in particular add up to an excellent interface for trying things out on screen. PageMaker falls short, though, with those who want to type in specs rather than dragging things around, and it's short on the object-creation and object-manipulation tools long familiar in draw programs. You can't ask PageMaker to move a page element to the right 3 points, for instance, align page elements automatically, or duplicate an element multiple times in a given direction. There's no grouping; rotation is available only for unthreaded text blocks, and then only in 90-degree increments; and you're limited in line weights and shades to the choices on the menu.

While earlier versions had some pretty serious typographic limitations, PageMaker 4 addresses them admirably. You may end up several dialog boxes deep, but if you want to control type, version 4 provides almost every tool you need. The one thing missing is a built-in tracking editor à la QuarkXPress or Design Studio — derigueur for the typographically compulsive. Its style sheets (see Figure 2-1) are among the best on the market and they work seamlessly with Microsoft Word's styles — a key advantage in production environments.

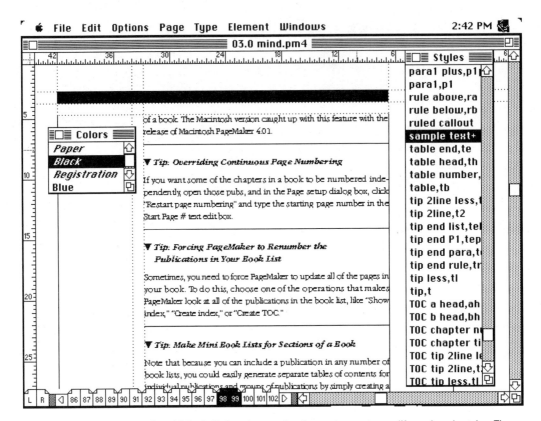

Figure 2-1: PageMaker's Style palette makes it easy to create, modify, and apply styles. The Colors palette serves the same purpose when you're working with color.

There's a whole bevy of new long document ("Book") features in PageMaker 4 that set it apart from the other design-intensive players, and make it more like the long-document programs. Automatic table-of-contents and excellent index generation, inline graphics that flow with text as in most Mac word processors (hallelujah!), a Story Editor (see Figure 2-2) for word processing – style editing, top-notch search-and-replace (including finding and changing text attributes), and a handy spelling checker put PageMaker beyond the layout-only region.

At $795, PageMaker is near the top of the page-makeup price spectrum, but in many ways it's worth every penny. Aldus is well known for its impressive tech support, customer service, documentation, and special items like tech notes. Along with a solid, well-rounded program, those factors add up to a friendly environment both for novices and for full-time page makers.

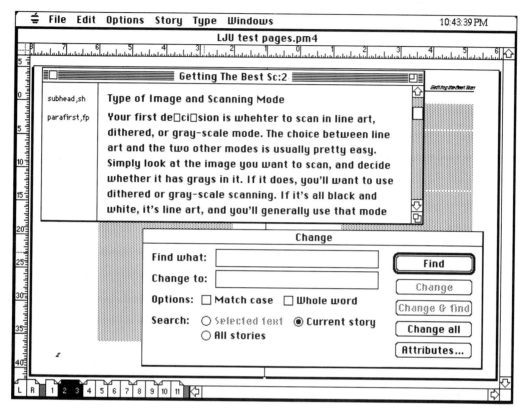

Figure 2-2: PageMaker's Story Editor makes it much easier to affect large-scale edits within a publication. From within the Story Editor you can use the spelling checker and the Find and Change feature.

QuarkXPress — power in page-makeup

Quark has now clearly solidified XPress's position as the leader in power features for page makeup, while also greatly enhancing its user interface — the sticking point that has kept so many people away from the program in the past.

The new package fulfills almost every wish on a QuarkXPress user's list. And when Quark implements a new feature, they go whole hog with it — what would be simply a bunch of bells and whistles becomes gongs and trumpets. XPress 3 is clearly the sports car of page makeup, compared to PageMaker's middle-of-the-road, station-wagon approach.

By far the biggest problem with previous versions of XPress has now been fixed: you can select multiple items, either by shift-clicking or by dragging a marquee. You

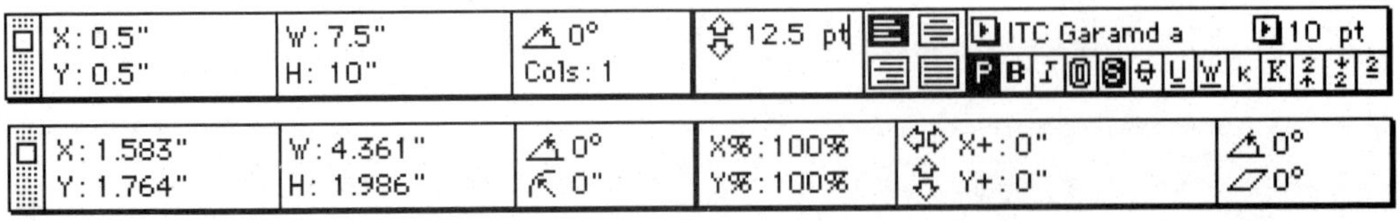

X: 0.5"	W: 7.5"	⊿ 0°	⬍ 12.5 pt	⊟⊟▶ITC Garamd a ▶10 pt
Y: 0.5"	H: 10"	Cols: 1		⊟⊟ P B I ⓞⓢ⧨U W K K ⇡ ⇣

X: 1.583"	W: 4.361"	⊿ 0°	X%: 100%	⬌ X+: 0"	⊿ 0°
Y: 1.764"	H: 1.986"	⟋ 0"	Y%: 100%	⬍ Y+: 0"	⟋ 0°

Figure 2-3: QuarkXPress's Measurements palette lets you change settings for selected items without using menus. The controls vary some depending on whether you have a text or picture box selected. Note that the setting on the left side affect the box, while the right side affects the contents of the box.

can group the multiple-selected items, align them (top, middle, bottom, left, center, right), align them with spacing (distribute them), and lock them so they can't be moved with the mouse.

The parent/child relationship between boxes (child boxes move with their parents and can't go outside them) used to be a problem too, and it's been fixed. Quark has renamed it Auto Constrain and demoted it from an inviolable constraint to a selectable option.

XPress 3 lets you work on an underlying pasteboard, so it's easy to drag items off the page and to create bleeds. Other interface improvements include the new Measurements palette (both this and the Tool palette are floating windows that you can reposition or close), which lets you see and change the specifications for any selected item — text, graphic, or imported picture — without resorting to multiple dialog boxes (see Figure 2-3). You can simply drag items between open documents (every program should offer this), and there's a customizable zoom tool in the toolbox now.

There are still a couple of wrinkles in this streamlined interface, however. The pasteboard is not common to all pages, for instance; it's just an area on which all the pages lie. So when you drag an item onto the pasteboard and then change pages, don't expect to see the item there waiting for you. Also, the pasteboard isn't very big; at the top and bottom there's less than an inch to store items (though the library, discussed below, makes up for these failings admirably).

You can't select objects that are behind other objects (which makes for a lot of layer shuffling), and there's no grabber hand for moving the page view around. The new Live Scroll Bars help some (the page moves interactively as you move the scroll bar), but of course they won't move your view diagonally.

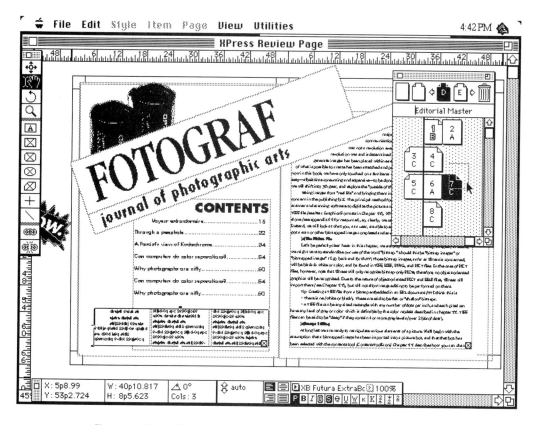

Figure 2-4: QuarkXPress 3.0 offers free rotation, polygonal picture boxes, automatic drop caps, and automatic trapping of XPress-created color elements. The Document Layout palette lets you move pages around within the document and build multi-page spreads.

XPress's Master Pages feature (which used to be called Default Pages) has been revamped to allow up to 127 master pages per document. You can use any master page for any document page, and changes to master pages now retroactively adjust pages that have already been created except, optionally, those elements that you've changed locally.

The Document Layout palette makes manipulating pages within a document a breeze. You can add, delete, or move pages within a document by dragging icons around (see Figure 2-4). Page spreads of two or more pages can easily be created, and items such as pictures, rules, or text boxes can straddle pages.

Figure 2-5: You can build multiple libraries in QuarkXPress containing up to 2,000 entries, and each of those entries can contain multiple items. You can attach a one-line description to each item, and optionally only see those entries with a given description.

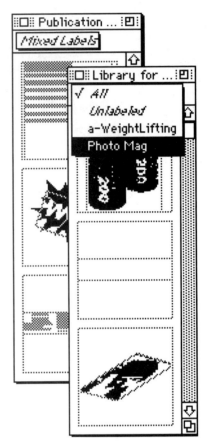

The new Library feature lets you store up to 2,000 commonly used page elements (or sets of multiple elements, grouped or ungrouped) in a library file (see Figure 2-5). You move elements in and out of the library by simply dragging, or by cutting and pasting. You can label each element and choose which groupings to view with a pop-up menu (so everything with the name *sidebar* could be displayed in a scrolling list, for example).

QuarkXPress's capable spelling checker and search/replace function now work globally, so you can search, replace, or check an entire document. The program is too cumbersome to be used effectively as a word processor, however (you can't simply scroll through a document), so don't expect to do more than light editing and copy processing.

Tops in typographics

On the type side, typesetters and professional publishers have long favored QuarkXPress for its powerful typographics, including its ability to render Type 3 PostScript fonts on screen (what ATM does for Type 1 fonts). Now, along with added precision (to .001 point or .005 em for most measurements), comes the ability to create automatic drop caps of any size. You just specify the number of characters to drop, and the number of lines to drop them. Also new is the ability to align text within a text block at the top, center, or bottom, or justify it vertically — adding space between paragraphs to make the text fit the box. You can specify the maximum space between paragraphs, but can't specify different maximum values for different paragraphs (or paragraph styles), which makes the feature much less useful.

QuarkXPress 3 provides increased control over widows and orphans, keeping lines and paragraphs together, and style types, such as the particular scaling ratios for small caps, super- and subscript, and superior type (this is a document-level preference). In many ways, however, the most awaited new feature is the free rotation of text boxes to the tenth of a degree.

Quark's Picture boxes have always been round or square; now they can be polygons. There are five canned shapes, or you can create one of your own (sorry, still no Bezier curves). There's free rotation of pictures (independently of the boxes containing them) to one-tenth of a degree, horizontal skewing, and scaling to one-tenth of 1 percent in either direction. Also new is the ability to greek pictures, precisely set the offset of an image (where the picture falls in the picture box), and check what pictures are in a document.

XPress can automatically check for and reimport pictures that have been modified externally (with an option to check with you first). Another great improvement is the separation of the transparency and the text runaround options; you can now have transparent or opaque boxes, with runaround or without.

You can now specify paragraph rules above and/or below paragraphs and the rules move with the paragraph as text reflows. You can insert floating boxes (text and/or graphics) that move just like any other character in the text but can hold any element or group of elements.

The color separation advantage

XPress has stood out for some time in its ability to generate process separations of its color pages, including color EPS graphics from FreeHand and Illustrator (though not including color bitmaps). Version 3 adds the ability to create traps (slight overprinting areas that prevent white lines from appearing between abutting colors), either automatically or according to your specifications. XPress's trapping only works for XPress type and graphics, though (you have to trap EPS graphics in their source programs).

XPress 3 can produce full-color page separations that include color TIFF images by separating the TIFFs in advance into DCS (Desktop Color Separation) files with programs like Adobe Photoshop or Preprint's SpectraSepsQX. And QuarkXPress will save pages in Aldus's OPI (Open Prepress Interface) format for separation by prepress systems or Aldus PrePrint.

Quark was not nicknamed Quirk for nothing: each upgrade since the program's first release has had to go through several versions and subversions before all the bugs got ironed out. This time has been no different. The thing about Quark, though, is that the company always comes through and fixes mistakes; it just takes time. The latest version, 3.1, is quite solid.

Also somewhat quirky are the three manuals that come with the program. Most of the answers are there, but they're scattered throughout the books. And some important issues, such as how to do color separations of color TIFFs, are not even touched upon.

If you can afford top dollar ($795 — same as PageMaker) and want the best tools for complex designs, including rotated items and color, QuarkXPress is your best bet.

ReadySetGo — the poor stepchild of page makeup on the Mac

If you exclude the no-longer-extant LetraPublisher (*née* MacPublisher), then it's fair to say that ReadySetGo has always been the poor stepchild of Macintosh page makeup. While it's loaded with features, very usable, and fully capable of producing top-notch pages, it doesn't offer PageMaker's seductive interface or QuarkXPress's awesome power. Nor does it compete with the pricing of the low-end page layout programs Publish It! Easy, Personal Press, and Springboard Publisher. At $495, it is less expensive than the power players, but not by such a huge amount (especially when you're talking discounted prices). PageMaker and QuarkXPress are better choices.

Design Studio — direct descendant of ReadySetGo

Realizing that ReadySetGo falls into a pretty deep hole between the two big page-makeup mountains, Letraset developed Design Studio, which looks a lot like ReadySetGo, but with interface improvements that make it attractive to the Page-Maker design-on-the-screen crowd, power tools that QuarkXpress users will admire (or in some cases, envy), and tools all its own that designers will crave. It's the same price as its two main competitors — $795.

Design Studio is a direct descendant of ReadySetGo. That's immediately apparent. ReadySetGo users who were asked to pay $325 to "migrate" to Design Studio may think it should have been an upgrade, but Letraset didn't. In any case, it's a major improvement. The new tools won't be so attractive to the general business users and production publishers that many of PageMaker 4.0's new features address, it's missing some power tools that production publishers love in QuarkXPress, and there are some clunky implementations and limitations that limit the program's usability.

The limitations have mostly to do with memory. If you rotate more than a few objects, you can expect Design Studio to refuse, citing low memory. The undo function is also very limited: it can't undo rotations, for instance.

Design Studio has a pasteboard underneath pages as in PageMaker, so you can drag items off the page and drag them back on to other pages. You can see items move as you drag them around (but not as you scale them), and you can set up column and ruler guides much as you do in PageMaker.

Design Studio offers most of the typographic control you could ask for — kerning, tracking, sub- and superscripts (including custom baseline shifts), vertical alignment and justification, and excellent hyphenation controls. There's even a feature for automatically building fractions. It's missing justification controls, however.

Design Studio's other big shortcoming lies in its style sheets, which it inherited directly from ReadySetGo. You can build styles that include both paragraph and character formatting and apply them to any selection of text, but when you apply the style, any local formatting (like italics) is removed from the styled text. And once you've applied a style, you can't apply local formatting to the same text without first removing the style. It's wrongheaded, infuriating, and in a program that's otherwise impressive, disappointing.

In addition, Design Studio has trouble importing Word's hanging indents. Most other things about this program are great, starting with irregularly shaped text and graphics frames (see Figure 2-6). These frames crop your graphics and shape your text to more than a dozen different odd shapes. And you can rotate any page element in one-degree increments (see Figure 2-7).

The Annexes feature allows for add-on menu items and features; included Annexes let you edit kerning and tracking tables, get a list of fonts and pictures used, and strip downloaded fonts from Design Studio's printed-to-disk PostScript. Upcoming annexes include DesignScript ($125), a page-layout command language that will let traditional composition systems and databases spec fully laid-out pages, and an annex for creating process separations.

Design Studio lives up to its name (and its $795 price); it's a full-blown designer's tool, appropriate for people designing pages day in and day out. Its poor style sheets, memory limitations, and lack of Undo for many functions make it much less useful for production publishers than PageMaker or QuarkXPress, though, and casual users will probably balk at its complexity.

Ventura Publisher — advanced features for long documents

For years, Ventura Publisher has been the one good reason to use an IBM PC. And for all those years, rumors have been flying that Xerox had a Mac version in the works. Well, it's finally here, and even though it's pretty much the same as Ventura 2.0, which came out in 1988, it boasts features that Mac publishers have only dreamed of (with the exception of a few FrameMaker and Interleaf users) — cross-references, autonumbering, footnotes, equations, anchored (floating)

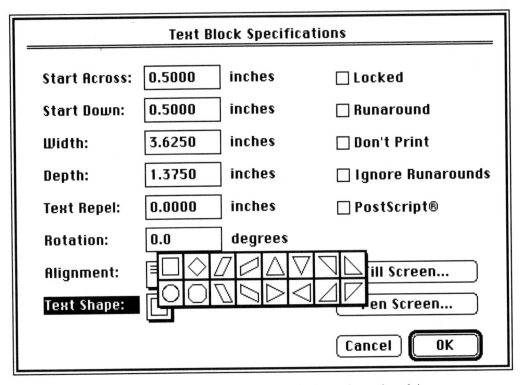

Figure 2-6: Design Studio offers text and graphics frames in a variety of shapes.

frames, spreadsheet-style tables, variables, markers, live running heads (as in a dictionary), and style sheets that never end.

Page makeup with style to spare

Style sheets are the heart and soul of Ventura. Almost all the formatting you do in Ventura is via paragraph styles. You use the Tagging tool to select one or more paragraphs (you can select multiple noncontiguous paragraphs on a page). Then you click in the Tags palette (see Figure 2-8) to apply a style to those paragraphs. Any time you change the formatting for a given type of paragraph — Subhead, for instance — you change the formatting for all paragraphs tagged with that style. The range of controls you have over a style exceeds anything we've seen on the Mac to date (see Figure 2-9).

You can specify that a paragraph should fall at the top, middle, or bottom of a frame; set it the width of the column or the width of the text frame (great for wide headlines above multicolumn copy); indent the first lines either absolutely or relative

Figure 2-7: With Design Studio's Rotate tool you can create wild text and graphics effects.

to the previous paragraph; set different left and right indents for left and right pages; rotate a paragraph in 90-degree increments; specify line spacing, space below, and space above a paragraph (if you choose, Ventura will ignore space above when the paragraph falls at the top of a column); and specify column and page breaks before a paragraph. You can specify line breaks before the paragraph, after it, both, or neither (this enables you to place two paragraphs on the same line — perfect for run-in heads).

You can specify up to three ruling lines (you specify their thickness and distance apart) above, below, or around a paragraph; they can be the width of the text, the paragraph margins, the column, the frame, or a custom width. Ventura allows for up to 16 tab stops, with your choice of leader character and leader spacing. There are automatic drop caps and bullets (you specify the number of lines for drop caps, the size of the indent for bullets, and the type specs for both drop caps and bullets). You can control tracking, hyphenation, and justification parameters, and specify the amount of spacing to allow above, below, and within the paragraph for vertical justification.

Ventura differs from other Mac page-layout programs in one significant way: it only provides links to imported text files, rather than actually importing a copy of the text. So when you change the text on the page, Ventura changes the source

Figure 2-8: The Tags palette in Ventura Publisher lets you quickly apply styles to paragraphs selected with the Tag tool. The styles at the bottom, starting with Z_ are generated styles that Ventura creates and applies when you create one of its automatic items, such as headers, footers, and captions.

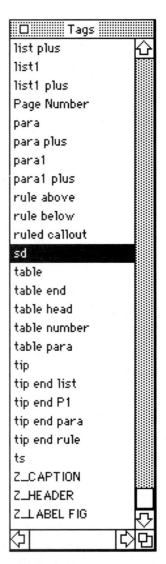

file itself. In fact, if you simply import a file into a Ventura chapter and then save the chapter, it completely alters the text file (see Figure 2-10). It strips out any formatting except for type style, instead inserting codes and tags that invoke Ventura's formatting controls.

Ventura removes Microsoft Word's style tags when it's importing (and won't import Word files in Fast Save format), converting all the formatting to its own coding system. WordBridge, a program that is included with Ventura Mac, converts styled Word documents to text files tagged for Ventura, with accompanying style sheets. It won't read Fast Save format either, however.

The spelling checker in Ventura is pretty good, with smart suggestions for correcting misspelled words. It brings up the same words repeatedly, however, rather than learning once you've told it to ignore the word.

Ventura addresses the two most difficult typesetting problems — tables and equations — with an impressive set of tools. The Tables function allows for spreadsheet-type tables in which the cells expand downward to accommodate multiple lines of text. You can join multiple cells together to make a single cell, and take advantage of all Ventura's styles and typographic controls. You can only have one paragraph per cell, but given that, Ventura's table function is the best available on the Mac.

Ventura's equation editor is competent, though not the math-publishing behemoth you'll find in FrameMaker. It lets you build good-looking equations — simple or complex — without too much arcane coding. There's one bug here, though: if your Symbol font doesn't have the correct font ID, trying to insert an equation crashes the whole program.

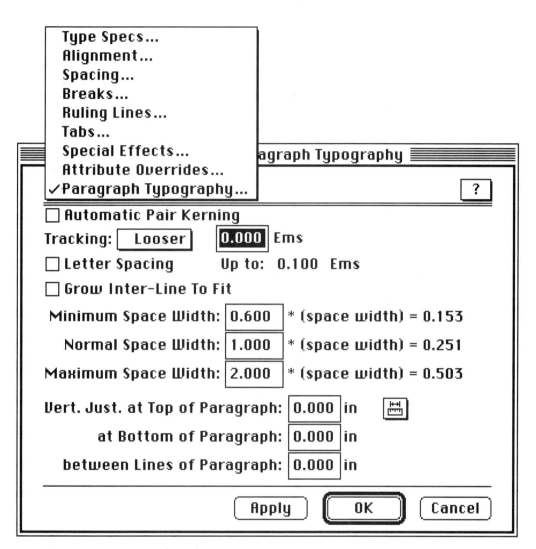

Type Specs...
Alignment...
Spacing...
Breaks...
Ruling Lines...
Tabs...
Special Effects...
Attribute Overrides...
✓**Paragraph Typography...**

agraph Typography

?

☐ **Automatic Pair Kerning**

Tracking: ☐ **Looser**   **0.000** Ems

☐ **Letter Spacing**   Up to: 0.100 Ems

☐ **Grow Inter-Line To Fit**

Minimum Space Width: 0.600 * (space width) = 0.153

Normal Space Width: 1.000 * (space width) = 0.251

Maximum Space Width: 2.000 * (space width) = 0.503

Vert. Just. at Top of Paragraph: 0.000 in

at Bottom of Paragraph: 0.000 in

between Lines of Paragraph: 0.000 in

Apply   OK   Cancel

Figure 2-9: Ventura offers an impressive array of controls over paragraph styles. The Paragraph Typography dialog box, shown here, is only one of nine dialog boxes that control styled paragraphs. You can jump between those dialog boxes using a pop-up menu.

You can anchor frames (containing either text or graphics) to an anchor point in the text, and the frame can either float directly above or below the anchor point, stay in a fixed place on the page but move from page to page as the text flows, or float within the text line itself. There's no command to float anchored frames to the top or bottom of the page, however.

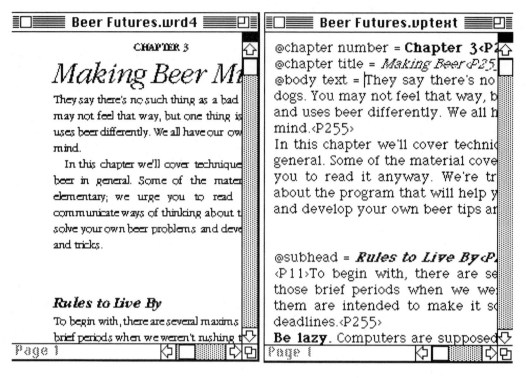

Figure 2-10: When you import a formatted text file into Ventura Publisher (in this case, from Microsoft Word), it converts it to a tagged and coded document, stripping out all formatting except type style changes (bold, italic, etc.). Ventura doesn't normally pick up paragraph styles from Microsoft Word; this file was run through WordBridge first, so style names were converted to paragraph tags, and the style formatting was converted to a Ventura style sheet.

Ventura's autonumbering maintains counters for chapters, pages, tables, and figures. It can start numbering these at the beginning of a chapter, or continue the numbering from the previous chapter.

You can cross-reference either within or across chapters in Ventura by inserting a reference to a named frame anchor or marker (a marker is a named position in the text put there for the sake of cross-referencing). While it involves creating a written list of markers and anchors to refer to (you can't just choose a name from a pop-up menu), it's effective if you do build a list and are careful to type the names correctly in the dialog boxes.

Footnotes are straightforward; you insert a footnote reference, and Ventura creates a frame for you to type the footnote. When the reference moves, the footnote moves with it. Ventura numbers footnotes from the beginning of the chapter or the beginning of the page, but it doesn't handle end notes. You can create tables of contents, figure lists, and the like by specifying which tags to gather into the list, and which chapters to gather them from.

To create an index, you enter index entries in the text. You can have two levels of entry, with sort keys for each (See and See Also references are available). Unlike PageMaker, however, you can't see a list of existing index topics and choose one. You have to type the entry properly each and every time.

Ventura provides basic tools for drawing lines, boxes (square- or round-cornered), and circles, as well as boxed text. These graphics are attached to frames, so when you move the frame, all the graphics move with it. This is especially useful for annotating a figure with call-outs and arrows.

The online help, though innovative in providing a pop-up menu with several help choices in every dialog box, is so concise as to be almost useless. Technical support was available, technically competent, and helpful when I called them, but you get only 60 days of support when you buy Ventura, starting with your first call. Additional support is $150 per year.

While Ventura is a good port from the IBM, several things reveal that it is at heart not a Mac program. It won't use any font whose screen font name exceeds thirty characters. Double-clicking with the text tool doesn't select a word — until you release the second click. Holding down Shift while using the cursor keys does not select adjacent characters; it jumps to adjacent pages. The Apply button in dialog boxes applies changes permanently; Cancel doesn't retract them. And you can't change type specs (shift to italic, for instance), then start typing — you have to type text, select it, then change the type specs. These are little things, but they are annoying, they slow you down, and they demonstrate Ventura's non-Mac origins.

Those origins do allow for good transfer of files between the PC and the Mac. The Copy All Files command moves all the necessary files — including font-width tables — between the two machines, though you often have to update pointers, telling Ventura where to find files.

A few other problems are the fault of the program design itself. There's no search and replace. There's no pasteboard. You can only create spot-color separations — not process color. You can only rotate text, and only in 90-degree increments. There's no grabber hand for scrolling around the page, so you're forever using the scroll bars. And Ventura constantly redraws the whole page, even when you just apply a style to a paragraph. It even redraws the page when you open a dialog box.

Ventura is a better production tool than FrameMaker, its closest competitor on the Mac, and it takes a different approach. Ventura is designed to integrate material from many sources, while FrameMaker is set up so that documents are created in the program from writing through editing to production.

Given that Ventura Publisher hasn't changed since 1988, it is a remarkable program. The Mac version is still young, however, and doesn't fit into the Macintosh environment with complete ease. Occasional page makers are better off with one of the more free-form programs like QuarkXPress, PageMaker, or Publish It! Easy. But for people who aren't afraid of numerous, deep dialog boxes, who can afford a top-dollar program (yes, yet again, $795), who plan their publications in advance, and especially those who are producing long, structured documents, I highly recommend Ventura.

FrameMaker — page layout using common live files

At first glance, the Macintosh version of FrameMaker 2.1 (the publishing favorite on Unix-based Sun and NeXT machines) looks like another page-layout program, albeit with more-than-impressive features for long, structured documents (see Figure 2-11). With cross-referencing, footnotes, indexing, auto-numbering, and anchored frames, FrameMaker looks like the long-document and technical production tool that Mac users have been awaiting for so long.

Page layout for authoring and document processing

FrameMaker is not a page-layout program in the sense that Mac users understand that term. First and foremost, it doesn't import formatted text files (it does import graphic files in all the major formats). You can open formatted Word and MacWrite files, and FrameMaker converts them into FrameMaker documents; from there you can cut and paste the formatted text into your FrameMaker publication. But you can't just import the formatted text. FrameMaker is designed as an authoring or document processing tool, with the idea that writers work in FrameMaker from the beginning. They write the documents; build all their cross-references, captions, callouts, and index entries; spell check, search and replace, and so on — without ever resorting to importing or exporting. Last-minute changes are simplified because everyone — in writing, editorial, and production — works on a single, live document. This means that FrameMaker is at its best on a server-based network, so everyone can get at the master files. You can even use it on a mixed network with Sun and NeXT workstations.

The trade-off, of course, is that for FrameMaker to work seamlessly, everyone working on the job needs a copy of the program (at $795 each), and must learn to use it. Bringing new writers up to speed takes quite a bit of training, and with projects that involve outside and contract writers, the cost of the program and the training can be prohibitive in both time and money.

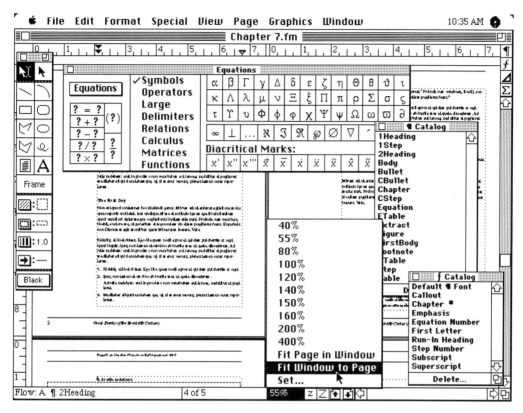

Figure 2-11: FrameMaker's four palettes give you access to tools for drawing and equation building, and to the catalogs of character and paragraph styles. The info bar at the bottom of the window shows the name of the "flow," the tag of the currently selected paragraph, the page number, and zoom magnification.

Robust features for creating documents

Given that essential difference between FrameMaker and other Mac page-makeup programs — it's not designed for importing documents, but for creating them — it's easy to rave about the program's features: a laundry list of abilities long awaited by Mac long-document publishers.

There's an adequate set of drawing tools (even including Bezier curves), and very robust word processing. You'll find automatic cross-referencing, footnotes, indexing, figure lists, tables of contents, autonumbering, equation generation (and analysis), definable variables, floating (anchored) frames, even hypertext capabilities (FrameMaker's impressive — though not context-sensitive — hypertext help system is simply a FrameMaker document in its own right).

You can create any number of variables for text that is still up in the air. If a product is still unnamed, for instance, or has a code name, you can insert a variable called "ProductName" and assign a value of "CodeName." When the product name is finalized, just change the value for the variable, and FrameMaker updates it throughout the document. You can even insert formatting instructions as part of the value.

Cross-references are equally robust. You can refer to heads, figures, page numbers, section numbers, or any combination; FrameMaker even lets you jump to the cross-reference location or search for unresolved cross-references. The indexing function is powerful, though not nearly as easy to use as PageMaker's. You can't see all your existing index topics and simply choose one; you must enter the topic correctly each time, or rely on simple word indexing.

FrameMaker works with flows of text — continuous stories that jump from column to column and page to page. You can name the different flows in your document and assign different properties to each flow. You can set up baseline synchronization, for instance, so baselines of type align from column to column.

FrameMaker's feathering option for vertical justification is slightly more sophisticated than QuarkXPress's. You can specify the maximum interline and interparagraph spacing, but not for individual paragraphs or paragraph styles — only for a complete flow.

FrameMaker offers character styles in addition to the more familiar paragraph styles, which makes it much easier to format run-in heads and other consistently formatted characters that aren't whole paragraphs. You can apply formatting changes in several ways (see Figure 2-12), but you can't base one style on another; if you decide to change the typeface for your body copy, you have to go through and edit all your styles — first paragraphs, bullet lists, numbered lists, and so on — rather than having the change ripple through all the styles automatically.

Within styles, you can define formatting using all of FrameMaker's impressive specification tools — indents, tabs, spacing, leading, alignment, hyphenation and justification, typeface, size, spread (the amount of spacing between letters), and automatic numbering (using any of several numbering schemes).

You can specify that a frame you've previously created on the "reference page" should automatically be inserted above or below any paragraph (or style of paragraph). Those frames can contain just about anything — from a simple line to a complex text-and-graphic conglomeration.

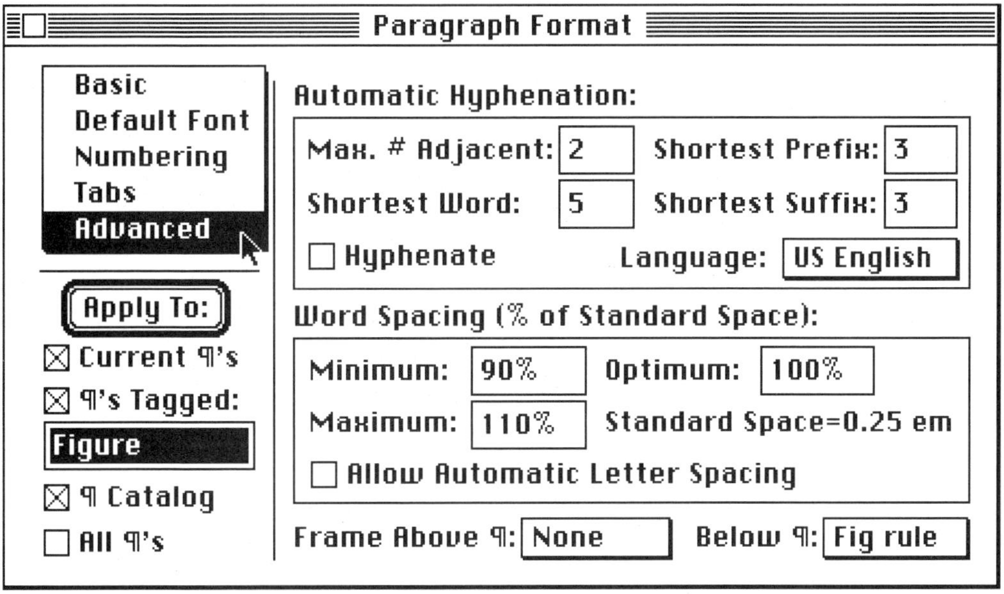

Paragraph Format	
Basic **Default Font** **Numbering** **Tabs** **Advanced**	**Automatic Hyphenation:**

Max. # Adjacent: `2`   Shortest Prefix: `3`

Shortest Word: `5`   Shortest Suffix: `3`

☐ Hyphenate   Language: `US English`

Word Spacing (% of Standard Space):

Minimum: `90%`   Optimum: `100%`

Maximum: `110%`   Standard Space=0.25 em

☐ Allow Automatic Letter Spacing

Frame Above ¶: `None`   Below ¶: `Fig rule`

Apply To:

☒ Current ¶'s

☒ ¶'s Tagged:

Figure

☒ ¶ Catalog

☐ All ¶'s

Figure 2-12: There are five dialog boxes controlling the format of a paragraph in FrameMaker, all accessed via the Paragraph Format option. You can apply changes to selected paragraphs, to tagged paragraphs, to the style itself (the ¶ catalog), or to all paragraphs in the document.

You can also attach frames to text at any location; they're called anchored frames (see Figure 2-13). These frames can float to the top of the column on which their anchor falls, the bottom, within the line, right after the line, or even adjacent to the paragraph outside the column on the left or right, or on the inside or outside of the page.

Anchored frames have at least one failing however: floating illustrations in a multicolumn layout are limited to the width of a single column; otherwise they overprint on adjacent columns. Illustrations wider than a column must be placed and moved manually as the document repaginates.

With all this long-document automation power, you can hardly expect FrameMaker to shine for short, design-intensive documents. And it doesn't. There's no manual kerning, for instance (there is automatic pair kerning), much less automatic tracking. EPS graphics appear contained in opaque white bounding boxes, making them hard to position on top of other elements, though the boxes are transparent on printout.

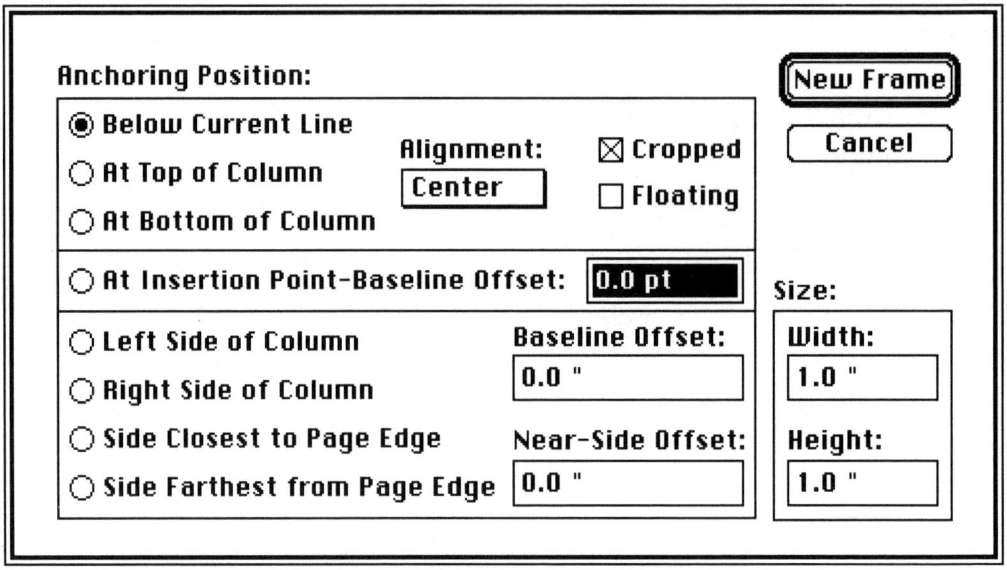

Anchoring Position:

- ⦿ **Below Current Line**
- ○ **At Top of Column**
- ○ **At Bottom of Column**

Alignment: ☒ **Cropped**
Center   ☐ **Floating**

New Frame

Cancel

- ○ **At Insertion Point-Baseline Offset:**   **0.0 pt**   **Size:**
- ○ **Left Side of Column**   **Baseline Offset:**   **Width:**
- ○ **Right Side of Column**   **0.0 "**   **1.0 "**
- ○ **Side Closest to Page Edge**   **Near-Side Offset:**   **Height:**
- ○ **Side Farthest from Page Edge**   **0.0 "**   **1.0 "**

Figure 2-13: FrameMaker offers great flexibility in where it positions floating frames in relation to their anchor points within text.

You can use up to eight predefined spot colors in a document, and while there are good controls for which of those colors display and print, printing options for high-quality film output are quite limited.

FrameMaker's tech support is accessible (I talked to a person on my very first call — no waiting, no call back), and seems well informed. That's good, because this is a big, complex program that many potential users (writers and editors, for instance) may find daunting. FrameMaker's manuals — ten of them, all well indexed — do an acceptable job of showing you how to use the features of the program, but they're a bit short on conceptual explanations. There's no overview, for instance, of what a marker is — just a terse definition and several specific usage examples.

You should plan on using at least a 68020-based Mac to run FrameMaker; it's pretty sluggish on an SE, especially with large documents. It holds all the text in open documents in memory for the sake of speed, and will simply not open or handle chapters that exceed available memory. Plan on giving it 3MB or 4MB under MultiFinder in order to work with documents totaling around 150 pages.

FrameMaker is a poor choice for short-document designers, and for book publishers and others with stringent typographic requirements, it's worth thinking twice before buying FrameMaker. But given the concept behind its design — that everyone from writers to production workers use FrameMaker and work on a common live file — this program is magnificent. It's very solid, makes excellent use of the Macintosh interface (these folks got religion), and brings features to the Macintosh that we've never seen before, or in some cases even dreamed of.

Interleaf Publisher 3.5 — the long-document, technical program

Interleaf Publisher — all 700 files and 9MB of it — is an obvious stranger to the Mac world. It doesn't use the Macintosh interface, for instance; the desktop, mouse clicks, menus, and dialog boxes are all different from what you'd expect. It doesn't use Apple's print manager, so it won't print on non-PostScript printers. It will use installed fonts, but if you have too many installed, it runs out of menu space (with my system, it stops around Palatino). It doesn't download fonts automatically; anything that's not already in your printer you have to download manually. It ignores Adobe Type Manager. There's no zooming, except when you're creating graphics. Finally, it must be installed on the start-up disk, and only recognizes that disk.

OK. Interleaf Publisher is not, at heart, a Mac program. Nor is it typographically sophisticated (trust me). So what is it?

Interleaf is a long-document technical-publishing program that runs on a variety of workstation platforms — Mac, IBM, and several Unix boxes — with special strengths for technical publishing. It's more like a mega-powered WYSIWYG word processor than a page-makeup program. It's a tool for day-in and day-out page makers — especially producers of documentation — who move thousands of black-and-white pages a year, don't care much about typographic sophistication, and have the full-blown systems you need for that kind of work.

Interleaf lets you automate production to a greater degree than other Mac programs. There's automatic figure numbering, cross-referencing, graphics that float with anchors in the text, indexing, table-of-contents generation, vertical justification, column balancing (so the columns on the last page of a multicolumn document are equal length), and a robust "diagramming" environment (including draw tools and business graphics).

To take advantage of Interleaf's powers, though, you'll need a very sophisti-cated operator — preferably one who doesn't balk at a bit of programming. With that kind of proficiency (and the programming tools — be they BASIC or Unix programs), you can automate publishing tasks to the point that Interleaf will automatically build your weekly report for you, reading, filtering, cleaning up, and formatting files from several sources, all untouched by human hands.

While Interleaf offers features you won't find in other Mac programs, it goes beyond being uncomfortable in the Mac environment; it's actively hostile. It imposes enough penalties that you have to wonder why you aren't using a Unix platform — a Sun workstation or the like — with all the multiprocessing, multitasking, and myriad utilities that Unix provides.

For really big black-and-white projects — especially technical material — Interleaf Publisher for the Mac is worth a look, but only for sophisticated, full-time page makers in multiplatform environments who don't need great typo-graphics, but do need to spend some of their time using other Mac applications.

Springboard Publisher — the affordable alternative

Are you looking for a page-makeup program under $200? Springboard Publisher may be it. It's no toy, and I've seen it in ads for under $100 (which is where it starts getting attractive). For that price you can't expect many power tools, but if you occasionally need to produce reports, brochures, newsletters, or the like, you'll find the basic tools you need here.

You can create text and graphics frames; lay out columns of type easily; wrap type around graphics automatically; draw lines, boxes, and ovals; edit and create bitmapped art (72 dpi) right on the page; and number pages automatically. There's an ingenious dialog for linking text frames (it's not as easy as clicking on successive frames, but it works nicely; see Figure 2-14), and a separate typing window that makes larger edits much easier than editing on the page (you can still edit on the page, of course).

So what's missing? You're limited to full-point increments for type and leading; you can't edit when you're zoomed out; can't zoom with a Command-click; don't have a pasteboard or a grabber hand for moving the page around; must shift to a separate mode to create and modify lines, boxes, and ovals; and — you may find this to be Springboard Publisher's worst flaw — you can't fill frames, rectangles, or circles with grays. You can only apply grays and patterns to the lines around frames, or fill frames with 72-dpi bitmapped patterns.

Aside from the fill problem, Springboard Publisher doesn't have any obviously fatal design flaws. It's a capable little program for the casual page maker, it comes with Smart Art, an excellent graphics utility from Adobe Systems, and the $199 price is hard to beat.

Personal Press — strictly for beginners

When Aldus Corporation, the creators of PageMaker, bought Silicon Beach Software last year, one of the properties the company picked up was a page-layout program called Personal Press, designed for beginning and occasional page makers

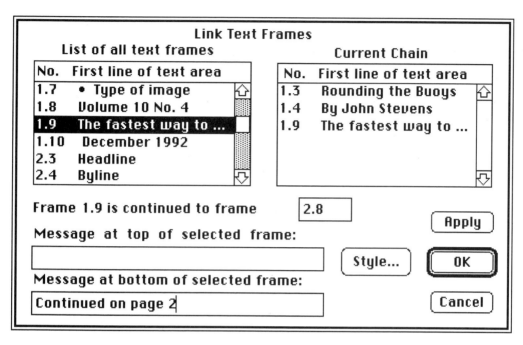

Figure 2-14: Springboard's Link Text Frames dialog box makes it easy to connect one text frame to another, and to attach continued lines at the top and bottom of frames.

and priced at $299. The program draws on many of the strengths of Silicon Beach's other programs (notably SuperPaint and Digital Darkroom), and even adds a little of Aldus's prowess in the form of import filters.

One notable interface innovation is Personal Press's use of Proxies (see Figure 2-15). Almost every dialog box lets you see a representation of the changes you're making on the actual text or graphic you're working on, so you can try things out before you click OK. Another innovation is the facility for placing Posted Notes on any page, containing the date, time, and any notes you want to pass on to your workgroup cohorts. You can hide or show the Posted Notes, and print them out as well.

Personal Press is lacking the now-ubiquitous pasteboard — a place for storing items temporarily off the page. To make up for this, it provides a Workbook — a scrapbook-like window in which you can store page elements.

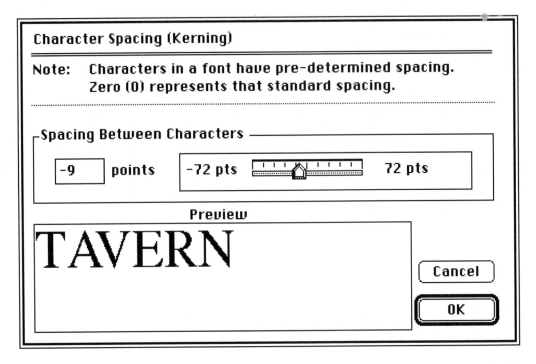

Figure 2-15: Most of Personal Press's dialog boxes let you see a Proxy — a representation of what your text or graphic will look like after you've made changes.

There are tools for creating boxes — containers for text and graphics — as well as lines and ovals, and tools to place the time, date, or page number anywhere on the page (though not within a line of text). You can specify the elements' sizes and positions either numerically or with the mouse, make them visible or not, locked or not, and printable or not, and as with most programs, you can apply lines and fills to those elements.

There's a wide variety of line and fill patterns (familiar from Silicon Beach's SuperPaint), though you can't specify a simple percentage tint. The greatest problem, though, is that you can't specify a line thickness smaller than one point, which almost guarantees that publications will look amateurish.

Personal Press offers nice control over how page elements are stacked; in addition to the normal Send to Back and Bring to Front commands, you can shuffle elements back and forth one layer at a time, nudge elements, and align them. There's a very flexible Replicate function, and an Equals tool makes it easy to make two objects the same size and shape.

Like its cousin PageMaker, Personal Press lets you have only one publication open at a time, and though you can import formatted stories into Personal Press from PageMaker publications (for those who are coming down in the world), you can't import stories from other Personal Press publications.

You can either import text into boxes in Personal Press or type right on the page. Once the text is there you can bring a well-designed spelling checker and thesaurus to bear. You can only edit text at 100 percent magnification, however; when you choose the text tool, Personal Press automatically takes you to 100% view, and all the text boxes come to the front, obscuring graphic objects that were in front of them.

The type-formatting controls are rudimentary, which is perhaps to be expected in a low-end page layout program (though it's not true of Publish It! Easy). You can specify type size, leading, word spacing, and kerning in 1-point increments, but there's no automatic kerning, which would be an obvious way to help novice users create good-looking publications. Personal Press's style sheets (named sets of formatting attributes that you can apply to selected text) are also pretty rudimentary; they only include character formatting — no paragraph formatting such as indents and tabs.

You can import most Macintosh graphics into Personal Press — the Big Four (PICT, EPS, TIFF, and Paint), plus SuperPaint and Digital Darkroom PICT, and Digital Darkroom archives. Once you've imported the graphics, you can scale them to a given size (though not a percentage) or scale them to fill the graphic box either proportionally or nonproportionally.

Personal Press's AutoCreate feature is designed to let novices build documents quickly based on the provided templates. A separate manual describes the templates ("you need four stories and three graphics for this newsletter"), so you can just choose the boxes and choose the text and graphics that are to fill them. Personal Press then builds the publication, pulling the files into the template.

The templates have one key flaw, however: they don't include style sheets (the lack of paragraph formatting in styles would be sorely missed if the templates had any style sheets). So once you've flowed the text in, you're on your own for specing the type. The templates aren't very attractive in the first place, and most users will find they need to adjust them considerably to make them work with their contents, so their utility is questionable.

The manuals and online help for Personal Press are excellent — providing both step-by-step guidance and big-picture understanding. The features in the program are generally well implemented, but it sports an odd mix of power-user features (notably the Replicate and Image Control features) that beginning page

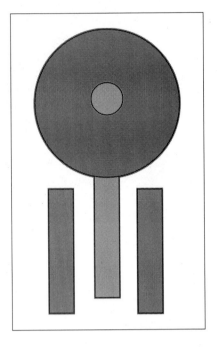

Figure 2-16: This sample shows filled shapes from Personal Press as printed on an Apple LaserWriter. Note how the fills extend beyond the boundaries of the shapes.

makers won't find much use for, and limitations (1-point minimum line weight, lack of automatic kerning) that make it hard for novices to produce good-looking documents. Though features such as Proxies and Posted Notes are great innovations, they don't make up for those more basic failings.

The old software adage "never marry a program with 1.0 in its name" holds true here. There's at least one serious problem with printing — the fills of boxes often hang outside of the box (see Figure 2-16) — and Personal Press crashed a lot on me unless I kept my system stripped down.

The program also needs work in fine-tuning the design and feature list to suit the newcomers to page makeup to whom it's being marketed.

In choosing between Personal Press, which makes it easy to create bad pages, and its less expensive competitor, Publish It! Easy, which makes it possible (and not difficult) to create good pages, I would definitely opt for Publish It! Easy.

Publish It! Easy — a lot of bang for the buck

When writing about Publish It, it's always a challenge to avoid dropping into a straight feature list. Many people refer to it as the Swiss army knife of desktop publishing, and since it includes robust tools for page layout, text editing, drawing, and painting, that moniker is appropriate.

Almost in the same breath, though, people tend to bemoan Publish It's clunky, cluttered interface. It's hard to avoid with so many features, but it makes the program hard to use. Timeworks has addressed those complaints admirably in a pared-down, streamlined, inexpensive ($249.95) version of Publish It by the name of Publish It! Easy.

While removing features was one method of simplifying the program, Timeworks hasn't stripped it of its jack-of-all-trades ambience. It still has a more-than-impressive toolbox and feature list — enough to keep most nonprofessional page makers very happy. Its tools for drawing, object alignment, and rotation (anything, in 1-degree increments), in particular, put it ahead of some of the big guns.

There's good text editing, including Find and Change (based on and/or including character formatting), spell-checking, and even a thesaurus (Thesaurus•Rex). Text formatting includes most of the controls that casual users need, plus some nice bells and whistles like automatic and manual kerning (in full-point increments), baseline shifts, and expanded or condensed type (1 percent increments). There are import filters for MacWrite, Microsoft Word (versions 3 and 4), WordPerfect (Macintosh), WriteNow, and even Microsoft Excel. Hyphenation is a batch, rather than an interactive process — select the text and use the Insert Hyphens command — but it's quite speedy and pretty smart.

Publish It! Easy imports all the standard graphics files, including gray-scale TIFF. It only offers seven standard colors, and though you can print to a color printer, don't expect spot color overlays; printing is basic and limited.

The most important changes aren't really in what's missing, they're in the interface. More than anything, Publish It! Easy stands out for its interactiveness. It's great for casual users who often find themselves trying things out on the page rather than plotting everything in advance the way professionals do. As you resize a text frame, for instance, the text reflows inside the frame interactively; it doesn't wait for you to release the mouse button. Most of its dialog boxes let you see the results of your changes before you click OK to close the box. And several palettes make it easy to get at the profusion of tools (see Figure 2-17).

The text library (see Figure 2-18) is perhaps the most innovative feature. You can adjust almost every text-formatting command — font, size, leading, kerning, etc. — by clicking to select it in the library.

If you change your mind, just click on Undo/Redo, and you get a list of your changes to that frame's text, so you can choose which to undo and redo. It's not totally selective, though; if you undo the second-to-last change, for instance, you also undo the last one. When you come back to that frame later, your undo/redo list is still there.

Publish It! Easy is one of the few page-makeup programs that actually let you see objects move as you drag them around on the page. Bear in mind, though, that you'll need more than a single megabyte (or else a stripped-down system) to make this effective.

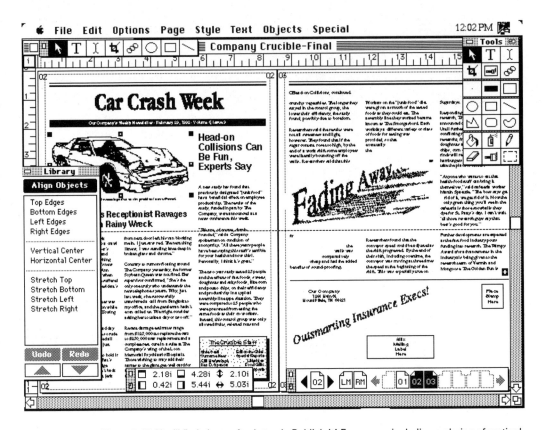

Figure 2-17: You'll find plenty of palettes in Publish It! Easy, even including a choice of vertical or horizontal toolboxes. You can shrink or enlarge them with the zoom boxes, and turn them on and off selectively.

So what's wrong with Publish It! Easy? Not a whole lot, especially considering the low (and heavily discounted) price tag. There are limitations — like its restriction to integral point sizes — that aren't a great problem for general business users, but some other things are more than annoying. The ruler guides (one horizontal and one vertical per document) are just as clunky and unusable as in its older brother; you can't create custom page sizes — just the standard letter, legal, and so on, in the print dialog box. There are no "continued on" lines and no style sheets.

Publish It! Easy is also a bit slow in some operations (such as text selection), but — this is surprising — most operations are not a whole lot slower on a Mac Plus than on a II (hyphenation and other batch operations are notable exceptions). It runs

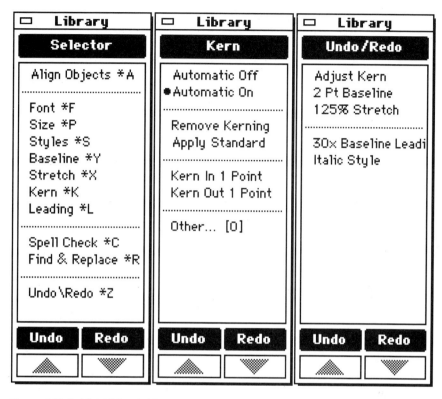

Figure 2-18: Publish It! Easy's Library palette lets you make most of your changes to text formatting without resorting to menus and dialog boxes. Click on any item in the Selector and you can control that aspect of text formatting. Click on Undo/Redo and you can selectively undo changes you've made in that text frame.

well on Pluses and SEs, and weighs in at less than 290K on disk, plus space for the dictionary, thesaurus, and so on.

The problems with Publish It! Easy are annoyances more than fatal flaws. It is a heck of a lot of page-layout program for a great price. It's a much better value than Springboard Publisher or Personal Press.

RagTime 3 — combined strength for business users

You may well have heard of RagTime before. It's very popular in Europe, and has been introduced (or at least announced) twice before in the States. For various reasons the distribution arrangements fell apart, and for this third attempt with RagTime 3, MacVonk (the Dutch creator) has set up a U.S. subsidiary to publish the product.

At first glance, RagTime 3 looks like a page-layout program with spreadsheet and graphing features. You do all your work on pages that scroll down the screen like a filmstrip, and you can zoom in and out as in page-layout programs. When you get to know it, though, you realize that RagTime is more like integrated programs such as Microsoft Works — but more integrated. The best description for RagTime might be business document processor. It offers most of the tools business users need to produce reports, proposals, memos, newsletters, and reasonably complex, intelligent forms.

There are five modes in RagTime — the basic page-layout mode, in which you create frames to contain text, text spreadsheets, graphs, and pictures — and modes for working with each of those frame types. The menus and tool bars change depending on which mode you're using (see Figure 2-19).

Unlike Works, which requires you to change between modes and copy and paste elements into the word processor, RagTime puts everything right on the page. If you click on a spreadsheet frame, you're in spreadsheet mode. Click on a text frame, and you're in text mode.

You can reference information from a spreadsheet frame from any point in the text or another spreadsheet, so when the first spreadsheet changes, the reference is updated. Charts also update automatically when their source spreadsheets change. These are not warm links — they're hot.

Frame creation is simple and intuitive, though it would be greatly improved by the addition of rulers and guides as in most page-layout programs. To create a frame you just draw a box (sorry, rectangles only) with the frame tool and decide what type of frame it is. You can also draw lines, but no circles. Frames can have rounded corners, lines can have arrowhead ends, and any line or box can have a drop shadow (there's no control over the appearance of arrowheads and shadows, however). Options let you wrap text around frames, make frames transparent, and anchor frames to text so they move when text reflows.

You can build very complex pages and save them as Forms, so you can simply tear off a new form when you need one — great for sales and expense reports, calendars, and the like.

The basic frame, not surprisingly, is the text frame, in which you can enter and format text. It's unfortunate that, despite its impressive strengths in other areas, RagTime's word processing (arguably the most important feature) is somewhat lacking. It's competent, but far from a top-flight word processor. It provides search-and-replace, spell checking, and hyphenation in more than half a dozen languages (most dictionaries haven't been released yet in the U.S.), but there's no

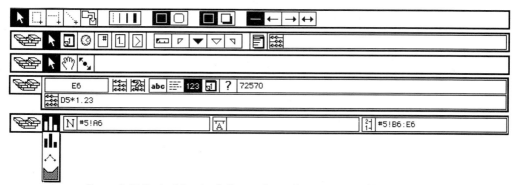

Figure 2-19: Each of Ragtime's five modes — frame, text, graphic, spreadsheet, and graph — uses a different toolbox. The menus also change according to what mode you're in.

index or table-of-contents generation, footnoting, figure numbering, or outlining, and sorting is only available within spreadsheets.

RagTime offers the basics in text formatting, with all adjustments in full-point increments (except manual kerning, which works in quarter points). Character formatting includes custom sizes up to 999 points, fractional spacing, colored and tinted type, condensed and expanded type (which actually just alters letter spacing), and adjustable sub- and superscripts. You can build all of these attributes into a Type Macro so they're easy to apply, and you can search for and change character formats throughout a document. Though these features come close, they aren't as powerful as true style sheets because they don't affect paragraph formatting.

Paragraph formatting is accomplished through rulers in the text that apply to ensuing paragraphs, up to the next ruler. They let you control leading (fixed or automatic, in one-point increments), alignment (left, right, center, justified), left and right margins, first-line indents, and tabs (right, left, center, and decimal, with or without leader characters of your choice). You can cut and paste rulers, and adjust attributes for the current ruler or all following rulers. The rulers are quite small, but an ingenious pop-up measurement tells you where your indents and tabs are positioned as you drag them (see Figure 2-20).

RagTime will import graphics in all the usual formats — PICT, EPS, Paint, and TIFF (including gray scale and 24-bit color TIFF, within memory limits). You can size and crop as you'd expect in a page-makeup program, apply colors to colorize black-and-white art, and adjust gray and color levels for multibit TIFF images.

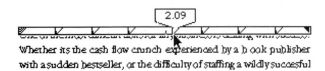

Whether its the cash flow crunch experienced by a book publisher
with a sudden bestseller, or the difficulty of staffing a wildly successful

---

Line Spacing

◉ **Fixed Spacing**
   in Points: `13`

Automatic Spacing:

○ 1 Line   +/- `0`   Points
○ 1 1/2 Lines
○ 2 Lines

Paragraph Spacing

○ **Fixed Spacing in Points:**

above: `0`   **below:** `0`

Automatic Spacing:

○ 1 Line
◉ 1 1/2 Lines
○ 2 Lines

☐ **No distance between text and upper/lower frame borders.**

Tab Fill Character: `.`   [**OK**]   [**Cancel**]

Figure 2-20: Ragtime's rulers determine paragraph formatting. You can adjust indents and tabs by dragging with the mouse, and line spacing via the ruler dialog box.

Live spreadsheet power

RagTime's Spreadsheet mode offers impressive powers, with many or most of the features (but somewhat less speed) than stand-alone spreadsheets like Excel and Wingz. You'll find a heady array of arithmetic, logical, scientific, date, data, and financial functions. There's a Button function that lets you turn a cell into a functioning button that is activated when you click on it. Even mail merging is accomplished through functions in spreadsheets, which makes this important feature quite difficult to learn, but flexible in execution.

A special type of cell — wraparound text — lets you type running text in a cell without using carriage returns and constantly adjusting the cell height manually. You can format text within a wraparound cell just as you can other text, including paragraph ruler formatting.

The most important feature of these spreadsheets, though, is that they are live, right on the page, and you can reference values in those spreadsheets from elsewhere in the document, or even from other RagTime documents. For the bulk of business documents, RagTime's spreadsheet powers are more than ample.

To build a graph based on spreadsheet data, you simply select the cells you want to graph and paste them into a graph frame. While you're limited to bar, pie, and fever graphs, the number of controls for each results in a lot of flexibility. Change the source spreadsheet values, and the graph changes accordingly (you can also freeze the values for the graph).

One of RagTime's best features is its strong support of multiple paper bins on specific printers. You can print the first sheet from one bin (letterhead, for instance) and ensuing sheets from another. You can print alternating pages for two-sided printing, with good control to allow for paper-feed variations between printers.

RagTime is not quite as strong as its competitors in any one area, especially in word processing, but its combined strengths, particularly in page layout, put it well beyond Microsoft Works and the like for most business users. Works still wins for its database, which is much easier than RagTime's spreadsheet data functions, for mail merging, and for drawing tools, but RagTime is much better at assembling complete, live documents. If you want to learn only one program, and need spreadsheets, graphs, graphics, basic word processing, and reasonable page-makeup tools, you won't go wrong spending $599 on RagTime 3.

Multi-Ad Creator — the multilayout approach

You probably haven't heard of Multi-Ad Creator. Even though the first version of this single-page layout program was impressive, it didn't get much play in the press or the page-makeup community. That may be remedied with the newer versions which are, in simple terms, great. There is one possibly fatal flaw, however — it only handles single pages.

If you're familiar with the PageMaker interface, or are looking for a program that equals it, you'll be comfortable in Multi-Ad Creator. The pasteboard, ruler guides, command-click zooming, grabber hand, flowing text blocks, placing conventions (no need to create frames first), and block-to-block text flow are all similar to PageMaker's functions, but in most cases, better. These people have been taking notes. You can't see objects (just bounding boxes) while you're moving or scaling them, though, with the exception of Creator-created graphics.

While all these features are attractive to designers, Creator's multilayout approach is a downright godsend. You can design the same page — with the same elements — many different ways, and store all the layouts in one document. No more Save As with a dozen cryptically named files on disk. You can flip through your alternate layouts, see them side-by-side, or print them all. Creator will even *suggest* layouts, based on rules you specify.

Creator's typographics are good, but it's missing automatic tracking, forced justification (surprising and unfortunate), and control over justification parameters. The style sheets, however, are the best designed and implemented of any Mac program I've seen (see Figure 2-21).

You can set up both paragraph and character styles, and paragraph styles can specify any character style for the paragraph text (and yes, local formatting overrides styles). There are even Style Models that automatically apply styles to successive paragraphs or text regions as they hit the page. Creator does not import Word's styles, however, or any paragraph formatting — only character formatting (less of a problem in a single-page environment).

There's a good complement of draw tools in Creator, including polygons and comic-book-style starbursts, but not including a Bezier-curve tool (smoothed polygons are the substitute). You can automatically wrap text inside or outside any of these shapes (but you can't crop or clip pictures within them), and even ask Creator to copy-fit for you — adjusting type size and rewrapping text iteratively within a frame until it gets it to fit. Creator will produce either spot-color overlays or process separations — including separations of scanned color images, even 32-bit files.

The trade-off for all this power is somewhat sluggish performance. The price ($795) and slow speed (requiring a 68020 or better) put this program out of the ballpark for anyone except full-time designers and those with ample budgets. And if you do any multipage work, you'll need one of the other programs in addition to this one (PageMaker's a good choice because of the similar interface). If you have the budget, though, and do much advertising design or production, Multi-Ad Creator is a top choice.

Choosing and using

So which program should you buy and use? Choose QuarkXPress for design intensive production work, especially for color. PageMaker's a top choice for designers who like to try out designs on screen. Multi-Ad Creator is great for full-time ad designers, though you should probably also have PageMaker or QuarkXPress around for multipage documents (and you might want FreeHand or Illustrator for the more demanding illustrative and color jobs).

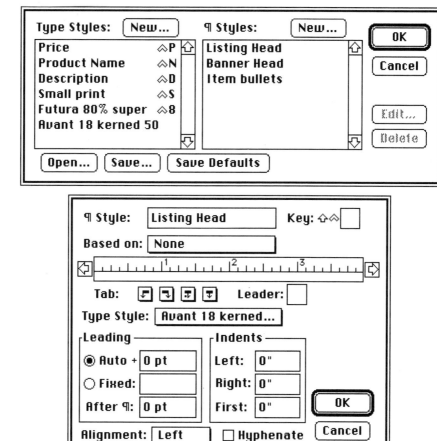

Figure 2-21: Multi-Ad Creator provides both character and paragraph styles. You can use a character style as the basis for the type formatting of a paragraph style.

For long-document publishers who don't mind deep dialog boxes and planning everything in advance, choose Ventura Publisher. If you can only have one program for both long-document and design intensive work, buy PageMaker. If your whole workgroup — writers, editors, and production people — is going to be set up in one program, FrameMaker is very attractive, given the high price.

For occasional page makers, the top choice is Publish It! Easy. It has an impressive toolbox and better controls than either Personal Press or Springboard Publisher. And if what you really want is a multipurpose business document processor disguised as a page-layout program (and you're not worried about what everyone else uses), choose RagTime.

Summary

✔ At $795, PageMaker is near the top of the page-makeup price spectrum, but in many ways it's worth every penny. Aldus is well known for its impressive tech support, customer service, documentation, and special items like tech notes. Along with a solid, well-rounded program, those factors add up to a friendly environment both for novices and for full-time page makers.

✔ If you can afford top dollar ($795, same as PageMaker) and want the best tools for complex designs, including rotated items and color, QuarkXPress is your best bet.

✔ Design Studio lives up to its name (and its $795 price); it's a full-blown designer's tool, appropriate for people designing pages day in and day out. Its poor style sheets, memory limitations, and lack of Undo for many functions make it much less useful for production publishers than PageMaker or QuarkXPress, though, and casual users will probably balk at its complexity.

✔ Although the Mac version of Ventura Publisher is still young and doesn't fit into the Macintosh environment with complete ease, it is still a remarkable program. Occasional page makers are better off with one of the more free-form programs like QuarkXPress, PageMaker, or Publish It! Easy. But for people who aren't afraid of numerous, deep dialog boxes, who can afford a top-dollar program (yes, yet again, $795), who plan their publications in advance, and especially those who are producing long, structured documents, I highly recommend Ventura.

✔ Given the concept behind its design — that everyone from writers to production workers use FrameMaker and work on a common live file — this program is magnificent. It's very solid, makes excellent use of the Macintosh interface (these folks got religion), and brings features to the Macintosh that we've never seen before.

✔ For really big black-and-white projects — especially technical material — Interleaf Publisher for the Mac is worth a look, but only for sophisticated, full-time page makers in multiplatform environments who don't need great typographics, but do need to spend some of their time using other Mac applications.

✔ Aside from not being able to fill shapes with gray, Springboard Publisher doesn't have any obviously fatal design flaws. It's a capable little program for the casual page maker, it comes with Smart Art, an excellent graphics utility from Adobe Systems, and the $199 price is hard to beat.

✔ With Personal Press, the old adage, "never marry a program with 1.0 in it's name," holds true. In choosing between Personal Press, which makes it easy to create bad pages, and its less expensive competitor, Publish It! Easy, which makes it possible (and not difficult) to create good pages, I would definitely opt for Publish It! Easy.

✔ Publish It! Easy stands out for its interactiveness. It's great for casual users who often find themselves trying things out on the page rather than planning everything in advance. Overall, it's a heck of a lot of page-layout program for a great price.

✔ If you want to learn only one program and need spreadsheets, graphs, graphics, basic word processing, and reasonable page-makeup tools, you won't go wrong spending $599 on RagTime 3.

✔ Multi-Ad Creator is an impressive layout program with its main flaw being that it only handles single pages. If you have the budget, though, and do much advertising design or production, Multi-Ad Creator is a top choice.

Where to buy

DesignStudio, $795
Letraset, Nielsen, & Bainbridge
40 Eisenhower Dr.
Paramus, NJ 07653
201-845-6100

FrameMaker, $795
Frame Technology
1010 Rincon Circle
San Jose, CA 95131
408-433-3311

Interleaf Publisher, $995
Interleaf, Inc.
Prospect Place
9 Hillside Ave.
Waltham, MA 02154
617-290-0710

Multi-Ad Creator, $795
Multi-Ad Services
1720 W. Detweiller Dr.
Peoria, IL 61615
309-692-1530

PageMaker, $795
Aldus Corp.
411 First Ave. S
Seattle, WA 98104
206-622-5500

Personal Press, $299
Aldus Corp.
411 First Ave. S
Seattle, WA 98104
206-622-5500

Publish It, $249.95
Timeworks, Inc.
625 Academy Dr.
Northbrook, IL 60062
708-559-1310
708-559-1399 (FAX)

Publish It! Easy 1.10, $249.95
Timeworks, Inc.
625 Academy Dr.
Northbrook, IL 60062
708-559-1310
708-559-1399 (FAX)

QuarkXPress, $795
Quark, Inc.
300 South Jackson
Denver, CO 80209
303-934-2211

RagTime, $599
RagTime USA
702 Marshall St.
Redwood City, CA 94063
415-780-1800

ReadySetGo, $295
Letraset, Nielsen, & Bainbridge
40 Eisenhower Dr.
Paramus, NJ 07653
201-845-6100

Springboard Publisher, $199
Spinnaker Software
201 Broadway
Cambridge, MA 02139
617-494-1200
800-826-0706
617-494-1219 (FAX)

Ventura Publisher, $795
Ventura Software Inc.
A Xerox Company
15715 Innovation Drive
San Diego, CA 92128
800-822-8221 (upgrades only)

Chapter 3
Fonts

by Erfert Fenton

In this chapter...

- ✐ Becoming familiar with basic font terminology.
- ✐ Practical exercises for installing fonts with the Font/ DA Mover, ATM, Suitcase II, and MasterJuggler.
- ✐ Organizing font menus with font utilities.
- ✐ A look at type design and type effects programs.

No matter which applications you use on your Macintosh, they all share a common element — fonts. Your exposure to fonts might be minimal if you work primarily with spreadsheets or databases, but if you use a word processor, page-layout application, presentation program, or any application that produces documents that will be seen by others, you should learn how to make the most of Macintosh fonts. This chapter introduces you to basic font terminology, explains how to install and organize your fonts, and describes dozens of utilities that let you do everything from reorder a font menu to add special effects to type.

Types of type: a brief history of Mac fonts

These days, there are two species of Macintosh fonts: bitmapped fonts and outline fonts. Within the category of outline fonts you'll encounter two subspecies: PostScript and TrueType. Let's take a look at each kind.

Bitmapped fonts

Bitmapped fonts are characters made up of a map of dots, or *bits* in computer parlance. (The term bit is short for *binary digit* — the ones and zeros that determine whether a dot on the screen is turned on or off.) The characters you see on the Mac's screen are bitmapped characters. Bitmapped characters are displayed and printed at a resolution of 72 dots per inch — the resolution of the Mac's display. Therefore, what you see on the screen is what you get on paper (see Figure 3-1). A few tricks can be employed to improve the appearance of printed bitmaps — you can check the Smoothing option in an application's Page Setup dialog box, or ask a dot-matrix printer such as the Image-Writer II to print at Best quality, which doubles the printed output's resolution. Bitmapped fonts are available from Casady & Greene, Dubl-Click Software, and other companies, as well as from Mac user groups and online services. You can make your own bitmapped fonts with Altsys Corporation's Fontastic.

Outline fonts

When the Macintosh was introduced, bitmapped fonts were the only game in town. The fonts that came with the Mac, as well as those offered by various vendors, were certainly superior to the ungainly glyphs of pre-Mac computers, but they didn't exactly set the typographic world on fire. Enter Apple's Laser-

About the author

Erfert Fenton has been writing and editing for *Macworld* since its premier issue in 1984. She has a B.A. in Fine Arts from the University of Colorado, and graduated with honors from the "Computer Writers' School of Hard Knocks," which included stints at Osborne/ McGraw Hill and *PC World* magazine. She regularly writes feature articles and reviews for *Macworld*; her article on typesetting service bureaus won a 1989 Maggie award. She is also the author of *The Macintosh Font Book* (Peachpit Press, 1989) and coauthor of *Canned Art: Clip Art for the Macintosh* (Peachpit Press, 1990).

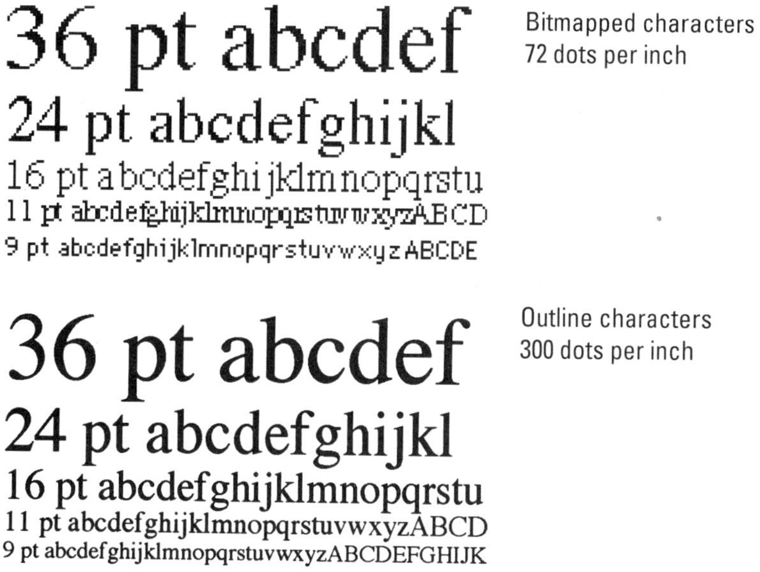

36 pt abcdef

Bitmapped characters
72 dots per inch

24 pt abcdefghijkl

16 pt abcdefghijklmnopqrstu

11 pt abcdefghijklmnopqrstuvwxyzABCD

9 pt abcdefghijklmnopqrstuvwxyzABCDE

36 pt abcdef

Outline characters
300 dots per inch

24 pt abcdefghijkl

16 pt abcdefghijklmnopqrstu

11 pt abcdefghijklmnopqrstuvwxyzABCD

9 pt abcdefghijklmnopqrstuvwxyzABCDEFGHIJK

Figure 3-1: Bitmapped characters (top) are displayed and printed at 72 dpi; PostScript outline fonts (bottom) can be scaled to any size and can be displayed and printed at 300 dpi.

Writer printer in 1985. The LaserWriter introduced a new type of type — *Post-Script outline fonts*. The LaserWriter included a built-in programming language called PostScript, which Apple licensed from Adobe Systems. PostScript could scale fonts to any size via a master outline; instead of installing a bit-mapped font for every size to be printed, a user could simply select any size and let PostScript handle the scaling. PostScript font outlines are made up of Bezier curves, which consist of points on a path and separate control points outside the path; PostScript characters are shown in Figure 3-1. In addition to offering virtually unlimited font sizes, the LaserWriter had a resolution of 300 dots per inch (dpi) — a vast improvement over the 72-dpi resolution of bitmapped fonts. Better still, the LaserWriter's PostScript let you produce graphics as well as text, ushering in the era of desktop publishing.

The original LaserWriter included 13 built-in fonts; later versions came with 35. But even 35 fonts weren't enough for many publishers, especially when you consider that each style or weight (Helvetica Plain, Helvetica Bold, Helvetica Italic, and Helvetica Bold Italic, for example) was counted as a separate font. Several font foundries soon filled the void with *downloadable fonts*, PostScript fonts that could be installed on the Mac and sent to the LaserWriter. (In most cases, applications automatically download fonts, which means the fonts you use in a document are simply sent to the printer. To improve printing speed, you can use a utility like Adobe's Font Downloader or Apple's LaserWriter Font Utility to manually download one or more fonts to the printer. Unlike automatically downloaded fonts, manually downloaded fonts stay in the printer's memory until it's turned off.)

Established type companies such as Linotype (now known as Linotype-Hell) offered downloadable PostScript fonts, as well as small upstarts like Casadyware (later called Casady & Greene). Altsys came out with Fontographer, a $500 type-creation program that put type design into the hands of individuals and started a cottage industry of digital type designers. But there was a difference between the downloadable fonts offered by Linotype and those offered by individual designers and small type shops; Linotype's fonts contained programming instructions called hints, which subtly altered character shapes to make them look good when printed at 300 dpi. Linotype and other type foundries licensed Adobe's font-creation tools, allowing them to produce hinted fonts. Fonts made with Adobe's technology were also *encrypted,* which meant that users couldn't access character outlines and edit or reshape them. Adobe-licensed fonts were called *Type 1 fonts,* while those created by other manufacturers were called *Type 3 fonts* (Type 2 fonts disappeared somewhere in the process of PostScript font evolution).

PostScript continued to evolve over the years and quickly became an imaging and printing standard. Linotype introduced a series of *imagesetters* that, like the LaserWriter, output PostScript text and graphics, but at a much higher resolution — 1,250 or 2,470 dpi. Other manufacturers, including Varityper and Compugraphic, introduced high-resolution PostScript imagesetters as well, and desktop publishing began to compete with traditional typesetting.

In the late 1980s, a number of printer companies introduced *PostScript clone* printers (or *PostScript-compatible* printers, as the companies preferred to call them), with versions of PostScript licensed from developers other than Adobe. The first clones had trouble printing Adobe's Type 1 PostScript fonts, so they offered built-in fonts from other companies, notably Bitstream. (By now, most clone printers can process Adobe fonts.)

PostScript was sailing along smoothly as the established printing standard until 1989, when Apple dropped a bombshell — the company was working on its own outline font format, code-named Royal (the new format is now called *TrueType*). This news caused considerable consternation in the font-using community. Many applauded Apple for offering developers an "open" font format, as opposed to Adobe's proprietary font-creation tools. PostScript font fans — from desktop publishers with modest font collections to typesetting service bureau owners with tens of thousands of dollars invested in PostScript technology — gnashed their teeth at the prospect of dealing with a new format. Many heated discussions ensued, and for several months you couldn't pick up a computer magazine without reading about font wars. Adobe relinquished some ground by publishing the specifications for its Type 1 format, but stole some of TrueType's thunder by introducing Adobe Type Manager (ATM), a utility that automatically scaled fonts to virtually any size for screen display or non-PostScript printing.

> ❝ *Now that some of the dust of battle has settled, it looks like PostScript and True-Type fonts are destined to coexist.* ❞

Now that some of the dust of battle has settled, it looks like PostScript and TrueType fonts are destined to coexist. TrueType scaling is included with Apple's System 7; you simply install TrueType fonts and the Mac automatically scales them to any size you select. TrueType fonts can also be sent to inexpensive printers such as the Apple StyleWriter (the StyleWriter costs so little because it doesn't contain PostScript; the Mac and TrueType, rather than built-in printer software, do all the font-scaling work). But System 7 and non-PostScript printers like the StyleWriter work with ATM and PostScript fonts as well. PostScript font owners don't need to replace or upgrade their current fonts, as many feared. You can even mix PostScript and TrueType fonts in the same document, if you're so inclined, and print the document on a PostScript or non-PostScript printer. And if you want to standardize your font format, you can use a utility such as Altsys's Metamorphosis Professional or Ares Software's FontMonger to convert fonts from PostScript to TrueType format, or vice versa.

Font installation

Installing TrueType fonts under System 7 is pretty easy; you simply drag an icon into the System Folder and click a button. The font is placed in the Mac's System file. To remove a font, you simply open the System file and drag the font icon out. TrueType fonts reside in a single icon; system software scales the TrueType outline for screen display and printing.

But not everyone will use TrueType or System 7; owners of older Macs (with less than 2MB of memory), users who choose not to upgrade to System 7, or those who have existing collections of PostScript fonts will have to employ the old-fashioned method of installation, which involves installing both bitmapped (screen) fonts and outline (printer) fonts. Times change, so be sure to read the documentation that comes with new fonts or printers, but for now, here are several font-installation strategies.

Three basic font-installation scenarios are presented here. A fourth scenario combines the utilities presented in the first three. The first scenario is a bare-bones approach using only the Font/DA Mover, for those who are still waiting for

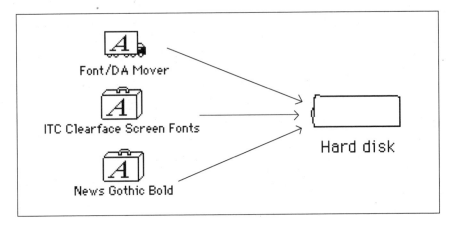

Figure 3-2: The Font/DA Mover and appropriate screen-font suitcases must be installed on your hard disk to copy the fonts you will use into the System Folder.

System 7 or don't intend to upgrade, and don't want to spend any money on extra utilities. The second scenario introduces Adobe Type Manager, which allows you to save space on your hard disk by installing a minimal number of screen fonts. The final scenario deals with font/DA extenders, which save time, disk space, and Font/DA Mover hassles by enabling you to turn screen fonts on and off without installing them in your System file.

For the following exercises, we'll install a set of PostScript fonts for a hypothetical newsletter: Adobe's ITC Clearface Regular, at 12 points, for the text; Clearface Bold Italic, at 10 points, for figure titles; Clearface Regular Italic, at 10 points, for figure captions; and Bitstream's News Gothic Bold, at 18 and 14 points, for two levels of headings. The exercises assume you have a hard drive, Font/DA Mover version 3.8 or later, and several PostScript fonts.

Scenario 1: Font/DA Mover

Apple's Font/DA Mover lets you install selected sizes of screen fonts into the Mac's System file, where they are then available to any application. Screen fonts come packed in an icon that looks like a suitcase. (Note: If you have System 6.0.7 or later, you can use TrueType fonts with Font/DA Mover 4.1 or later and Apple's TrueType INIT.)

1. Place a copy of the Font/DA Mover on your hard disk. Copy a screen-font suitcase for each font you'll be installing on your hard disk (see Figure 3-2). (Adobe and Bitstream arrange their screen fonts differently; Adobe's Clearface family resides in a single suitcase, while the screen fonts in Bitstream's

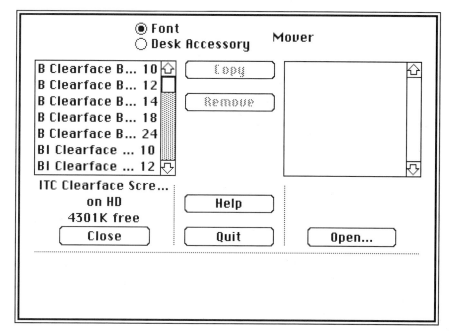

Figure 3-3: When you double-click the Clearface suitcase, the Font/DA Mover window displays the fonts in that suitcase.

MacFontware packages reside in a separate suitcase for each style. Therefore, in this example you'd copy the ITC Clearface suitcase — which contains plain, italic, bold, and bold italic — and the News Gothic Bold suitcase onto your hard disk.)

2. Double-click the Clearface suitcase icon. The Font/DA Mover window appears, with the fonts in that suitcase listed in the left-hand column (see Figure 3-3). Beneath the column, the Font/DA Mover displays the suitcase name and the name of the disk it's on (in this case, your hard disk).

3. Click the Open button beneath the right-hand column. A list of the files and folders on your hard disk appears. The Font/DA Mover installs fonts in your Mac's System file, so your first task is to find that file. Locate the System Folder in the list of files and folders, double-click it to open it, then double-click System to open the System file. A list of the screen fonts installed in your System file appears in the right-hand column of the Font/DA Mover. Beneath the column, the Font/DA Mover displays the file name (System) and the name of the disk it's on (in this case, your hard drive) as shown in Figure 3-4.

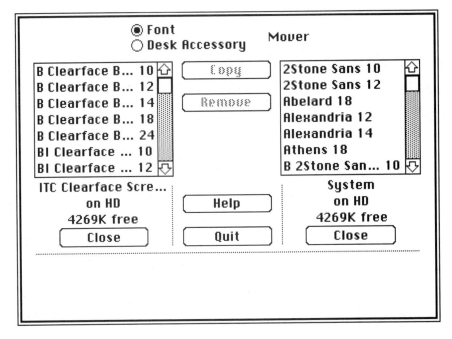

Figure 3-4: Once you have found the System Folder in the right-hand column of the Font/DA Mover, double-click it to open it, then double-click System to see the screen fonts installed in your System file.

4. In the left-hand column, click on the names of the font weights and sizes you wish to install, in this case Clearface Regular 12-point (Clearface Re... 12), Clearface Regular Italic 10-point (I Clearface R... 10), and Clearface Bold Italic 10-point (BI Clearface... 10). Hold down the Shift key as you select different fonts to select several at once, or hold down the mouse button and drag across a contiguous group of names.

When you've selected all the screen fonts you want to install, click the Copy button. Note that the arrows (>>) on the Copy button point toward the destination of the screen fonts — in this case, the System file (see Figure 3-5).

To install screen fonts from additional suitcases (in this example, Bitstream's News Gothic Bold), click the Close button below the left-hand column and select the appropriate suitcase from the list that appears. Repeat the procedure just described to install the additional font. When you've installed all the screen fonts you need, click the Quit button to return to the desktop.

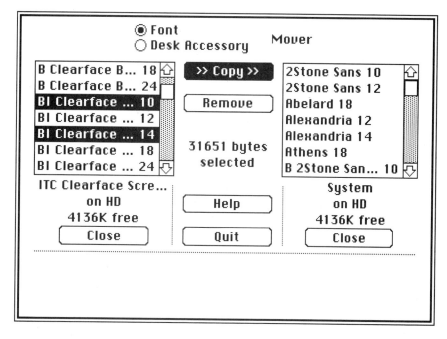

Figure 3-5: Selecting the screen fonts you want from the left-hand column of the Font/DA Mover and clicking Copy will install those fonts into the System file.

5. Now that you've installed the screen fonts you need, you can throw away your copies of the font suitcases, which are just taking up space on your hard drive. By installing only the sizes you need for the newsletter, you've conserved a considerable amount of disk space; the two suitcases in this example would take up a total of 818K if you installed every size and style in them, but installing only the fonts you need uses only 25K. If you need additional sizes or weights later, you can add them with the Font/DA Mover.

Note: You don't have to install a particular font size for that size to print correctly on a PostScript printer, but for the sake of on-screen readability you'll probably want to install all the sizes you'll be using. If a size isn't available, the Mac's built-in QuickDraw routines will create a rough approximation of characters in that size for screen display.)

6. Now that you've installed the appropriate screen fonts, it's time to install their corresponding printer fonts. *Install* is perhaps too intimidating a word; all you need to do is drag the printer font icon for each font into your System Folder (see Figure 3-6).

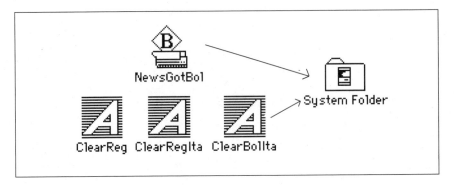

Figure 3-6: To install printer fonts onto your hard disk, drag the font icon for each font you want — in this case NewsGotBol, ClearReg, ClearRegIta, and ClearBolIta — into the System Folder.

Leave the printer fonts loose in the System Folder; if you place printer font icons into another folder within the System Folder, the Mac won't be able to locate them when it's time to print.

Note: You may notice a folder called "AFM" on the disk your fonts came on. AFM (Adobe Font Metrics) files contain font metrics and kerning information that's used by a few applications. Unless an application's manual tells you to install AFM files, you can ignore them.

Scenario 2: Adobe Type Manager

Using the Font/DA Mover to install all the screen font sizes you need is the cheapest way to go, since the Font/DA Mover is included with Apple's system software utilities. But if you use dozens of fonts, you'll be saving money but squandering disk space by using the Font/DA Mover. If you add Adobe Type Manager to your font utilities collection, you can install only a single size of each font and let ATM scale the characters for screen display and QuickDraw printing (Adobe suggests you install two sizes per font — say, 10 and 12 point — for optimum scaling).

Because ATM scales fonts to virtually any size, not only do you have to install fewer screen fonts to display typical sizes like 18 and 24 point, but you can also view previously undisplayable sizes like 38 or 55 point. And ATM saves owners of QuickDraw printers such as the LaserWriter II SC or the GCC Personal Laser Printer the trouble of installing the correct sizes of bitmapped fonts to be scaled by the printer.

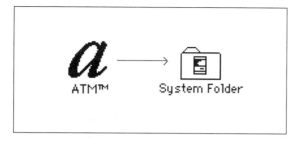

Figure 3-7: Dragging the ATM icon into the System Folder and restarting your Mac installs Adobe Type Manager onto your hard disk.

While the original release of ATM supported only Adobe Type 1 PostScript fonts, a subsequent release took care of that limitation; ATM now supports Type 1 fonts from other manufacturers also. And while some users complained that ATM's on-the-fly font scaling was more like on-the-crawl, the recently-released version 2.0 offers improved speed; version 2.0 is about twice as fast as the previous version.

1. ATM is a cdev (control panel device). To install it, you just drag the ATM icon into the System Folder and restart your Mac (see Figure 3-7). You can turn ATM on and off from the Control Panel and adjust the size of its font cache — a larger cache makes for faster scaling.

2. With ATM installed, use the Font/DA Mover as you did in the first exercise, but this time install only the 10- and 12-point sizes for each font you wish to place in the System file (see Figure 3-8).

   (If you're not a big fan of the Font/DA Mover, you're in luck. ATM 2.0 includes an INIT called Font Porter that lets you simply drag a suitcase icon into the System Folder to install screen fonts. When you restart your Mac, all the fonts in the suitcase are automatically loaded. Although this method does away with the Font/DA Mover, it also does away with one of the bonuses of ATM — saving disk space by installing a minimal number of screen fonts. As a compromise move, you might want to bite the bullet and use the Font/DA Mover to create custom suitcases filled with just the 10- and 12-point sizes of the fonts you use for particular projects, then install each suitcase with Font Porter when you need it. Scenario 4 shows you how to make a custom suitcase with Font/DA Mover.)

3. For each screen font you installed, drag the associated printer font into the System Folder (see Figure 3-9). ATM gets its scaling information from the printer font, so the printer font must be in the System Folder for ATM to work.

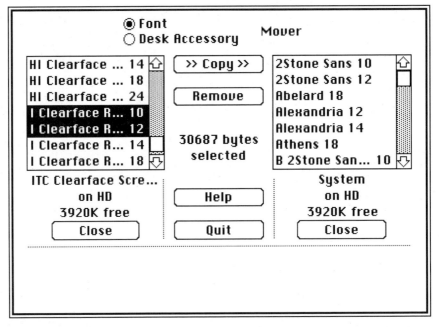

Figure 3-8: With ATM installed, you install fonts with the Font/DA Mover as before, but this time you need only select 10- and 12-point sizes for each font you want.

4. With ATM installed, bitmapped fonts will be smoothly scaled to virtually any size, including fractional point sizes if an application supports them. Although characters look blocky at small sizes because of the Mac's 72-dpi screen resolution, even small sizes look good when printed on a QuickDraw or PostScript printer (see Figure 3-10).

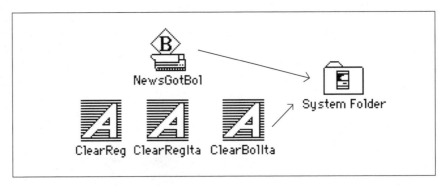

Figure 3-9: For each screen font installed, drag the associated printer font into the System Folder (ATM gets its scaling information from the printer font).

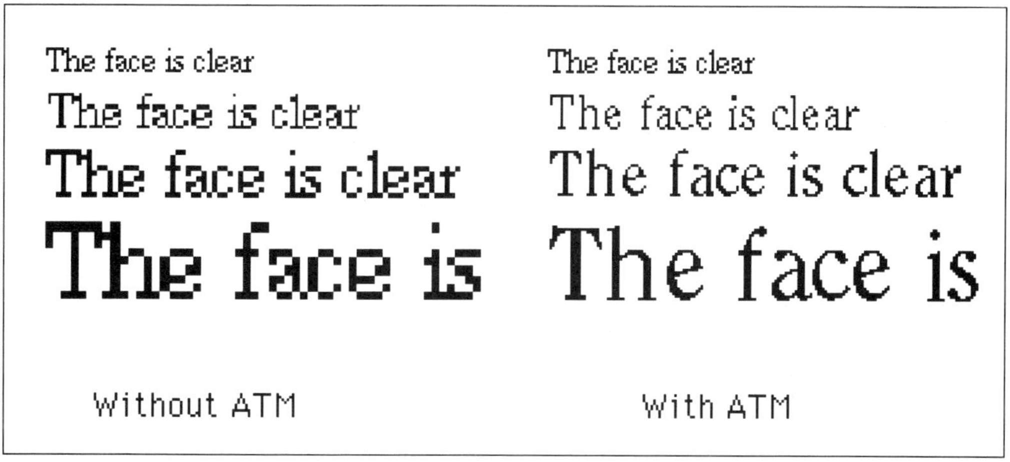

The face is clear | The face is clear

The face is clear | The face is clear

The face is clear | The face is clear

The face is | The face is

Without ATM | With ATM

Figure 3-10: ATM smoothly scales bitmapped fonts to virtually any size.

Scenario 3: Suitcase II or MasterJuggler

Another way to avoid the Font/DA Mover is to use a font/DA extender such as Fifth Generation Systems' Suitcase II or ALSoft's MasterJuggler. These wonderful utilities let you access dozens of suitcases full of fonts (or desk accessories) without installing them in your System file. Like ATM's Font Porter, these utilities won't save you disk space, but they'll save you trouble since you can add or remove fonts without going through the tedious process of adding or deleting them from the System file.

Suitcase II and MasterJuggler are very similar, so the following instructions can be applied to either utility. Both programs include several companion utilities for viewing fonts, resolving font ID number conflicts, and managing Fkeys, DAs, and sounds.

1. Suitcase II and MasterJuggler are INITs; drag the utility's icon into the System Folder, restart your Mac, and it's up and running (see Figure 3-11).

2. From within Suitcase II/MasterJuggler, which is from the Apple menu, you can open the font suitcases you wish to access.

Font suitcases can be large — from around 200K to 600K apiece. Suitcase II or MasterJuggler can compress fonts by as much as 50 percent or so; the program automatically decompresses a suitcase when you use the fonts it contains.

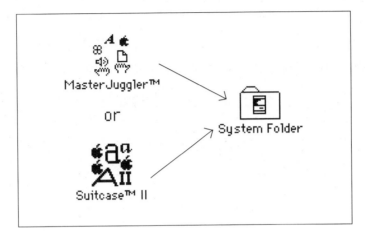

Figure 3-11: To install INITs such as Suitcase II and MasterJuggler, drag the icon into the System Folder and restart your Mac.

3. If you've finished a project and won't be using a particular suitcase for awhile, you can close it in Suitcase II/MasterJuggler and then remove your copy of the suitcase from your hard disk to reclaim disk space.

Scenario 4: the best of all three worlds

This exercise combines the capabilities of the Font/DA Mover, ATM, and Suitcase II/MasterJuggler to optimize font installation on your hard disk. This scenario is designed to simplify adding and removing fonts, save disk space by installing the minimum number of fonts possible, and avoid font ID number conflicts.

The first step, which entails removing most of the fonts from your System file, may seem puzzling, but there's a reason for it. You're performing this step to prevent font ID number conflicts, those annoying glitches that occur when two fonts are assigned the same ID number. Symptoms of font ID conflicts include installed fonts that fail to show up in a program's Font menu, or a document typed in one font that prints in another. Fonts installed in the System file have priority over fonts in a suitcase accessed by Suitcase II or MasterJuggler. If you remove the fonts from your system file, then a font in the System can't elbow its way in front of one in a suitcase.

1. We'll start with some housekeeping. Double-click on the Font/DA Mover icon to list the fonts in your System file. Before you proceed, make sure you have the originals of all the fonts you see listed, because you're about to throw away the ones you see here.

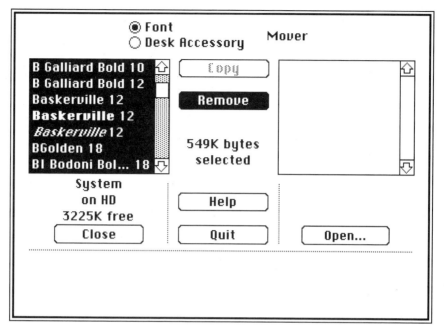

Figure 3-12: To remove fonts from the system, select the fonts — in the left-hand column — you don't want and click Remove.

Select the fonts you want to remove from the System — ideally, you should select all of the fonts listed (note that the Font/DA Mover won't let you throw away Chicago 12, Geneva 9 and 12, and Monaco 9, which are required for System operation). Remember, you can sweep the cursor across a group of adjoining names, or Shift-click to select several names at once.

When you've selected all the fonts you want to delete, click the Remove button (see Figure 3-12). The Mac chugs away, and the fonts are deleted from the System file.

2. Quit the Font/DA Mover and return to the desktop. Copy the suitcase icons for all the fonts you'll be using onto your hard disk. To save yourself another round of disk insertions, copy the necessary printer fonts into the System Folder as well (see Figure 3-13).

3. Double-click on one of the suitcases to open the Font/DA Mover. As in Scenario 1, the fonts in that suitcase will be listed in the left-hand column. To make a new font suitcase, first click the Open button beneath the right-hand column (see Figure 3-14).

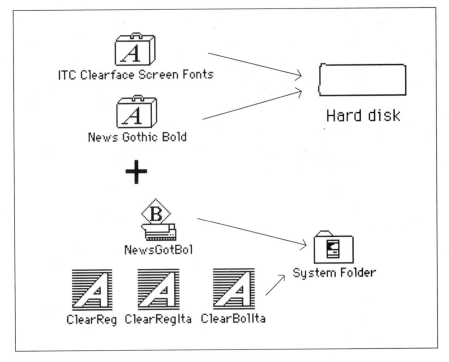

Figure 3-13: Copying the screen fonts and printer fonts to your hard disk together will save you a disk-insertion step.

4. In the dialog box that appears, click the New button. In the window that subsequently appears, type the name you wish to assign your custom suitcase. For example, you might want to make a suitcase that holds all the fonts for your monthly newsletter; type "Newsletter Fonts" and click Create (see Figure 3-15).

5. In the Font/DA Mover's left-hand column, shift-click the 10- and 12-point sizes for the fonts you want to install. Next, click the Copy button to add the fonts to your new suitcase (see Figure 3-16). Click the Close button beneath the left-hand column, and open another suitcase from the list that appears. Repeat step 3 for all the fonts you wish to install for your newsletter set, closing and opening suitcases in the left-hand column.

When you've installed all the fonts you need in your Newsletter Fonts suitcase, click the Close button beneath the right-hand column, then create additional suitcases for other projects if you wish.

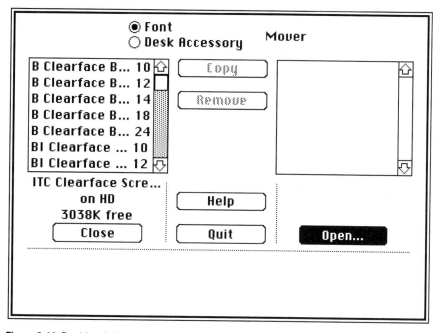

Figure 3-14: Double-clicking on one of the font suitcases opens the Font/DA Mover. To begin making a new font suitcase, click the Open button.

6. When you've created all the suitcases you need, click Quit to return to the desktop. Throw away the overstuffed suitcase icons you opened to pack your custom suitcases. Now, install ATM and Suitcase II or MasterJuggler, as

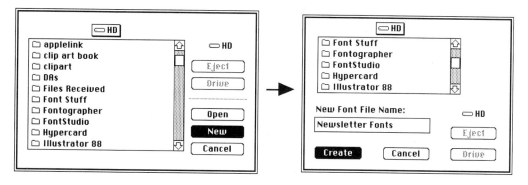

Figure 3-15: To create a new font suitcase (1) click the New button, and (2) type the name you want to use for the custom suitcase in the subsequent window, pressing the Create button to implement.

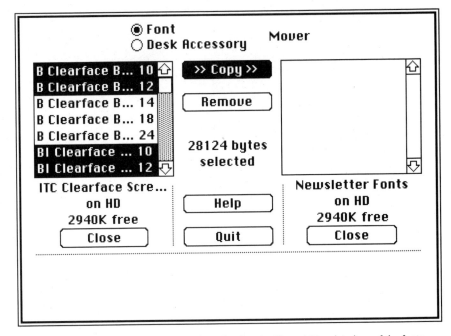

Figure 3-16: Add fonts to a new suitcase by selecting the 10- and 12-point sizes of the fonts you want and clicking the Copy button.

described in the previous sections, and restart your Mac. Open the custom suitcases you need with Suitcase II or MasterJuggler, start up a word processor or page-layout program, and you're ready to create a document. The fonts in the suitcases you selected will appear in the program's Font menu, and ATM will take care of scaling the characters.

The hard disk route

If you use a large number of downloadable fonts, you should consider the advantages of accessing them from a hard disk. The latest version (4.0) of Adobe's Font Downloader lets you download a batch of fonts to a hard disk attached to a PostScript printer's SCSI port.

The fonts on the printer's hard disk can be downloaded much faster than fonts downloaded from the Mac's disk drive to a PostScript printer over AppleTalk. According to an Adobe representative, a complicated print job could run up to 30 percent faster on a disk-based PostScript printer, since no download time is required — it's as if the fonts resided in the printer. When fonts reside on a printer's hard disk PostScript is able to access only the characters it needs to render, rather than downloading an entire font, saving a considerable amount of memory and speeding up printing. Disk-based printers can also have several megabytes available for caching character bitmaps (storing character shapes once they've been rendered, rather than throwing them away and building them from an outline over and over), which also speeds up printing.

Font management

If you install a large number of fonts, you might be dismayed to find yourself scrolling down a seemingly endless font menu. Before you give up on using Zapf Chancery, take a look at the following options for organizing your font menu.

Take control of your font menu

Mention the Futura family and you'll strike terror into the heart of anyone who hates yard-long font menus. Adobe's version of Futura, for example, boasts 20 members, from Futura Light to Futura Extra Bold, with plenty of styles and weights in between. Choosing among 20 family members is hard enough, but with Adobe's naming strategy, the Futura family is scattered throughout a font menu under monikers like CXB Futura Co. (Futura Condensed Extra Bold) and OCXB Futura Co. (Futura Condensed Extra Bold Oblique). Wouldn't it be swell if you could access all the weights you needed under the main listing Futura? Fortunately, you have several options for doing so.

The simplest solution is to buy font families that have been merged by the manufacturer. Bitstream's MacFontware packages, for example, typically come in the standard styles roman (plain, in Mac parlance), italic (or oblique), bold, and bold italic. When you install a Bitstream font family, only the family name (Baskerville, for example) appears in your applications' font menus. But selecting Bold, Italic, or Bold and Italic from the Style menu will summon the correct screen font in the selected style. If you're not sure whether a company's fonts are merged, check with that company.

Both Suitcase II and MasterJuggler include utilities that let you place styles under a single family name, doing away with crowded font menus. For simple font families that consist of plain, bold, italic, and bold italic styles, Suitcase II's Font Harmony utility will merge the styles so they appear under a single family name; styles are then accessed from a program's Style menu. MasterJuggler's Font/DA Utility takes a different approach, allowing you to rename fonts. Therefore, you could name your fonts Futura CO, Futura CXB, and so on, making them all appear alphabetically under the main heading Futura.

SHOPPING TIPS

If a font family doesn't come merged, and if you don't feel like fiddling with a utility to merge it, you can take the easy way out and use Adobe's new Type Reunion INIT. Drag the Type Reunion icon into the System Folder and restart. That's all. When you open an application, you'll find that the Font menu lists a single name for each font family. If the font has several styles, a style submenu pops up when you select the main font name. Although Type Reunion is an additional investment, it's a worthwhile one if you want to have your font families automatically consolidated. Eastgate Systems' Fontina offers another option for organizing a font menu. Fontina also consolidates font-family members, but takes a different approach than Type Reunion's submenus; Fontina fills the entire screen with columns of alphabetized font names.

Creating and editing typefaces

If you can't find just the font you need among the more than 6,000 available for the Mac, you might want to create your own. If you don't have the energy to create an entire face, you can use a type effects program to modify existing outline fonts.

Type design programs

These days, you can choose among four Mac-based type-creation programs. Three of the programs — Altsys's Fontographer, Letraset's FontStudio, and Kingsley/ATF's ATF Type Designer I — are in the $500-$600 range, and offer a relatively similar set of features. These programs let you construct characters out of Bezier curves, creating character outlines from curve, corner, and tangent points (see Figure 3-17). You can draw characters from scratch or trace them from scanned templates. The programs then generate bitmapped screen fonts and PostScript or TrueType outline fonts.

Another font-creation program, URW's Ikarus-M employs a different approach. With Ikarus-M, you use a dedicated digitizing tablet and a mouse with cross hairs to trace drawings of characters. Ikarus-M uses a different type of curve than the other font-creation programs — unlike Bezier curves, which have control points outside of the character path; all the points in an Ikarus-M character fall on the path itself. Ikarus-M is an excellent tool for professional type designers, but at $3,000 (including the digitizing tablet and raster-to-vector conversion software), it probably won't make it to the desks of beginning type designers.

Type effects programs

Want to add a color, gray scale, or pattern to a letter? A shadow or perspective effect to a word? How about placing a line of text on a curving path, or altering a letter's outline for your logo? You can do all of the above — and more — with a variety of special-effects programs for fonts. The following summaries will give you an idea of what type-effects programs can do.

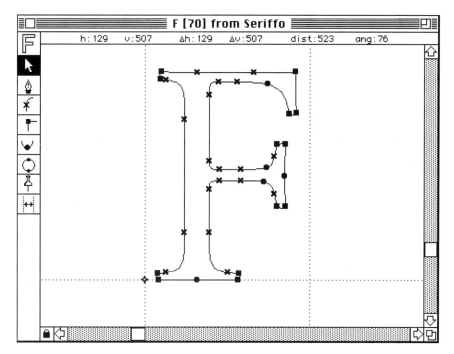

Figure 3-17: Type design programs such as Altsys's Fontographer, Letraset's FontStudio, and Kingsley/ATF's ATF Type Designer I let you construct characters out of Bezier curves.

Effects Specialist (Postcraft International, $179.95)

Provides a library of 120 color effects, which can be altered in a number of ways. Effects run the gamut from basic gradient fills to outlines shaped like railroad tracks. Effects can also be rotated, skewed, or stretched. Imports bitmapped or PostScript Type 3 fonts. Exports PICT or EPS (see Figure 3-18).

LetraStudio (Letraset USA, $495)

Lets you manipulate Type 1, Type 3, or LetraFont-format characters. Surround characters with one of the program's "envelopes" and stretch, skew, rotate, or otherwise distort letters or words. Also lets you set text on a curving path. Exports PICT or EPS (see Figure 3-18).

TypeStyler (Broderbund Software, $199.95)

Lets you import Type 1 or Type 3 PostScript fonts and reshape characters, add fill patterns or colors, and apply effects such as rotation, perspective, and shadows. Drawing tools let you combine text with graphic elements. Exports as PICT, EPS, or Paint (see Figure 3-18).

Effects Specialist (Postcraft International, $179.95)

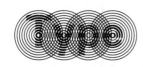

Provides a library of 120 color effects that can be altered in a number of ways. Effects run the gamut from basic gradient fills to outlines shaped like railroad tracks. Effects can also be rotated, skewed, or stretched. Imports bitmapped and Type 3 PostScript fonts. Exports PICT and EPS.

TypeStyler (Brøderbund Software, $199.95)

Lets you import Type 1 and Type 3 PostScript fonts and reshape characters; add fill patterns or colors; and apply such effects as rotation, perspective, and shadows. Provides tools for combining text with graphic elements. Exports PICT, EPS, and paint.

LetraStudio (Letraset USA, $495)

Lets you import and manipulate Type 1, Type 3, and LetraFont-format characters. You surround characters with one of the program's *envelopes* to stretch, skew, rotate, or otherwise distort letters or words. Also lets you set text on a curving path. Exports PICT and EPS.

Smart Art I–IV (Adobe Systems, $99 each)

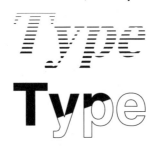

Prefab effects include variations on perspective, arc, shadows, and rotated or slanted text. Imports Type 3 and Type 1 PostScript fonts. Exports EPS and PICT.

Figure 3-18: You can alter text — place text on a curving path, add color to a letter, and so on — with a variety of special-effects type programs.

Smart Art (Adobe Systems, $99)

Prefab effects include variations on perspective, arc, shadows, and rotated or slanted text. Imports Type 1 or Type 3 PostScript; exports EPS or PICT (see Figure 3-18).

ParaFont (Design Science, $99)

Alters character outlines of existing Type 1 or Type 3 PostScript fonts to automatically create special characters such as fractions, small caps, oldstyle numerals, and oblique, condensed, or expanded letters. Changes are saved as a custom PostScript font (see Figure 3-19).

FontMonger (Ares Software, $99.95)

Uses existing fonts to create oblique letters, small caps, fractions, and superior and inferior characters. Converts among PostScript Type 1 and Type 3 and

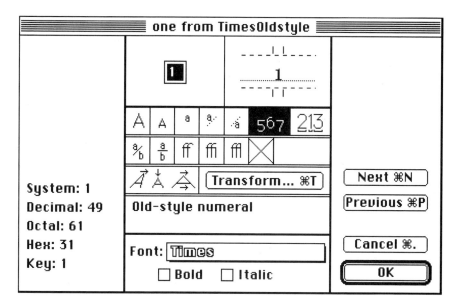

Figure 3-19: Design Science's ParaFont allows you to automatically create special characters by altering the character's outline.

TrueType formats. Lets you combine characters from several fonts into a single, composite font.

Macintosh fonts have come a long way since 1984. In less than five years they have made a quantum leap from chunky bitmaps to typeset-quality text. And the evolution of Mac fonts shows no sign of slowing down. Soon we'll see refinements like *optical scaling,* the creation of different proportions depending on the selected point size. Print quality is bound to go up, and printer prices are bound to go down. With innovative companies like Apple and Adobe involved in font technology, the next five years will surely bring about developments typographers have never even dreamed of.

Summary

✔ There are two types of Macintosh fonts: bitmapped fonts and outline fonts. Bitmapped fonts are characters made up of a map of bits (characters you see on the Mac's screen at 72 dpi). PostScript outline fonts are made up of Bezier curves that can be scaled to any size via a master outline. Apple's version of an outline font is TrueType which allows the Mac to scale fonts to any size you select.

✔ Using the Font/DA Mover to install all the screen fonts sizes you need is the cheapest way to go, since the Font/DA Mover is included with Apple's system software utilities.

✔ To save disk space, Adobe Type Manager (ATM) allows you to install only a single size of each font and let ATM scale the characters for screen display and printing.

✔ You can access dozens of suitcases full of fonts without installing them in the System file with Fifth Generation Systems's Suitcase II and ALSoft's MasterJuggler.

✔ The Font/DA Mover, ATM, and Suitcase II/MasterJuggler can be used in combination to simplify adding and removing fonts, save disk space, and avoid font ID number conflicts.

✔ Mac-based type-creation programs such as Altsys's Fontographer allow you to construct characters out of Bezier curves, creating character outlines from curve, corner, and tangent points.

✔ There are a variety of special-effects programs for fonts that allow you to add color or pattern to a letter, place a line of text on a curving path, and alter a letter's outline for your logo, for example.

Where to buy

Adobe Illustrator, $595
Adobe Systems, Inc.
1585 Charleston
P.O. Box 7900
Mountain View, CA 94039-7900
415-961-4400
800-833-6687

Aldus FreeHand, $595
Aldus Corporation
411 First Avenue, South
Seattle, WA 98104-2871
206-622-5500

ATF Type Designer I, $549
Kingsley/ATF Type Corp.
2559-2 East Broadway
Tucson, AZ 85716
602-325-5884
800-289-8973

Effects Specialist, $179.95
Postcraft International, Inc.
27811 Hopkins Ave., Ste. 6
Valencia, CA 91355
805-257-1797

Evolution, $99
Image Club Graphics, Inc.
1902 11th Street SE, Ste. 5
Calgary, Alberta
Canada T2G3G2
403-262-8008
800-661-9410 (U.S.)

FontMonger, $99.95
Ares Software Corp.
561 Pilgrim, Ste. D
Foster City, CA 94404
415-578-9090

Fontographer, $495
Altsys Corporation
269 West Renner Road
Richardson, TX 75080
214-680-2060

FontStudio, $595
Letraset USA
40 Eisenhower Dr.
Paramus, NJ 07653
201-845-6100
800-343-8973

Ikarus-M, $1,575 ($3,425 for pkg.)
URW
1 Tara Blvd., Ste. 210
Nashua, NH 03062
603-882-7445

LetraStudio, $495
Letraset USA
40 Eisenhower Dr.
Paramus, NJ 07653
201-845-6100
800-343-8973

Metamorphosis, $149
Altsys Corporation
269 West Renner Road
Richardson, TX 75080
214-680-2060

ParaFont, $99
Design Science, Inc.
4028 East Broadway
Long Beach, CA 90803
213-433-0685
213-433-6969 (FAX)

Smart Art, $99
Adobe Systems, Inc.
1585 Charleston
P.O. Box 7900
Mountain View, CA 94039-7900
415-961-4400
800-833-6687

TypeStyler, $199.95
Broderbund Software, Inc.
P.O. Box 12947
San Rafael, CA 94913-2947
800-521-6263

Chapter 4
Macintosh Databases

by Charles Seiter

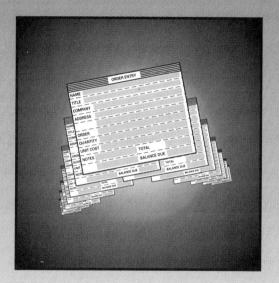

In this chapter...

- ✔ Using the database in your spreadsheet.
- ✔ Mailing and recordkeeping with list managers.
- ✔ The relational database: what you get for your money.
- ✔ Details on FoxBASE, 4D, Helix, and Omnis.
- ✔ Finding a third-party custom application.
- ✔ SQL database connection: Oracle and others.

Databases are a unique category of software, a category that represents the full range of complexity in commercial programs. At the simplest level, there are DAs that you can learn to use in a few minutes to manage mailing lists. At the other extreme are programmable relational databases that require long-term commitment to master. Finally, there are databases with programmable interfaces to mainframe products based on SQL (Structured Query Language) which you are unlikely to need unless you are a professional database expert.

If you buy a word processor with page-layout features but never learn how to use them, it probably won't make the word processor harder to use in daily life — for all its features, Microsoft Word 4.0 isn't much more difficult than the original MacWrite. The same is true of advanced features, such as macros, in spreadsheets, as many happy Excel non-macro-users can attest.

This convenient circumstance does not apply to databases. While flat-file databases are just tables, relational databases are nearly the most complex products ever sold to innocent consumers. Experience shows that, unless you must plunge in immediately to work out the data system of a fairly complicated business, you should probably get the simplest product that will meet your needs and figure that you will export your data to a more complex product later. Although the vendors of high-end programmable relational databases these days include a variety of templates and canned examples with their products to help beginners, in general you're more likely to succeed if you start with a simple product and then work your way up when necessary.

Although I'll review most Mac products on the market, the most important piece of database information is one you will provide: What's the data? Before we peruse the catalog of databases, see if you can find yourself somewhere in these caricatures of database users. You'll find that the section headings of this chapter match up with the descriptions.

Nothing fancy: "I just need to keep a list of names, phone numbers, and addresses that I use all the time. It would be nice if I could merge names and addresses into letters without too much trouble, too."

Basic data: "I have some phone-book data but I also need to keep track of money and

About the author

Charles Seiter received a Ph.D. from CalTech, took a job as a chemistry professor, and after seven years strayed away from this into the field of scientific instrument design. Over the years he has written eight computer books, one of which brought him into contact with the staff at *Macworld*, and since 1986 he has been a *Macworld* contributing editor specializing in databases, programming languages, and science/engineering topics. Because neither instrument design nor writing for *Macworld* requires much physical presence, he lives in obscure but picturesque locations in Northern California and may thus be reached on AppleLink at macworld2.

prepare reports. I don't want to learn to program, but I do need to run up some subtotals and totals from time to time, maybe a few hours per week."

Business land: "I have customers, invoices, contacts to track, bills to send out — all the paperwork associated with a business. Right now I spend at least 10 to 15 hours per week on data handling. By next year I'll have a number of people reporting to me doing full-time data processing."

Blue connections: "I work in an office full of PCs where most people work with applications developed in dBASE. I think it will be easier for me to use the existing programs than to start from scratch."

Big-time connections: "The networked VAXs in my building use a big SQL-based minicomputer database. I'm supposed to get a group of Macs connected to this system."

If your needs fall somewhere within this rather broad range, there's a Mac product or products for you. Despite the inherent complexity of relational databases, you should at least be encouraged to know that all Mac databases, partly because of adaptation to the Mac interface and partly because of user insistence, are significantly easier to use than their counterparts on other computers.

Flat-file databases — nothing fancy

The simplest databases are flat-file databases. Flat files are just tables — each column heading defines a database field (such as last name or phone number), and each row constitutes a database record. For this reason, the database functions in spreadsheets (Microsoft Excel, Wingz, Full Impact), are quite sufficient if you only want to keep small mailing lists or phone books. The spreadsheets have straight-forward commands for browsing and sorting your records, and can export your database tables as tab-delimited flat files if you want to perform a mail-merge with a word processor file (all Mac word processors except WordPerfect use tab-delimited files directly).

> 66 *While flat-file databases are just tables, relational databases are nearly the most complex products ever sold to innocent consumers.* 99

The problem with this simple plan is that you may not own a spreadsheet or may need the convenience of a DA for your list-style database. In this case, you may want to consider Retriever ($199.95, Exodus Software) or DAtabase ($129.95, Preferred Publishers). The decision between these two is a matter of taste rather than functionality. Both run on a 512K Mac or higher, and both do an excellent job at list management. DAtabase can also accommodate picture fields, besides text and numbers, while Retriever has a particularly easy-to-learn iconic interface (see Figure 4-1).

 File   Edit   View   Special   Retriever

	Retriever™	

Status
File Name: "Part. MUG list"   Last Modified: 4/8/88

Rec	User Group Name	User Group Ph..	City	ST
3	M A V G	516-735-6960	Bethpage	NY
4	BCS Mac User Group	617-367-8080	Boston	MA
5	Boston Computer Society	617-367-8080	Boston	MA
6	Boulder Macintosh Meeting	303-444-3051	Boulder	CO
7	Macintosh User Group	814-362-7791	Bradford	PA
8	Mac Valley Users Group	818-848-1277	Burbank	CA
9	Mac Users Group-Harvard University	—	Cambridge	MA
10	Club Mac of Monterey	408-625-0333	Carmel	CA
11	Charlotte Apple Computer Club	704-553-2300	Charlotte	NC
12	Charlotte Apple Computer Club	704-553-2300	Charlotte	NC
13	Summit Mac Users Group	201-635-1991	Chatham	NJ
14	South Jersey Mac Users	609-589-0500	Cherry Hill	NJ
15	Apple-Siders		Cincinnati	OH
16	MACincinnati		Cincinnati	OH

| 61 | | | | |

Name
num70
rad ic
rad/c
Radius
Radius
ret/h
retre
retrie
speed
speed

Figure 4-1: The little icons at upper-right in the Retriever screen are the only tools you need to navigate this database.

If you're keeping name lists for personal files or a club or church group, either product will work; if you need a database for business reasons, either one will run out of gas by about Wednesday afternoon of your first week of use.

A specialized database DA that has been specifically designed just to be a motorized address book is Intouch ($69.95, Advanced Software). If you know in advance that your data consists exclusively of names, phone numbers, and addresses, this little database has lots of nice touches (easy envelope and label printing, multipage note capability for each name) to make life easy.

Basic data

The next step up in database sophistication is the general purpose flat-file database, a larger application invariably calling for at least a 1MB Mac, hard drive optional. As I noted earlier, a flat file is just a table, enabling a flat-file product such as Panorama ($395, ProVue Development Corp.) to be designed around a basic spreadsheet with advanced sorting and searching features (see Figure 4-2).

🍎 File Edit Font Size Search Sort Math Outline

	Math menu
Total	⌘T
Average	⌘J
Count	
Minimum	
Maximum	
Running Total	
Running Difference	
Equation...	⌘=
Fill...	
Empty Fill...	
Sequence...	
Propagate	⌘P
Unpropagate	
Propagate Up	
Unpropagate Up	

Presidential Ele...

Year	State	Electoral Vote For Democrat	E... F...		Popular Vote or Republican
1976, Carter vs. Ford	WI	11			1,004,987
1976, Carter vs. Ford	WV	6			314,726
1976, Carter vs. Ford	WY	0			92,717
•1976, Carter vs. Ford		297			9,148,940
1988, Dukakis vs. Bush	AK	0			102,381
1988, Dukakis vs. Bush	AL	0			809,450
1988, Dukakis vs. Bush	AR	0			463,377
1988, Dukakis vs. Bush	AZ	0			692,139
1988, Dukakis vs. Bush	CA	0			4,749,894
1988, Dukakis vs. Bush	CO	0			727,633
1988, Dukakis vs. Bush	CT	0			739,612
1988, Dukakis vs. Bush	DC	3			25,732
1988, Dukakis vs. Bush	DE	0			130,581
1988, Dukakis vs. Bush	FL	0			2,519,517
1988, Dukakis vs. Bush	GA	0			1,067,291
1988, Dukakis vs. Bush	HA	4	0	192,364	158,625
1988, Dukakis vs. Bush	IA	8	0	666,728	541,936
1988, Dukakis vs. Bush	ID	0	4	147,384	253,461

Figure 4-2: Panorama is basically a spreadsheet (note the long list of math options) with an array of database facilities represented by the icon palette at left.

Although Panorama features an excellent report generator, drawing facilities, and forms designer, perhaps its real bid for your consideration comes from speed — its efficient tabular organization lets it sort and search large files (50K and up) in seconds rather than the minutes typical for its competitors.

A flatfile doesn't have to look like a table, however. One example that's been around since the earliest Mac days (and it's still blissfully compact, at an application size of 168K) is RecordHolder Plus ($99.95, Software Discoveries). Here each record in the database typically looks like a full page of data (see Figure 4-3) rather than a single row in a table.

This makes data entry more convenient, and RecordHolder, playing on this strength, has many data-entry options (error checking, radio buttons, check boxes) to make entry of new records as accurate as possible. Yet another program with many of these features is MyAdvancedDatabase ($59.95, MySoftware Co.). At its basic level, this product simply presents users with a set of data cards to be filled in; at a more advanced level the user can program different types of cards and formats.

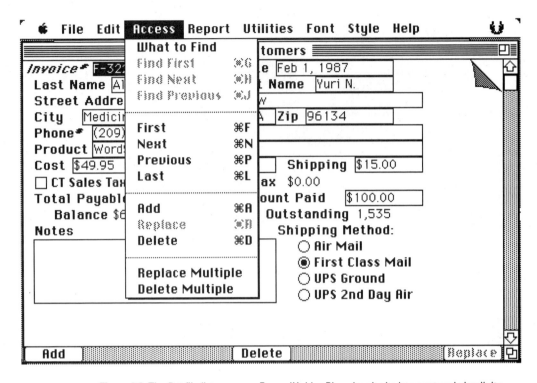

Figure 4-3: The flat-file list manager RecordHolder Plus, despite its low cost and simplicity, provides a particularly effective set of features to speed and check data entry.

Tables and pages of data are really just different views of the same information, and the popular flat-file database Microsoft File ($195, Microsoft) makes this explicit by having a command that switches between the two views. In Form view, the user designs the data page that holds a single record; in List view a large stretch of data can be browsed in table format. A version of Form view is also used to specify the data fields to be used in making merged documents; as you might expect, it's no accident that File is a champion at mail merge with Microsoft Word.

One of the points that distinguishes File from the slightly humbler database built into the all-in-one product Microsoft Works ($249, Microsoft) is File's large array of forms designed to accommodate standard office supplies for labels and laser printers (see Figure 4-4).

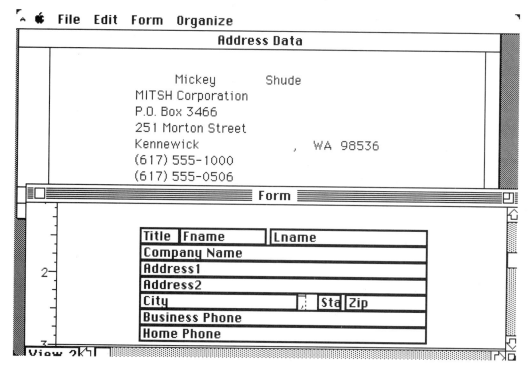

Figure 4-4: Microsoft File contains an assortment of templates for office use. This example shows a label template designed to fit Avery Label Form 4116 for printing stick-on labels on a laser printer.

Another feature useful for printing labels is a set of Custom Setup/Print Custom commands to accommodate odd smaller paper sizes on ImageWriters and LaserWriters. Beyond this, the current version of File (2.0) offers Memo as a field type; Memo fields can hold up to 32K characters and, probably because of this, are not searchable, unlike text fields. File also supports networks (Microsoft expects you to buy a copy of File for each workstation) but doesn't explicitly handle access privileges — these are managed with standard AppleShare privilege-tagging of folders by folder owners. And finally, an attempt at simulating advanced database capabilities in File is the inclusion of a macro program called AutoMac III (Genesis Micro Software).

Microsoft felt obliged to upgrade the earlier version of File so as not to disgrace itself utterly in the face of competition from flat-file market leader FileMaker

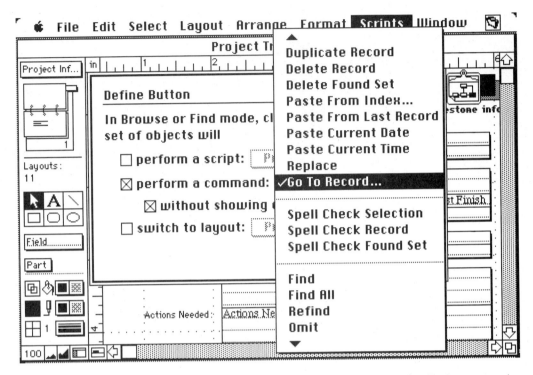

Figure 4-5: FileMaker Pro's dazzling macro (called Script in FileMaker) facility lets you attach buttons to database views to call up any automated tasks with a double-click.

Pro ($299, Claris Corporation). FileMaker Pro has an outstanding macro facility for automating database tasks (see Figures 4-5 and 4-6), a reputation for precise and easy form design, good network support, and a generally high level of refinement. Because it started with an impressive feature set as the original FileMaker, and added more through several generations (FileMaker II, IV, and Pro) without compromising its basically simple design, it has become the only flat-file product that can compete as a business-management tool with the relational databases.

In fact, FileMaker approaches relational database capabilities with its Link command, which lets the program look up data in files other than its currently active file.

Now, however, we turn to the big programs that constitute the center of the Mac database universe.

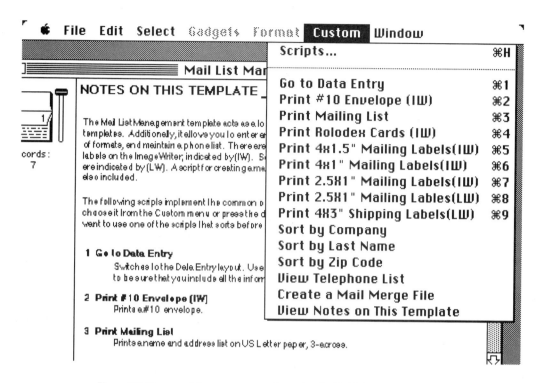

Figure 4-6: Since scripts are so easy to formulate in FileMaker, all sorts of chores can be relegated to specific named scripts — Claris provides a generous assortment.

Business land

Relational databases are the systems with enough flexibility to accommodate the data needs of complex businesses. In principle, they don't necessarily appear to be especially baffling: relational rules allow flat tables to be linked by key fields that are common to one or more tables. Since it's possible to create a network of links, however, with both one-to-one and one-to-many links among different types of data tables, it's usually not clear to beginners what data structure or structures should be used. Compounding the possible confusion is the array of programming facilities built into the leading relational databases. These range from effective but unusual icon-based programming to near-Pascal syntax; these programming features require serious study in their own right.

> ❝ *Relational databases are the systems with enough flexibility to accommodate the data needs of complex businesses.* ❞

Since a relational database is expected to be a viable business tool, the best-selling Mac databases are programmable, customizable, multiuser-capable products with provision for remote data access. The main products that fit this description are 4th Dimension, FoxBase Pro, Double Helix 3.5, and Omnis 5; they represent the state of the database art in relational information systems. At the end of this section I will also comment on two relational, but nonprogrammable databases, FileForce and dBase Mac, products that appear to have secured market niches but which also seem to lack the broad appeal of the others. All of these products claim to run on 1MB Macintoshes; in practice you'll want at least 2MB and a hard drive to do serious work.

Double Helix 3.5

Helix ($695, Odesta Corporation) is one of the longest-lived Mac products, having outlived early competitors like FileVision and MacLion. Over the years it has picked up more features and speed but remains the most idiosyncratic database for the Mac or any other computer.

Odesta designed Double Helix to be a programmable relational database that nonprogrammers can use relatively easily. It has a distinctive style (see Figure 4-7) in which you manipulate icons that stand for database elements — nowhere in Helix do you type in text commands, and at the end of your efforts there's no "program" in the conventional sense.

In Double Helix, fields are represented by one kind of icon, indexes by another, and layouts for data entry or reporting by another kind. Most Helix programming is done with tiles which represent operations on fields — you stick one or more fields onto a tile and it produces a result in another field or in a display. More complex tasks are handled by Sequences, which are essentially macros composed of commands chosen from a selection list. The numerous Helix icons seem bewildering to people familiar with text-oriented programming languages, but programming newcomers go farther faster in Helix than in traditional systems.

There are two other consequences of Helix's graphical programming mode. First, application screens for data entry and retrieval tend to be more complex and graphically detailed than those built up with text-based programming. Also, Double Helix's unique coding style may allow you to do things unintentionally, but foolproofs your work against system crashes or lockups — it yields applications that almost never bomb or freeze.

For the experienced developer, Double Helix allows rapid and unlimited customization of applications. It's common for Helix developers to coach database clients in making on-the-spot modifications to finished applications over the telephone — it's the only full-strength relational database for which such a

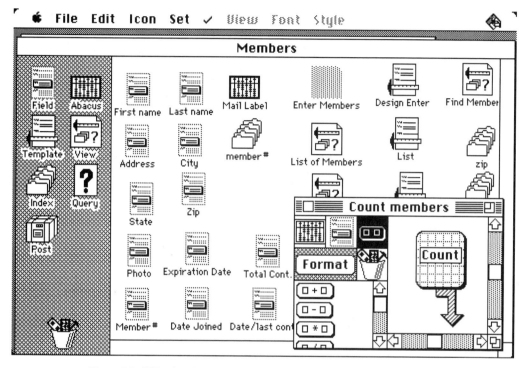

Figure 4-7: All Double Helix programming is accomplished by dragging and connecting an assortment of icons that stand for commands (such as Count in this figure).

statement could be made. At the User code level in an application, it's possible to change the users and user names, data layouts, and fields in the datafiles (relations) themselves. Most Double Helix applications are open in this way, which implies both that modification will be simple, and that single-user execution speeds will never be as optimized as they might be in a database that preprocesses command files. Odesta has nevertheless been working on the speed problem. In addition to internal speed improvements in frequently used commands, the Double Helix interface now gives constant hints on indexing important fields as they are entered or created. At the price of additional storage space for indexes (the file-card icons in Figure 4-7), searching on medium-size databases (5 to 10,000) records can be made faster.

Double Helix is also unusual in that it offers applications that are intrinsically multiuser. If an application is developed in Double Helix, users can run it under Multiuser Helix with no modification. Specifically, Odesta bundles client/server database-management software with Double Helix 3.5; it's the only Mac database really designed for client/server database management, which gives it a speed advantage in multiuser practice over its competitors (which use a peer-to-peer scheme).

Omnis

Omnis ($1,000, Blyth Software) is another Mac veteran — British developer Blyth has been a force in the American Mac market for five years, despite a brief corporate reorganization back in 1989. The first version was a plain alphanumeric database with a good reputation for speed and reliability. Omnis 5 has entered the modern Mac world: an application generator (Omnis Express) interfaces with buttons, arrows, and check boxes (see Figure 4-8) that activate underlying programs and XCMDs for reading HyperCard data.

Omnis programming differs from conventional programming in that its text-format commands are selected from sets of lists (this approach is also used for Double Helix's Sequences). This apparently minor constraint has some important consequences. First, it means that you can't compose a command sequence that will cross up the Omnis interpreter. Second, it means that you are protected from a variety of simple mistakes of the "missing semicolon" type that occur in conventional programming. This scheme works well if the command set is rich enough to allow most frequently required database chores to be accommodated with one or two commands. Omnis's highly evolved command set meets this condition; commands selected from lists allow placement of radio buttons and search arrows in interface screens, for example. For basic applications that can be beautified later, Omnis also includes Omnis 5 Express, an application generator in which you specify, in outline form, your database requirements and let the generator produce the working Omnis code.

The straightforward development tools and program foolproofing in Omnis produce quick results, and the application interfaces typically feature a respectable set of custom menus and HyperCard-like buttons for navigation. The event manager built into Omnis's developers' tools, according to Blyth, is the reason it's possible to quickly throw together a custom application that handles a profusion of open windows for different functions that nonetheless run without crashes. Network installation is simple, and Omnis applications are fast at routine searching.

4th Dimension

The launch of 4th Dimension ($795, Acius) was the biggest Mac event of its year (1988), as perhaps befits this large and complex product. In 4th Dimension it is possible to program nearly every function found in other Macintosh databases, and 4D offers other features (graphs, including sized-picture graphs, and an

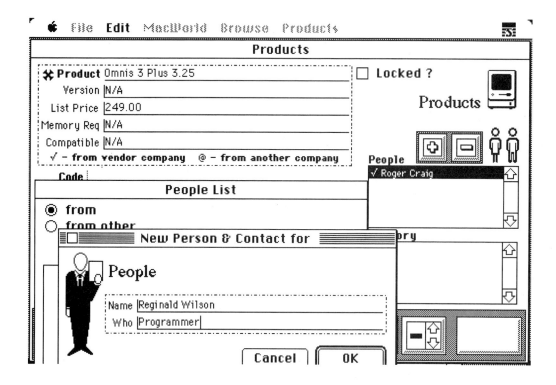

Figure 4-8: The Omnis applications generator lets you populate most views with buttons for database browsing or other activities. This makes for friendly end-user applications.

Oracle/SQL extension) no other database yet can match. For interface development, for example, besides the usual radio buttons and check boxes, 4D has invisible buttons, scrollable zones, thermometers, and rulers, to name a few. The 4D screen editor for layout creation offers an array of patterns, measuring tools, and layering controls that rival those of dedicated forms-generation programs.

The 4D programming language has easily the richest command set of any Mac database, and the programming environment even includes a symbolic debugger. To complete this picture, Acius now also offers, as add-ins, a compiler for performance improvement, a MacDraw-like drawing program, a spreadsheet module, and a general-purpose word processor.

Not everyone feels immediately at home in such splendid surroundings. The first version of 4D required an amount of procedural programming that neophytes often found daunting, so Acius introduced an application template called

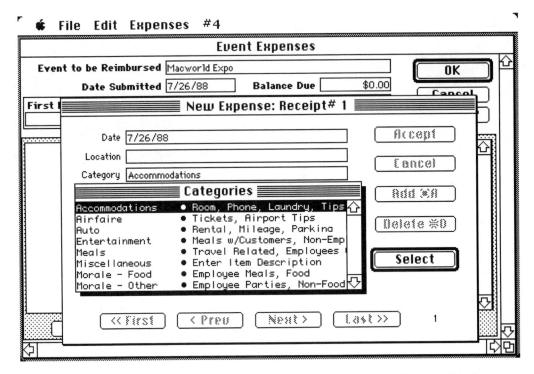

Figure 4-9: 4th Dimension is a complete Macintosh applications environment. This simple expense account database was generated from templates provided with 4D in about a half hour.

Skeleton to guide beginners. Many of the features of this earlier effort have been incorporated into 4D 2.0, which has a quite streamlined datafile setup (see Figure 4-9) and choices for establishing a record-manipulation menu. While effective use of all the features of 4D may require diligent study for months or longer, it's now possible, following the tutorial and the Quick Start documentation, to have a simple relational database working on your first day.

It's relatively easy to set up all the required types of files for a 4D application and then link files graphically; often, in fact, it's easier to answer all the requirements in an applications specification in 4D than in its competitors. Although in principle the drawing tools offered for layout creation can encourage lavish use of graphics in data entry and reporting layouts, most 4D interfaces tend to be simple for speed reasons. The 4D developers' environment has always been geared to developing applications that mesh with Macintosh users' intuition, and most applications reflect that direction (see Figure 4-10).

```
  é   File   Edit   Import │ Find │ View   Order   Report

                            by Name              ⌘F
                            by Category
  Products        4730 of 47 by Area
  Name                      by Date Verified                Version      Last Verif
  3238MA+                   by List Price
  3DWorks                   by Person's Last Name
  3DWorks!                  by Vendor
  3DWorks/RenderWorks       by Story                        N/A
  3DWorks/RenderWorks for                                   N/A
  3M Type 154 LaserPrinter
  4M Type 154 LaserPrinter  Show All             ⌘G
  512K-2MB                  Show Selected
  512K-2MB for the PC       Omit Selected
  512K-4MB
  512K-4MB for the PC       Custom Search
  9600 Baud v. 32 Full Rang  Bytcom                          N/A
  9600 Plus                  Smarteam, Inc.
```

Figure 4-10: 4th Dimension produces applications with the homely virtue that they contain no surprises for anyone familiar with the Mac interface. The database shown in this figure took a week to program but about five minutes to learn.

As 4D is the most highly evolved Mac database system, the large group of experienced programmers and consultants that work with 4D have produced a long list of distinguished, "real Mac" third-party applications. (Ask Acius for third-party literature.)

Fox Pro/Mac 2.0

FoxBase/Mac arrived on the Mac as an austere, fast, character-oriented database obviously translated directly from the IBM PC. At first FoxBase's main attraction was speed. This was not a negligible point in view of the languid performance of early "real Mac" databases, and over several years Fox has added, piece by piece, the features needed to generate applications that are recognizably Macintosh software (see Figure 4-11), giving us FoxPro/Mac ($495, Fox Software).

The product now has picture fields, interface screen radio buttons, a report generator, a screen formatter with a MacDraw-style toolbox, and coding templates. The templates, although not as convenient as Omnis's application generator, at least give developers a skeleton framework for programming instead of a bare screen.

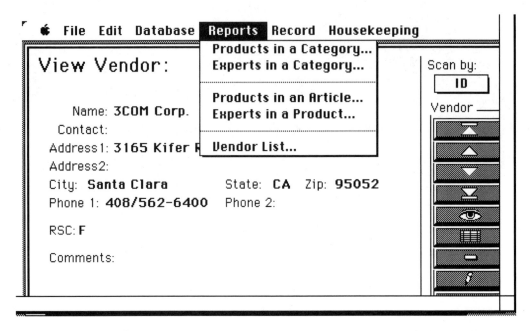

Figure 4-11: FoxPro Mac has the tools to equip a genuine, high-speed relational database with a HyperCard-like user interface.

The set of coding templates and their associated control language, called FoxCode, are the key to FoxPro/Mac applications. Templates and submodules, written in a Pascal-like syntax, generate screen tables encapsulating screen design in a series of editable text statements. The application generator generates the set of program (.prg) and format (.fmt) files that actually constitute an executable FoxPro/Mac program. This aspect of the Fox environment, while more typical of PC than of Mac practice, is an advantage for developers in that most of the program logic in FoxBASE custom applications translates from Mac to PC and back. FoxBase+/Mac, like Omnis 5, was specifically designed with mixed-platform, multiuser computing in mind — a typical office might have Macs and PCs running their respective versions of FoxPro on a network (multiuser FoxPro costs $695 per station).

One difference between Fox and its competitors' programming schemes is that an interpreter designed to execute FoxPro program files entails much less overhead than other styles. A Search command on a single database field issued from a FoxPro screen invokes, in a single step, a piece of optimized code that calls up the index for the search field and matches the query to field data in less time than a screen refresh. Part of the search speed and flexibility in a Fox application derives from the Keywords datafile, a 300K-plus, behemoth with no analog in the other databases. Another unique new feature is a patented searching technology, trademarked under the name Rushmore, that uses a special indexing code method to speed up disk-based searches on large databases by factors approaching one hundred. Fox was fast in the first place; now it's untouchable, at least in single-user mode.

The one disadvantage of the overall FoxPro approach is that it imposes so much responsibility for program correctness on the programmer — most of the constraints built into Double Helix or Omnis are not present. Thus an unfinished runtime application in FoxPro can generate a variety of error messages when it is started, as opposed to Double Helix, in which an unfinished application will simply lack intended features. It's not the best choice for jobs that must be completed in a hurry, but for applications in which you have the time and the training to do a careful programming job, FoxPro/Mac lets you build applications that will outperform those generated in any other Mac relational database.

No programs?

Two other relational databases for the Mac offer a wide range of features, but for simplicity, lack a programming language. That is, a developer or user can design a database, establish relational links, and generate reports, but the limitations of the product can't be worked around by programming. Perhaps for this reason, these programs have been less successful commercially than the Big Four described above.

dBase Mac was originally developed for Ashton-Tate (the dBase company) but eventually spun off to a group sponsored by many of the original programming staff (under the name nuBASE for the Mac it's $295 from New Era Software). Although it never attained the popularity Ashton-Tate expected, it's a remarkably complete and powerful product.

FileForce ($395, Acius) was first advertised as a sort of 4D Lite, a full-featured relational database with the programming language removed (see Figure 4-12).

It's an appealing package for a small office with three to six connected Macs; at this level of use in a business a relational database is important, but simplicity is equally important in practice, since there usually isn't a programmer available. Although the conceptual work of relational database design can't disappear altogether, the examples (lots of typical business databases, mailing lists, and labels), tutorials, and documentation in this package make you believe you're more likely to succeed in automating a small-office workload with FileForce than with its big brother 4D or with 4D's competitors. Acius has announced that Calc, Write, and Draw modules will be available for FileForce by 1992.

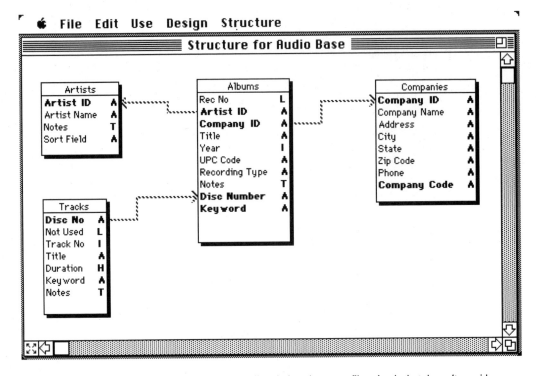

Figure 4-12: FileForce lets you handle relations between files simply, but doesn't provide a programming language for some types of advanced applications.

Blue connections

If you need to network to IBM PCs or to develop applications that run on both platforms, you have a simple set of choices. Both FoxPro and Omnis have versions that run on PC compatibles, but you should know that the Mac environment lets you program features that don't correspond to anything in the PC environment, so portability is not 100 percent. As Windows 3.0 variants of these programs appear on the PC side of the market, however, it's likely that environment compatibility will improve.

For programs developed on the PC trying to break into the Macintosh market, one useful product is dBASE IV Runtime PLUS ($195, Ashton-Tate). Basically it's a utility that lets the thousands of dBASE IV applications developed on PCs and other platforms (Unix, VMS) run without modification on the Mac. Although the ported application will likely appear somewhat spartan compared to more familiar Mac software, there are many vertical markets in which the savings from reusing a large code base are more important than interface details. Another virtue of dBASE IV Runtime PLUS is that it lets Macintosh users on a mixed network use an application simultaneously with other users on other types of computers.

Big-time connections

If you work in a business that uses larger computers (minis or mainframes), it's an odds-on bet that data on those computers is accessed using a data command language called Structured Query Language (SQL). Although SQL was originally developed by IBM as a standard, it was quickly adopted by a variety of database vendors and now is a success story if no longer exactly a standard in the strict sense of the term (nearly every database vendor uses specific, nonstandard extensions).

The Big Four all have some sort of provision for generating SQL commands, ranging from a 4D add-on that links 4th Dimension to the popular minicomputer database Oracle, to a SQL command translator built into the latest version of FoxPro/Mac. Most database vendors are also trying to accommodate Apple's own database access language (DAL); DAL-to-SQL translators are being prepared so that the originating Mac databases can issue queries to any other type of computer.

Two outstanding efforts in SQL connectivity should be mentioned, although this is a database area in which announcements are made almost weekly. Oracle for the Macintosh ($299 single, $699 network, Oracle Corp.), which works with SQL*Net for the Macintosh ($299, same source), is a large program (2MB RAM, 8MB on hard drive) that lets developers program a HyperCard front end to Oracle SQL databases. Since Oracle databases represent nearly half of all installed SQL activity, this is a significant Mac product.

A newer product, which will presumably acquire in subsequent versions the refinement it lacked upon introduction in 1991, is P•Ink ($695, MacVonk). This product ships as a software set that manages a SQL server and a collection of workstations, with modules to support access by Mac databases such as FoxPro/Mac and 4th Dimension that allow external code modules. While it's an ambitious first attempt to provide the first Mac SQL server, it's more a product for SQL developers than for typical Mac users.

Summary field

Databases on the Mac are an unusual software category. Unlike page layout, word processing, or spreadsheets, the market has never identified a single dominant product. Perhaps this is because Macintosh users demand more customization in databases than one product can readily exhibit, or perhaps it's because the trade-offs between database friendliness and database performance are particularly acute. In any case, it's not a lack of good products but rather an embarrassment of riches that keeps the Mac database area lively.

Summary

✓ For keeping simple mailing lists, there are specialized database DAs designed just for this function such as Advanced Software's Intouch.

✓ The simplest databases are flat-file databases which are tables where each column heading defines a database field and each row constitutes a database record.

✓ You'll need a relational database if your business has complex data needs requiring databases that are programmable, customizable, multiuser capable, and which also include remote data access.

✓ Programmable relational databases such as Acius's 4th Dimension can provide you with a rich command set, but also require long-term commitment to master.

✓ The leading Mac relational databases currently on the market include: Double Helix 3.5 (Odesta Corporation), which has a distinctive style in which you manipulate icons allowing nonprogrammers to use it easily; Omnis (Blyth Software), which has a different programming technique where text-format commands are selected from sets of lists, protecting you from making common programming errors; 4th Dimension (Acius), a large and complex program laden with features — graphs, Oracle/SQL extension, debugger — and the richest command set of any Mac database; and FoxPro/Mac 2.0 (Fox Software), designed specifically for mixed-platform, multiuser computing featuring templates and submodules that generate screen tables encapsulating screen design in a series of editable text statements.

✓ Structured Query Language (SQL) is a data command language that allows you to access data from large computers (minis or mainframes). Oracle Corporation's Oracle for the Macintosh, for example, is a program that allows for SQL connectivity by letting developers program a HyperCard front end to Oracle SQL databases.

Where to buy

4th Dimension, $795
Acius, Inc.
10351 Bubb Road
Cupertino, CA 95014
408-252-4444

DAtabase, $129.95
Preferred Publishers
1770 Moriah Woods Blvd., Ste. 14
Memphis, TN 38117
901-682-9676

dBASE IV Runtime PLUS, $195
Ashton-Tate
20101 Hamilton Ave.
Torrance, CA 90502
213-329-8000

Double Helix
Odesta Corp.
4084 Commercial Ave.
Northbrook, IL 60062
708-498-5615
800-323-5423

FileMaker Pro, $299
Claris Corp.
5201 Patrick Henry Dr.
Santa Clara, CA 95052
408-987-7000

FoxPro/Mac 2.0, $495
Fox Software
134 W. South Boundary
Perrysburg, OH 43551
419-874-0162
800-837-3692

Intouch, $69.95
Advanced Software
1095 E. Duane Ave., #103
Sunnyvale, CA 94086
408-733-0745
800-346-5392

Microsoft File, $195
Microsoft Corp.
One Microsoft Way
Redmond, WA 98052-6399
206-882-8080
800-426-9400

Microsoft Works, $249
Microsoft Corp.
One Microsoft Way
Redmond, WA 98052-6399
206-882-8080
800-426-9400

My Advanced Database, $59.95
My Software Co.
177 Jefferson Dr.
Menlo Park, CA 94025
415-325-9372
800-325-3508

nuBASE for the Mac, $295
New Era Software Group, Inc.
14540 SW 136th St., Ste. 204
Miami, FL 33186
305-255-5586
800-325-2604

Omnis, $1,000
Blyth Software
1065 E. Hillsdale Blvd.,Ste. 300
Foster City, CA 94404
415-571-0222
800-346-6647

Oracle for the Macintosh, $699
Oracle Corp.
500 Oracle Pkwy.
Redwood Shores, CA 94065
415-506-7000
800-ORACLE1

P•Ink, $695
MacVonk USA
313 Iona Ave.
Narberth, PA 19072
215-660-0606

Panorama, $395
ProVue Development Corp.
15180 Transistor Lane
Huntington Beach, CA 92649
714-892-8199

Retriever, $199.95
Exodus Software
800 Compton Road, Ste. 9240
Cincinnati, OH 45231
513-522-0011

Chapter 5

Managing Your Personal Finances on the Mac

by Alan Slay

In this chapter . . .

- ✔ A look at easy-to-use programs for writing checks and tracking your money.

- ✔ Going beyond check writing basics — investment tracking, tax planning, and determining insurance needs with personal financial managing software.

- ✔ A summary of the advantages and disadvantages of the best general tax programs.

- ✔ Tracking real estate investments, planning retirement, or saving for a large purchase with niche programs.

- ✔ Personal finance software that lets you write a will that will hold up in any court.

Almost everyone has money problems, with the most common complaint being not having enough. Your Macintosh can provide a great deal of help. A number of excellent programs enable you to budget, write checks and organize your checkbook, keep track of your assets and how much you owe, and provide valuable reports at tax preparation time — so you can work from a single report rather than search for information in a pile of receipts and notes you've accumulated over the year in various drawers and folders.

Some money programs even help overcome the "not enough" problem by helping you do such things as set and work toward financial goals, analyze and track investments, calculate how much your monthly payments on loans will be, and figure out how much you can afford when purchasing a house. There's even a program to record and analyze your gas and electric bills, and another that guides you in preparing your will. And there are also, of course, programs to help you through the happiest time of the year when you prepare your tax forms for your federal and state revenue services.

The basic, general personal finance programs

Probably the best place to begin reviewing the wide range of personal financial functions you can perform on your Mac is to look at the basic, general personal-financial programs.

The simplest bare-bones applications, and those most commonly used, are the basic electronic checkbook programs like Intuit's Quicken and Aatrix's Checkwriter II. With such programs you can, for example, easily call a check up on your screen, enter the necessary information, and then print the check (or store several checks in a queue and print them all at once). Deposits and cash withdrawals are handled in a similar manner using simple electronic versions of deposit slips and withdrawal forms. The advantage of these programs is simplicity and ease of use, and if you're not an individual who likes to go into fine details on your finances, such a basic program will likely serve your needs well.

About the author

Alan Slay is a free-lance writer specializing in financial software. He has over 25 years' experience with mainframes and microcomputers and has worked extensively in finance and accounting with several companies.

Of the two, I lean toward Quicken, because of its cleaner appearance and more professional appearing screens. But Aatrix is equally functional and offers a few menu features not available in Quicken, such as a screen to transfer money between accounts (see Figure 5-1).

One limitation of basic programs however, is that you can enter only two categories of transactions: income and expense. It's possible to track stocks and investments with these low-end programs, but it takes some manipulation.

Tables of Differential Features: Checkwriter Programs

	Checkfree	Checkwriter II	Dollars and Sense	MacMoney	Andrew Tobias Managing Your Money	Personal Finance	Quicken
Publisher	Checkfree Corp.	Aatrix Software	The Software Toolworks	Survivor Software Ltd.	MECA Software	Pop-Up Publishing	Intuit
Price	$29.95 +mo. fee ($9)	$59	$99.95	$119.95	$249	$35	$59.95
Version	1.5	3.1	5.0	3.51	3.0	1.0	1.5
Budgeting	✓	✓	✓	✓	✓		✓
Electronic check transmission	✓	✓					
Income/expense categories only	✓						
Inc/exp/asset/liab categories			✓	✓	✓	✓	
Loan/saving calculations				✓	✓		
Operates as desk accessory		✓					
Insurance need calculations					✓		
Retirement planning				✓	✓		
Dedicated investment tracking						✓	
Transfer between checking/saving accounts		✓	✓	✓	✓		
Tax estimator				✓	✓		
Mortgage refinancing calculations					✓		
Exports to MacIn Tax program	✓		✓	✓	✓		✓
Free, unlimited support	✓	✓		✓			✓
Comments:	Modem required for elec. pmt. of checks					Templates for Panorama database, which is required to run program	

Figure 5-1: Programs for investment management and analysis and what they offer.

Tables of Differential Features: Investment Tracking Programs

	Financial Decisions	Larry Rosen Programs	Market Manager Plus	M/S Excel Money Manager	Stock Watcher	The Investor	On Track	Wall Street Investor	Wall Street Watcher	Wealth builder
Publisher	Gen Micronics	Larry Rosen Co.	Dow Jones & Co., Inc.	Microsoft Press	Micro Trading S/W, Ltd.	Arminius Public & Products, Inc.	Palo Alto Software	Pro Plus S/W, Inc.	Micro Trading S/W, Inc.	Reality Technology
Version	3.0		2.0	(1989 publication)	1.99A	1989	1.0	3.02	3.0	1.1
Price	$65	$89 ea.	$299	$34.95	$195	$99	$99.95	$695	$495	$149
Update prices from publisher										✓ (Qtly.)
Update prices via modem			✓		✓	✓		✓	✓	
Automatic price update			✓		✓	✓			✓	
Automatic price update & charting				✓					✓	
Portfolio management & tracking		✓	✓	Limited	✓	✓		✓	✓	✓
Planning & tracking to reach goal	✓			Limited						✓
Checkbook management			✓			✓				
Buying vs. renting calculations				✓						
On-line trading with broker								✓		
Tracks stocks/dividends on calendar			✓							
Odd lot transactions put/call ratios									✓	
Comments:	Excel Template	5 programs: Bond analyzer, Int. calculator, Investment anal. Bond portf. mgr., mort. loan anal.		Excel templates			Excel template. Tracks liabilities, calculates loans and savings goals.			Quarterly updates: $99.95 to $174.95

Figure 5-1: Continued.

Tables of Differential Features: Tax Preparation Programs

	HyperTax Tutor	MacInTax	TurboTax
Publisher	Softstream Int.	Chipsoft, Inc.	Chipsoft, Inc.
Version	1989 version	1989 version	1989 version
Price	$99	$99 States: $69	$89 States: $49
Extensive list of forms included		✓	✓
Screen replicas of IRS forms	✓ (for inquiries only)	✓	✓
Forms linked for cross entering data		✓	✓
Explanation screens with IRS instructions	✓	✓	✓
Auto. transfer from worksheet to forms		✓	✓
Integrated state returns		✓ (14)	✓ (10)
Prints approved IRS forms on blank paper		✓	✓
Audit flags & IRS norms			✓
Forms guide to select needed forms		✓	✓
"What if" tax planning		✓	✓
Calculates depreciation & amortization			✓
Detailed itemization windows		✓	
Checks for possible errors		✓	✓
Cost of annual update		$50	50% discount
Tax savings suggestions	✓	✓	✓
Comments:	Hypertext format: click on form section for text for information		

Note: MacInTax offers supplementary if X: series that integrates with the main program: Personal Tax Analysis and Business Expense Reports at $79 per supplement.

Figure 5-1: Continued.

One alternative to the low-end programs is Pop-Up Publishing's templates for money management, similar in function to Quicken or Aatrix Checkwriter II. These templates work with the Panorama database, which is a spreadsheet-format database as opposed to a standard database such as Omnis 5 or Fourth Dimension. The set of templates is sold at the shareware price of $25, which makes it an attractive purchase if you already own Panorama. If not, you're better off going with Quicken or Checkwriter II.

The next step up in personal-finance programs includes such programs as Survivor Software's MacMoney and The Software Toolwork's Dollars and Sense. Besides offering income and expense categories, these programs also enable you to enter data for, and track, liabilities (the money you owe) and assets (the things you own, such as a house or car). If you take the time to complete all the data called for in these programs, you can produce a personal balance sheet that will tell you exactly what all your assets are worth, and list your liabilities in detail. The programs will then total your assets and liabilities and tell you exactly what your net worth is.

In addition, these programs can perform simple calculations. MacMoney for example, offers a screen to calculate how much your payments would be on a loan you're considering. You simply enter the amount you want to borrow, the interest rate, and how long you plan to take to pay the loan, and voilá — you are told exactly how much you'll have to pay each month. MacMoney is also used by many small businesses, and its publisher sells a separate companion program called InvoicIt for preparing customer invoices.

Dollars and Sense is similar in capabilities to MacMoney except that it does not have several features, such as the loan calculator, that MacMoney has added in its latest versions. Although Dollars and Sense is still an adequate midlevel personal money manager, it shows its years of neglect and needs to be updated to bring it up to the MacMoney level.

As with the low-end programs, you can also track stocks and investments in these programs. But with the low-end programs, the more complexities you add, the more difficult your record keeping becomes. Still as you learn to use the program, you may want to stretch it more and more and use it to perform additional functions.

At the high end of the personal financial management programs is MECA Software's Andrew Tobias' Managing Your Money. MYM does everything that the general programs do, plus you'll get specific screens for handling investments and taxes. The program is updated at least annually to provide for tax law changes, although (as the publisher indicates) not to the level of refinement provided in the dedicated tax-preparation programs.

MYM has separate, dedicated screens for stocks, bonds, and other investments. If you enter all your data and keep your figures current, not only will you be able to see what your investments are worth, but you'll also have excellent records on the age of these investments and how much you've made (or lost), and you'll have a dedicated data file detailing all the items in your financial portfolio. Such data is very important when you do your taxes, as the IRS requires these details when you declare, for example, capital gains or losses. In addition, MYM enables you to do such things as calculate loan payments, project the future value of investments and savings accounts, figure out how much insurance you'll need, and even get approximate projections on what you'll owe in income taxes so you can plan how you'll pay the various government agencies when taxes come due.

The obvious disadvantage of MYM is that you have to adopt data input and updating as a personal religion. If you're not prepared to dedicate yourself to the work needed to initiate and update these programs, you'll be much more comfortable (and feel less guilty) with a simpler program such as Quicken or MacMoney.

A variation on the general-financial management program is Checkfree Corporation's Checkfree, which provides electronic mailing of your checks. As a Checkfree subscriber (through your modem), your main interest will likely be entering your checks and having them delivered electronically, rather than mailing them out yourself. As a byproduct of this service you get a basic money-management program. Checkfree lets you keep your account balance current (what you send is what you're paying out of your account), and reconciling your account is simple and direct. The program also allows for budgeting, and exports data to Microsoft Excel and your word processing program.

Investment management applications

The next step beyond the basic, general programs is one of the most popular Mac add-on areas — investment management. There are a variety of programs available.

Wealthbuilder by *Money Magazine* provides a general planning and investment system for personal use. It allows you to enter assets manually or import the data from Andrew Tobias' Managing Your Money; establish your financial objectives based on your available assets; evaluate various investments through graphs comparing your potential investments to various standards (for instance inflation, the price of gold, the S&P 500); and then track your progress in reaching your goals. One limitation of Wealthbuilder is that you update current values of your investments through update disks prepared and sold by the publisher quarterly. You'll probably be paying for a lot of data you don't really need (or possibly not find some data you do need), and cumulative cost of these updates can mount up. On the other hand, the program is ideal for users without a modem, and it should meet your expectations if you are diligent in its use.

Another general program for investment management and analysis is Pro Plus Software's Wall Street Investor (see Figure 5-2). This program analyzes your investment portfolio and charts changes in stocks and bonds. Through your modem you may access a database of current financial data on thousands of

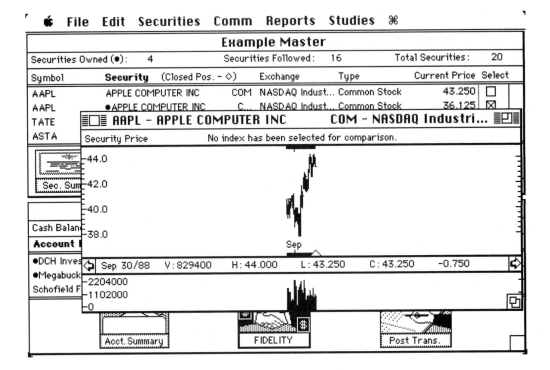

Figure 5-2: Wall Street Investor, as well as other investment management programs, offers text and graphs which help you record and track your investments. These programs also track stocks and bonds you are watching for possible purchase.

public companies, and even buy and sell securities online through various brokerage houses.

A similar program is Dow-Jones's Market Manager PLUS (from the publishers of the *Wall Street Journal*). This program also stores investment information and analyzes your portfolio in textual and graphic reports, and gives you access to Dow Jones News/Retrieval, from which you download information and price quotes.

Micro Trading Software offers its Wall Street Watcher and Stock Watcher programs. These are also investment charting programs, and Wall Street Watcher allows you to connect to Dow Jones News/Retrieval or CompuServe through your modem and automatically update and chart the value of your investments on a daily basis (or to manually update if you prefer).

A number of other portfolio-tracking programs give you access to commercial business databases in order to update your data. The Investor, for $99, allows you to track your portfolio of stocks, bonds, mutual funds, and so on, and gives you access to Dow Jones News/Retrieval as well. Larry Rosen, who has written several investment books, offers specialized, niche analysis products on separate 800K disks ($89 per disk) for tracking and analyzing stocks, bonds, and real estate. Mr. Rosen also offers programs to calculate the cost and yield of loans, as well as an analyzer that helps determine whether or not to refinance a mortgage loan.

Financial Decisions, another niche product is a $65 disk of 115 Excel templates published by GenMicronics. These templates enable you to plan goals (retirement, making a large purchase, and so on), and then project what your investments will yield toward meeting these goals.

Stephen L. Nelson's Money Manager offers a Microsoft Press booklet which contains 31 Excel templates that cover the gamut of investment analyses, such as Home Purchase vs. Rental, Tax Planning, Saving Plans, Life Insurance, Debt Management, Fixed vs. Variable Rate Loans, Real Estate, and Investment portfolios. The booklet even gets into such basics as balancing your checkbook. The book basically offers you, for $34.95, many features (through Excel templates) that Andrew Tobias' Managing Your Money gives you, less MYM's integrated check writing and financial reporting functions and Mr. Tobias' humorous commentaries.

The important thing to remember about Microsoft Excel (or Works) templates is that you can do many of these things yourself within the program, if you're so inclined. The advantage of the templates lies in paying someone else a relatively small amount to do the work for you. If your needs are specific and limited, an hour or less working with the program manual can likely give you what you need.

The specific-function investment-tracking programs are good buys if you need what they offer, such as planning for a goal or analyzing bonds (or other specific securities). I lean toward Stockwatcher as the best value at $195 since it offers a number of features found in its $495 companion program Wall Street Watcher at less than half the price. If you want the automatic updating/charting function of the more expensive program (Stockwatcher updates but doesn't chart), and you need to track puts and calls, for example, then Wall Street Watcher would be worth the extra cost. If the size of your investments doesn't justify more than a $100 investment in a tracking program, then I recommend the $99 package The Investor (see Figure 5-1).

Remember also that if you subscribe to an online service, such as Compu-Serve, you can access one of their brokerage houses and buy or sell securities at the additional hourly charge the service adds for this access.

Tax-preparation programs

Between January and April each year, the most popular Macintosh personal financial aid becomes the tax preparation program. I have been using these programs for the past seven years now, and frankly, I couldn't function without one. Income tax time used to be one of my most dreaded times of the year, but since I took a basic tax course (to give me more confidence) and adopted the personal computer for preparing my forms, tax time has been reduced to nothing more than an annual traumatic experience.

> **66** *Between January and April each year, the most popular Macintosh personal financial aid becomes the tax preparation program.* **99**

The most popular comprehensive tax preparation program on the Mac is Chipsoft's MacInTax. It offers a wide range of forms, and the forms that are not available from the IRS at publication date are provided in later updates after you mail in your registration. MacInTax also offers data import from several of the general personal finance programs, including Quicken and MacMoney. It offers many helpful features, such as linking the forms, so that entries on the Schedule A form, for example, are automatically totaled and carried over to the 1040. It also offers extensive help and explanation. MacInTax is an excellent program with good customer support. You really can't go wrong with this program.

There are a few critical elements in choosing a personal tax preparation program. The first is ease of use. Since you use the program once a year, it has to be easy to learn and relearn. The program must be direct and intuitive, or you spend more time looking up how to do things than you spend actually doing them. The other critical element is having the tax forms you need available in the package. Nothing is more frustrating than sitting down to devote a few hours to getting the onerous chore done and finding you have to hunt for some form that isn't in the package. Read the publisher's package carefully to see if it offers a wide range of forms, and, if possible, try the program to find out how easy it is for you to learn.

Another element that may be critical in choosing a personal tax program is the availability of your state's forms as a supplement to the federal program. This is a weakness in the Mac programs. MacInTax, for example, publishes a very limited number of state programs. If you live in New York or California, you should have no problem. But the Missouri and Wyoming people will have to do their state taxes manually until the publishers expand their offerings. The state supplements are sold separately, at just over half the price of the federal program; I recommend purchasing your state program if it's available.

These tax preparation programs have been enhanced each year to provide more and more help in preparing your forms, and with the way the tax laws have been bouncing around, you can't get too much help in this respect.

Chipsoft is expanding MacInTax with supplemental programs to aid in your tax planning, thus extending the annual traumatic experience into one that is ongoing throughout the year. On the other hand, many people prefer to spread the work over several months rather than gather everything at the last minute, and these supplementary programs could save you a good deal of time. MacInTax's Personal Tax Analyst series simulates situations that will affect your tax liability for the year and beyond, offering spreadsheet format that allows you to play with your projected data.

MacInTax also offers a Business Expense Reports supplement that enables business users to complete their expense reports and compile their business deduction forms simultaneously, thus eliminating the process of aggregating expenses for your tax forms (while also making sure your deduction ducks are all lined up in an auditable row).

A number of other programs can assist in preparing your taxes. Softstream International's HyperTax Tutor helps answer tax questions by allowing you to select a tax area (either in text or on a tax form), read the applicable tax laws for that area, and get tax-saving explanations and advice. The program works in hypertext, so while you're reading an explanation and find a highlighted term you don't understand, you can double-click it, get an explanation of the term, and then return to the original text. If you stumble on questions like What does the IRS consider a dependent? or Am I qualified for Head of Household?, the program is well worth the investment and is easier to navigate than the IRS or privately published tax booklets.

The Heizer software category

The Ray Heizer software catalog has an extensive array of personal financial templates for Excel and Works that makes it a category unto itself (see Figure 5-3). Heizer publishes specialized, nonintegrated niche personal finance programs at shareware prices from various authors.

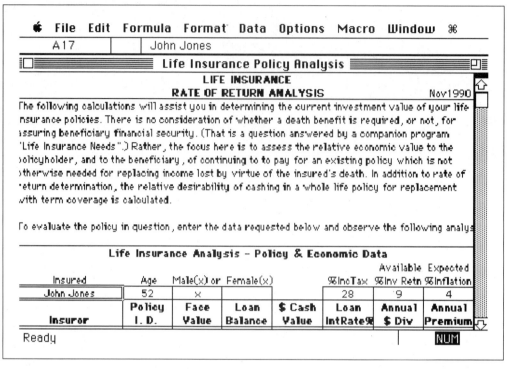

| File | Edit | Formula | Format | Data | Options | Macro | Window | ⌘ |

A17   John Jones

Life Insurance Policy Analysis

LIFE INSURANCE
RATE OF RETURN ANALYSIS   Nov1990

The following calculations will assist you in determining the current investment value of your life insurance policies. There is no consideration of whether a death benefit is required, or not, for assuring beneficiary financial security. (That is a question answered by a companion program "Life Insurance Needs".) Rather, the focus here is to assess the relative economic value to the policyholder, and to the beneficiary, of continuing to to pay for an existing policy which is not otherwise needed for replacing income lost by virtue of the insured's death. In addition to rate of return determination, the relative desirability of cashing in a whole life policy for replacement with term coverage is calculated.

To evaluate the policy in question, enter the data requested below and observe the following analysis

Life Insurance Analysis – Policy & Economic Data

Insured	Age	Male(x) or Female(x)			Available Expected
					%IncTax %Inv Retn %Inflation
John Jones	52	x			28 9 4

| Insuror | Policy I. D. | Face Value | Loan Balance | $ Cash Value | Loan IntRate% | Annual $ Div | Annual Premium |

Ready   NUM

Figure 5-3: Heizer Software's catalog lists a host of nonintegrated personal finance, and other Mac programs at shareware prices. This illustration is from the program that allows you to analyze a life insurance policy that you own, or are considering purchasing, in terms of its return on investment.

Heizer's financial programs include a check-writing program, a budgeting program, a daily income/expense log, a spreadsheet for recording and analyzing gas and electric bills, a program to analyze the advantages of insulating your house, a loan calculator, a life insurance policy analyzer, an analyzer for disability insurance needs, and a program to record an inventory of items in your home for insurance purposes, priced from $12 to $20 each. They also offer a personal financial-planning set, including tax planning, insurance needs, education financing, estate analysis, and asset management. This set of programs, priced from $14 to $36 separately, will set you back a total of only $96. Heizer also has applications for farm and ranch management, retirement, small-business finance and accounting, personal health, tax planning aids, sports, education, mathematics, clip art and religion. There is also a $15 program on mixing drinks, which could be appropriately used as a tax preparation supplement if you're so inclined.

Don't be misled by the low price of the Heizer programs. They're all first-rate products. Each delivers what its author promises and is a good value. You can get a catalog by contacting Heizer Software.

The last word in personal finance

When you have made your fortune through managing your personal finances well, tracked all your investments, and minimized your taxes, you are ready for the last personal finance program you will ever need — Nolo Press's WillMaker ($69.95). With this program you can leave property to your family, friends, and charities by making up to 28 separate bequests; name alternate beneficiaries if your first choices don't survive you; name a guardian to care for your children; and in case you're visited by three spirits some Christmas night, you can even cancel debts others owe you. According to its publisher, "wills generated by WillMaker have been used and found to be legal by thousands of lawyers since its publication in 1985."

WillMaker requires about an hour to prepare a will, and works by asking you a series of questions to which you enter the answers. The program then takes your answers and inserts them in your actual will document. The manual gives explicit instructions on legal details, such as how to get the signatures of witnesses, so that all legalities are provided for. The questions you answer are fairly easy to understand, and the publishers provide a quarterly newsletter and a technical support line to registered owners.

Nolo Press also has a companion program, For the Record ($59.95), which allows you to list your assets and liabilities and calculate your net worth to facilitate the processing of your estate and also help you for insurance purposes.

Summing up

If you're looking for a general checkwriter, Quicken or Checkwriter II will serve you best if you want maximum ease of use with minimum detail, plus Checkwriter II will work as a DA. For more detail, look at MacMoney and Dollars and Sense, and if you want to broaden into investments and insurance and/or tax planning, consider Managing Your Money (see Figure 5-1).

If Managing Your Money is not sophisticated enough, you should look at the niche programs for your specialized needs, or one of the dedicated investment programs. These programs cover a wide price range — from a Heizer program costing under $20 to the comprehensive programs selling in the $500 to $700 class. Look at the ones whose cost justifies the dollar-size of the investments it'll be handling. I consider Stockwatcher ($195) an especially good buy in the comprehensive program category (see Figure 5-1).

Summary

✔ For the person who wants a simple, easy-to-use check writer program, there are basic, no-frill applications like Quicken, Aatrix Checkwriter II, MacMoney, and Dollars and Sense.

✔ Programs like Andrew Tobias's Managing Your Money combine basic check writing with insurance planning and investment programs.

✔ Checkfree is an application that allows you to pay bills electronically.

✔ A variety of programs are available for investment planning and tracking, covering basic planning for such things as sending your children to college, to sophisticated programs that automatically download data daily and track and chart your individual stocks, bonds, and other investments.

✔ Different publishers offer specialized niche programs that track and analyze stocks, bonds, and real estate investments.

✔ Several publishers offer templates that can be used with Microsoft's Excel or Works programs to analyze life insurance, manage debt, and calculate whether you should buy or rent a home.

✔ The burden of tax preparation programs can significantly be lightened by using tax programs when it comes time to pay your federal and state income taxes.

Where to buy

Andrew Tobias' Managing Your Money, $249
MECA Software, Inc.
55 Walls Dr.
Fairfield, CT 06430
800-288-6322

Bond Portfolio Manager, $89
Larry Rosen Co.
7008 Springdale Road
Louisville, KY 40241
502-228-4343

Checkfree, $29.95
Checkfree Corp.
P.O. Box 987
Columbus, OH 43272-4320
614-898-6000

Checkwriter II, $59
Aatrix Software Inc.
P.O. Box 5359
Grand Forks, ND 58206-5359
701-746-6801

Complete Bond Analyzer, $89
Larry Rosen Co.
7008 Springdale Road
Louisville, KY 40241
502-228-4343

Dollars and Sense, $99.95
The Software Toolworks
60 Leveroni Court
Novato, CA 94949
415-883-3000

Financial and Intercut Calculator, $89
Larry Rosen Co.
7008 Springdale Road
Louisville, KY 40241
502-228-4343

Financial Decisions, $65
General Micronics
5900 Shore Blvd., #401
St. Petersburg, FL 33707
813-345-5020
603-664-9020

For the Record, $59.95
Nolo Press
950 Parker St.
Berkeley, CA 94710
415-549-1976

HyperTax Tutor, $99
Softstream International
10 Twin Ponds Road
South Dartmouth, MA 02748
508-991-4011

Investment Analysis for Stocks, Bonds, and Real Estate, $89
Larry Rosen Co.
7008 Springdale Road
Louisville, KY 40241
502-228-4343

The Investor, $99
Arminius Publications & Products Inc.
P.O. Box 1265
Merchantville, NJ 08109-0265
609-662-3420

MacInTax, $99
Chipsoft, Inc.
6330 Nancy Ridge Road, Ste. 103
San Diego, CA 92121
619-587-3939

Mac Money, $119.95
Survivor Software Ltd.
11222 La Cienega Blvd, Ste. 459
Inglewood, CA 90304
213-410-9527

Market Manager PLUS, $299
Dow Jones and Co. Inc.
P.O. Box 300
Princeton, NJ 08543-0300
609-520-4641

Microsoft Excel Money Manager by Stephen Nelson, $34.95
Microsoft Corp.
One Microsoft Way
Redmond, WA 98052-6399
800-426-9400

Mortgage Loan, $89
Larry Rosen Co.
7008 Springdale Road
Louisville, KY 40241
502-228-4343

Personal Finance Templates, $35
Pop-Up Publishing
5901 Warner Ave.
Huntington Beach, CA 92649
714-894-9930

Quicken, $59.95
Intuit
P.O. Box 3014
Menlo Park, CA 94026
415-322-0573
800-624-8742

The Ray Heizer software catalog
Heizer Software
1941 Oak Park Blvd., Ste. 30
P.O. Box 232019
Pleasant Hill, CA 94523
415-943-7667
800-888-7667

Stock Watcher, $195
Micro Trading Software Ltd.
Box 175
Wilton, CT 06897
203-762-7820

Wall Street Investor, $695
Pro Plus Software Inc.
2150 East Brown Road
Mesa, AZ 85213
602-461-3296

Wall Street Watcher, $495
Micro Trading Software Ltd.
Box 175
Wilton, CT 06897
203-762-7820

Wealth Builder, $149
Reality Technology
3624 Market St.
Philadelphia, PA 19104
215-387-6055

WillMaker 4.0, $69.95
Nolo Press
950 Parker St.
Berkeley, CA 94710
415-549-1976

Chapter 6
Picking a Printer

by Jim Heid

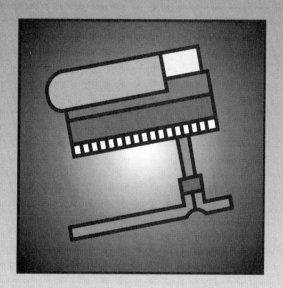

In this chapter...

- ✔ Four common printers — dot matrix, ink jet, laser, and color — and how they work.
- ✔ Choosing the right kind of printer for your needs.
- ✔ A detailed look at laser printers.
- ✔ Using a printer designed for an IBM PC with a Mac.
- ✔ Color printers: ready for prime time?

Whether you use the Mac to create mailing lists, desktop publications, business graphics, legal briefs, or novels, you'll need a way to commit your efforts to paper. This chapter looks at the types of printers available for the Mac, with a special focus on the most popular category — the laser printer. The prices listed here are suggested retail prices; keep in mind many dealers and mail-order houses offer discounts of between 10 to 25 percent off retail.

About the author

Jim Heid has been writing for *Macworld* since 1984, and has appeared in every issue since March 1985. In addition to features and reviews, he writes the monthly "Getting Started" column, which was recently nominated for an Excellence in Technology Communications award. He specializes in page printers, desktop publishing, typography, MIDI, and digital audio — a mix that exploits his background as a typographer, musician, and audio buff. (He grew up in his father's recording studio, which was Pittsburgh's first.)

Prior to writing for *Macworld,* he was Senior Technical Editor for *Kilobaud Microcomputing* magazine. He has been working with and writing about personal computers since the late 70s, when he computerized his home-built ham radio station with one of the first Radio Shack TRS-80s. He is the author of five books on Macintosh and IBM PC personal computing including *Inside the Apple Macintosh* (Brady, 1989) which he coauthored with Peter Norton, and *Macworld Complete Mac Handbook* (IDG Books Worldwide, 1991). He has spoken to user's groups in New York City and Los Angeles, at developer's con-ferences, and at Macworld Expos. He and his wife live on California's scenic Mendocino coast.

Printer categories

Macintosh printers fall into four general categories:

❖ *Dot matrix.* Printers such as Apple's Image-Writer II are successors to the typewriter — they create text and graphics by striking an inked ribbon. But where a typewriter uses preformed characters, a dot-matrix printer uses a grid — a matrix — of fine wires located in a *print head* that moves from left to right across the page. By firing these wires in specific patterns, the printer can produce graphics and text in any typestyle. Where print quality is concerned, dot-matrix printers are on the bottom of the totem pole. However, because they're *impact printers,* they can print on carbon or carbonless multipage business forms such as invoices — a feat the other printers discussed here can't match. Dot-matrix printers are also ideal for printing mailing labels, since they can accept *continuous-feed* paper stock (paper whose sheets are attached to each other, accordion-style). Price: $595.

❖ *Ink jet.* Apple's StyleWriter and Hewlett-Packard's DeskWriter are higher-class cousins of dot-matrix printers. Instead of using an inked ribbon and print wires to produce images, an ink-jet printer uses several dozen microscopic nozzles that spray extremely fine streams of ink at the paper (see Figure 6-1). Besides making the printer much quieter than its dot-matrix counterparts, this scheme allows for much finer print quality, or *resolution.* For

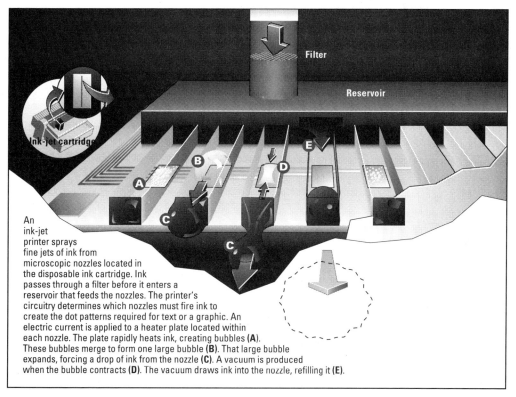

Filter

Reservoir

Ink-jet cartridge

An
ink-jet
printer sprays
fine jets of ink from
microscopic nozzles located in
the disposable ink cartridge. Ink
passes through a filter before it enters a
reservoir that feeds the nozzles. The printer's
circuitry determines which nozzles must fire ink to
create the dot patterns required for text or a graphic. An
electric current is applied to a heater plate located within
each nozzle. The plate rapidly heats ink, creating bubbles (**A**).
These bubbles merge to form one large bubble (**B**). That large bubble
expands, forcing a drop of ink from the nozzle (**C**). A vacuum is produced
when the bubble contracts (**D**). The vacuum draws ink into the nozzle, refilling it (**E**).

Figure 6-1: Inside an ink-jet printer.

example, the ImageWriter II has a maximum resolution of 144 dots per inch (dpi), while a StyleWriter can print 360 dpi. But ink jets have some distinct disadvantages — more about them shortly. Price: $599 to $729.

❖ *Laser.* The type of printer most people associate with the Mac, laser printers use photocopier-like mechanisms to produce text and graphics with 300-dpi resolution (see Figure 6-2). Laser printers are much faster than dot-matrix or ink-jet units — even the least-expensive models can print up to several pages per minute. Laser printers are also the preferred units for desktop publishing and proofing, since their resolution is high enough to accurately render the subtleties of typographic fonts and to print newspaper-quality halftones of scanned images. Price: $999 to over $10,000.

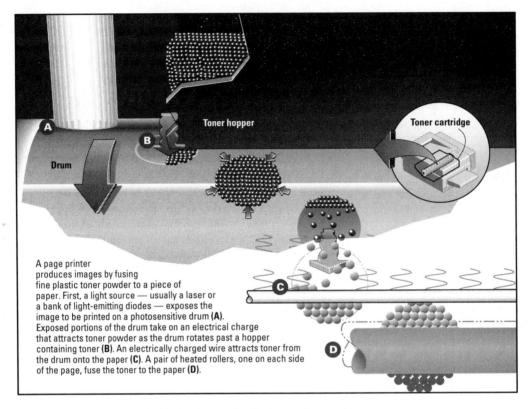

A page printer
produces images by fusing
fine plastic toner powder to a piece of
paper. First, a light source — usually a laser or
a bank of light-emitting diodes — exposes the
image to be printed on a photosensitive drum (**A**).
Exposed portions of the drum take on an electrical charge
that attracts toner powder as the drum rotates past a hopper
containing toner (**B**). An electrically charged wire attracts toner from
the drum onto the paper (**C**). A pair of heated rollers, one on each side
of the page, fuse the toner to the paper (**D**).

Figure 6-2: Inside the photocopier-like laser printer.

❖ *Color.* These specialized scribes use a variety of complex techniques to apply colored ink, dye, or wax to paper — usually to special paper, at that, although plain-paper color printers are becoming available. Low-end color printers are used for printing attention-getting overhead transparencies and business graphics. High-end units are often used for proofing color publications, scanned images, and illustrations that will be printed using four-color printing presses. For critical color publishing applications, however, most publishing pros still rely on photographic *cromalins* or *matchprints* produced by color-separation service bureaus. But because such prints often cost $50 to $100 each, many publishers use proofs from color printers first to look for obvious errors in color balance or placement. Price: from about $1,000 to $50,000 and up.

Dot-matrix printers — printing with impact

If you need to print on multipart forms or continuous-feed stock, a dot-matrix printer is the answer. There hasn't exactly been a population explosion in this product category, however — Apple's venerable ImageWriter has owned the market ever since it was introduced along with the original Mac. The current model, the ImageWriter II ($595) can also produce color images when equipped with a color ribbon.

The ImageWriter II can use two basic types of paper: *fanfold* (one continuous sheet, perforated so you can tear it into separate sheets after printing), and standard sheets that you roll into the printer's mechanism as though loading a typewriter. If you use single sheets often, you might consider the optional *cut-sheet feeder* ($225), which feeds single sheets automatically. You can also share an ImageWriter II on a network by adding the Apple's ImageWriter II/LQ LocalTalk Option ($139), a circuit board that plugs into the printer.

A few other firms currently offer or have offered dot-matrix printers for the Mac, but they aren't recommended — not because they're inferior to the ImageWriter II, but because software companies generally test their programs only with the most popular Mac printers. Buy an obscure printer, and you may encounter printing problems with your favorite programs. As any video buff who suffered through the Beta-versus-VHS wars of a few years ago will tell you, a product's popularity can influence its usefulness more than its quality and performance.

Ink-jet printers

As mentioned earlier, ink-jet printers are capable of much higher output resolution than dot-matrix units. But ink-jet output still isn't in the laser league. Up close, even the naked eye can discern sloppy character edges created by ink seeping into the paper's fibers as it dries. Scanned images and large black areas have a mottled look. You can minimize these flaws by photocopying printed pages, but handle them gently — ink-jet output can smear in its first few seconds of life.

> **" As any video buff who suffered through the Beta-versus-VHS wars of a few years ago will tell you, a product's popularity can influence its usefulness more than its quality and performance. "**

Today's ink-jet printers no longer require special paper, as did some pioneering models of the mid-80s, but they're still more finicky than lasers. Apple's StyleWriter and Hewlett-Packard's DeskWriter can't handle heavy card stocks and can't automatically feed multiple envelopes. And output quality varies dramatically depending on the quality of paper you use. You'll also wait longer to see it; most personal laser printers can churn out several pages in the time it takes an ink-jet to produce one.

StyleWriter vs. DeskWriter

Apple's StyleWriter and Hewlett-Packard's DeskWriter are the only two Mac-specific ink-jet printers that produce 300-dpi or sharper output. (GCC's three-pound, battery-powered $549 WriteMove prints 192 dpi.) The StyleWriter retails for $599. Shortly after the StyleWriter debuted, Hewlett-Packard cut the DeskWriter's retail price to $729.

DeskWriters manufactured after May 1990 are equipped with a LocalTalk connector, allowing them to be shared on a network. The StyleWriter can't be shared on a network; it connects via a serial cable to the Mac's modem or printer port. Neither printer supports background printing under MultiFinder or System 7, but both are compatible with third-party spoolers such as Fifth Generation Systems' SuperLaserSpool.

The DeskWriter includes four font families (Compugraphic versions of Helvetica, Times, Courier, and Symbol); an optional font pack includes seven additional families (the standard LaserWriter Plus mix). All fonts are outlines, and HP's easily installed driver software can scale them to any size up to 250-point. The printer also works so well with Adobe Type Manager (ATM) that some mail-order firms sell the pair together.

The StyleWriter includes the same four font families, but the fonts themselves are Apple TrueType outline fonts, which can be scaled to sizes larger than 250-point. The StyleWriter is also ATM-compatible.

In tests performed by Macworld Lab, the StyleWriter was about twice as slow as the DeskWriter. But where size and portability are concerned, it's no contest: the StyleWriter is definitely the lightweight champion.

The StyleWriter also has the edge where it counts: in output quality. Its 360-dpi resolution makes StyleWriter output noticeably sharper than that of a DeskWriter. Still, the StyleWriter falls short of the deep, rich blacks that laser printers provide. And water — even a moistened finger — causes StyleWriter output to smear.

The StyleWriter's lower price, TrueType fonts, and higher resolution make it the better printer, but the DeskWriter isn't out of the running. HP's latest inks are less prone to smearing than the StyleWriter's. And although the DeskWriter is far too slow to serve a large network, it could keep up with a couple of patient small-business or education users. If portability and resolution are less important to you than speed, water resistance, and network compatibility, the DeskWriter is the printer of choice.

Laser printers

If you've been longing for a laser printer but have been waiting to buy until prices fall, your day has come. 1990 was the year of the Volkslaser, as Apple, QMS, GCC Technologies, NEC, Texas Instruments, and others unveiled nearly a dozen new 300-dpi laser printers aimed at individuals and small businesses. For between $999 and $3,000, you can buy a printer that provides more fonts, better print quality, and faster performance than Apple's original $6,995 LaserWriter. These improvements in the price-to-performance ratio apply at the higher ends of the laser printer spectrum, too. High-performance workhorse printers that churn out ten or more pages per minute now start at about $4,000.

QuickDraw, PostScript, or both?

The first step toward finding the right laser printer involves choosing between printers that rely on Adobe Systems' PostScript page-description language, or on QuickDraw, the Mac's built-in library of text- and graphics-display routines.

Either a PostScript or a QuickDraw printer can handle text-oriented documents such as correspondence, manuscripts, and contracts. But for printing desktop publications, illustrations, scanned images, and other graphics-intensive jobs, choose a PostScript printer. Built-in networking features also make a PostScript printer almost essential if you have more than one computer (whether Mac or IBM PC), because you can share the printer with each machine by buying inexpensive LocalTalk connector kits.

> 66 *Overall, PostScript printers offer so many advantages — some technical, others side effects of PostScript's popularity — that it's hard to imagine choosing any other kind of printer.* 99

PostScript printers often operate more quickly because they relieve the Mac of most of the work involved in printing a page. Overall, PostScript printers offer so many advantages — some technical, others side effects of PostScript's popularity — that it's hard to imagine choosing any other kind of printer. Until you compare prices.

PostScript printers cost more than comparable QuickDraw printers, mostly because of their more sophisticated controller circuitry, but also because of the licensing and royalty fees Adobe Systems charges printer manufacturers. Some examples: GCC Technologies' QuickDraw-based PLP II retails for $999; its PostScript-driven cousin, the BLP Elite, sells for $1,599. Apple's Personal Laser-Writer LS lists for $1,299, while the Personal LaserWriter NT goes for $2,599. The extra cost is easier to justify if you plan to share the printer among several machines, but most people shopping for a personal printer don't have sharing in mind.

The good news is that the chasm in capabilities between PostScript and QuickDraw printers is narrowing. The release of Apple's TrueType fonts for System 6.0.7 and System 7 is one contributing factor, but overall — and ironically — Adobe deserves most of the credit. Its $99 Adobe Type Manager utility gives QuickDraw printers access to thousands of PostScript fonts, and lets them print those fonts in almost any size. And Adobe's TypeAlign program works with ATM to allow you to skew and distort text, attach it to a curving baseline, and create other exotic effects that previously were beyond QuickDraw's capabilities.

Even with TrueType, ATM, and TypeAlign, however, QuickDraw printers deliver inferior results with PostScript-oriented drawing programs such as Aldus FreeHand and Adobe Illustrator. But you can bridge even that gap by using PostScript emulation software such as QMS's UltraScript or Custom Applications' Freedom of Press. Printing via a PostScript emulator is almost always slower than using a true PostScript printer, but in the world of personal page printing, performance often takes a back seat to affordability.

Evaluating engines

Deciding between QuickDraw and PostScript is only half the job. *Print engines*, the mechanisms that shuttle paper and produce images on it, also vary widely.

The name *laser printer* derives from the use of lasers to expose images on photosensitive drums or belts, which then attract fine plastic toner powder and apply it to the paper. (Some of today's printers use alternative light sources such as banks of light-emitting diodes, but they're still often described as laser printers. Technically, the correct term for all these beasts is *page printer.*) As the paper leaves the printer, a pair of heated rollers melts the powder into place.

Like photocopiers, laser printers offer different paper-handling speeds and capacities. Most printer engines can push paper at a pace of four to ten pages per minute (ppm). Generally, however, you see these speeds only when printing multiple copies of the same document or very simple documents, such as manuscripts in the Courier font.

As for paper capacities, most printers provide one paper tray that holds between 100 and 250 sheets. Some printers, including Apple's Personal LaserWriter NT, QMS's PS-825, Qume's CrystalPrint Express, and HP's LaserJet IIIsi, provide two paper trays. Two trays allow you to easily mix letterhead and second sheets or envelopes, and they help cut down on feeding sessions.

Speaking of feeding, the printer's toner supply requires replacement every few thousand pages or so. Canon-built engines, found in Apple, Canon, QMS, and

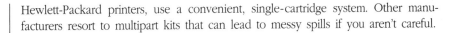

Hewlett-Packard printers, use a convenient, single-cartridge system. Other manufacturers resort to multipart kits that can lead to messy spills if you aren't careful.

Alas, the disposable cartridges used in Canon engines are an environmentalist's nightmare, each contributing several pounds of plastic to the local landfill. Happily, you can recycle cartridges — and save money in the process. (For recycling information, try the American Cartridge Recycling Association, 305-539-0701 or the International Computer Products Remanufacturing Association, 503-222-3215.)

What constitutes good performance?

As you can see, a printer's controller and its engine each play a role in determining general performance. For that reason, consider the types of documents you plan to print, then choose the printer whose controller and engine are best suited to them.

With QuickDraw printers such as Apple's Personal LaserWriter LS and SC and GCC's PLP II and IIs, your job is relatively easy. Because the Mac acts as the controller, the printer's speed at handling complex jobs containing lots of fonts and graphics will depend on the speed of the Mac. If complex jobs slow the printer to a crawl, you can boost performance by endowing the Mac with more memory or even an accelerator board upgrade. And the upgrades pay performance dividends even when you aren't printing.

With PostScript printers, the Mac's speed plays a very small role in determining performance, making the engine-controller balancing act more important. If you print short but complex documents — lots of fonts and sizes, large scanned images, PostScript graphics — a printer with a fast controller, such as the QMS-PS 410, will out-perform a printer with a slower controller but a fast engine, such as GCC's BLP IIs. For simple but lengthy documents — legal contracts, manuscripts, proposals, "personalized" form letters — a printer with a fast engine will serve you better.

> **66** *... a printer's controller and its engine each play a role in determining general performance ... consider the types of documents you plan to print, then choose the printer whose controller and engine are best suited to them.* **99**

Optimal control

Several factors influence the performance of a PostScript printer's controller. For starters, the type of central processing unit (CPU) used in the controller and the speed at which it runs govern how quickly the controller can perform the many calculations involved in producing a page. Nearly all personal PostScript printers use a Motorola 68000 CPU running at speeds of between 10 and 16MHz, although there are exceptions. QMS' swift little PS 410, for example, uses the faster 68020, often found in higher-priced lasers, including Apple's LaserWriter IINTX. A growing number of printers — Qume's CrystalPrint Publisher II and CrystalPrint Express, Epson's EPL-7500, and DataProducts' LZR-660, to name a few — use specialized RISC (reduced instruction-set computer) microprocessors that are designed to run faster than general-purpose processors such as the 68000 series.

The amount of internal memory the controller provides also influences performance. More memory allows faster performance with typographically complex documents because the printer can retain, or *cache,* a larger number of character bit maps, eliminating the need to reconstruct those characters from the original font outlines if they're needed again. More memory also allows the printer to hold more *downloadable* fonts, ones stored on the Mac's hard drive and transferred to the printer during the print job.

Built-in memory is also an important issue if you plan to mix downloadable PostScript fonts and TrueType outline fonts. In System 7, Apple's TrueType *rasterizing* software (which generates characters in the sizes needed for a given page) is downloaded to a PostScript printer's memory during the print job. The TrueType rasterizer requires about 50K of printer memory, leaving less room for downloadable PostScript fonts. The memory crunch will hit hardest in the base models of TI's microLasers, which contain just 1.5MB.

Adobe Systems is always refining and improving the PostScript interpreter software that it sells to printer vendors. The latest PostScript versions usually include Adobe Type Manager font rasterizer. All other things being equal, a printer that contains ATM routines prints text faster than one that doesn't.

(Incidentally, don't confuse the ATM rasterizing routines with the ATM utility mentioned earlier. The ATM utility runs on the Mac and provides sharp characters for the screen and for QuickDraw printers. ATM rasterizing software built into a PostScript printer's controller allows the printer to create characters more quickly.)

Send in the clones: low-budget PostScript

Then there are the PostScript clones — printers that understand PostScript, but use non-Adobe PostScript interpreters. In the personal printer market, PostScript clones include Abaton's LaserScript, Qume's CrystalPrint Publisher series, Microtek's TrueLaser, and Abaton's LaserScript LX. Clone vendors usually claim faster performance than Adobe PostScript printers, even high-end ones like Apple's LaserWriter IINTX.

Those claims don't always hold up. In my experience, PostScript clones are faster when printing typographically complex documents and object-oriented (MacDraw-type) graphics, but they're often slower when printing bit-mapped graphics, especially scanned images.

In the past, PostScript clones had serious problems handling *Type 1* down-loadable fonts, the downloadable font format used by Adobe and many other font developers. Type 1 fonts contain instructions that the printer's controller uses to optimize the appearance of each character at a given size. These instructions, also called *hints,* are encrypted, and clone developers were unwilling to crack the code, fearing lawsuits from Adobe.

Adobe recently has published most of the Type 1 specifications, however, and clone vendors have decrypted most hints. Today's PostScript clones still don't handle Adobe Type 1 fonts as skillfully as Adobe interpreters, but the differences are becoming difficult to discern, even under magnification.

PC patch jobs

Laser and ink-jet printers designed for the IBM PC world often cost considerably less than their Mac-specific cousins. If you're willing to stray from the pack and deal with occasional incompatibilities, you can get that laser look by using a PC printer with a Mac. You merely need the proper cable and driver software that the PC printer can understand.

For software, use a QuickDraw-based driver package such as JetLink Express or MacPrint, or a PostScript emulator such as QMS's UltraScript, Custom Applications's Freedom of Press, or TeleTypesetting's T-Script.

In the past, third-party PC printer drivers have had serious application compatibility problems. Fortunately, with the proliferation of QuickDraw-based laser and ink-jet printers, applications developers have begun to adapt to Apple's programming guidelines. But pages of caveats and workarounds still pollute the JetLink Express and MacPrint manuals, so verify compatibility with your favorite programs before you buy.

> 66 *If you're willing to stray from the pack and deal with occasional incompatibilities, you can get that laser look by using a PC printer with a Mac.* 99

A PostScript emulation program resides on your Mac's hard drive and acts as an intermediary between your programs and a non-PostScript printer. When you issue a Print command, the emulator saves on disk the PostScript instructions from the LaserWriter driver. The emulator's interpreter then takes over, translating the file into instructions your printer can understand. QMS UltraScript provides the best mix of performance and ease of use.

Laser printer picks

In the under-$3,000 class, one laser printer stands above the rest: the $2,795 QMS PS 410. The PS 410 combines the easy-to-set up Canon LX engine with a 16MHz, 68020-based controller that handles complex documents as swiftly as a

$5,999 LaserWriter IINTX. The PS 410 also includes excellent documentation and a package of support disks for both the Mac and IBM PC.

It's a superb printer for anyone who has both Macs and PCs, thanks to its ability to switch automatically between PostScript and HP LaserJet emulation mode depending on the type of data it receives. (QMS pioneered the emulation-sensing technique, now used in a few other PostScript printers. With most printers, though, you need to flick switches or send special software codes to change between PostScript and HP emulation.) In short, this little printer has it all — almost.

The PS 410 holds only 50 sheets of paper, unless you buy the optional 250-sheet tray for $195. Even then, however, you may find the printer's 4-ppm engine too slow for typographically simple documents or multiple copies of the same document. For such applications, I recommend GCC's $2,899 BLP IIs. Its controller is slower than the PS 410's, but its 8-ppm engine gives it the edge when engine speed counts most. Okidata's $2,599 OkiLaser 840 uses the identical engine but is slower.

The BLP IIs and its 4-ppm cousin, the $1,999 BLP II, are also the only personal PostScript printers that provide a SCSI connector for attaching a font-storage hard drive. Indeed, if you use droves of downloadable fonts, a BLP II with a hard drive could prove faster than the PS-410, as it would eliminate font-downloading time.

The PS 410 and the BLP series reside near the top of the personal printer price range. For a less costly PostScript-based machine, consider GCC's 4-ppm BLP Elite ($1,599) or TI's 6-ppm microLaser. Mail-order houses often discount the micro-Laser PS17, which (like the BLP Elite) contains 17 fonts, to as low as $1,399. I've found the 35-font version for $1749. The microLaser's swift controller and its 6-ppm engine provide balanced performance for any type of job.

Another solid performer in the under-$3,000 class is Dataproducts's $2,995 LZR-960. The LZR-660 is a 9-ppm printer built around a Weitek RISC processor, and it contains Adobe's Level 2 PostScript — which among other things, runs faster than the Level 1 PostScript in use today. The LZR-960 also provides a SCSI port for a font-storage hard drive. You might also consider Epson's $2,999 ELP-7500, which uses a 6-ppm Minolta engine and a controller containing a Weitek RISC processor (one of which also powers Qume's swift CrystalPrint Publisher II). But the Qume's a clone; the ELP-7500 uses an Adobe interpreter.

As for the QuickDraw printers, it's a tougher call. On paper, the $999 PLP II has the price edge over the $1,299 Personal LaserWriter LS. On the street, however, the two printers' prices may be closer, given that many Apple dealers offer discounts in the 20 percent ballpark. GCC has a smaller dealer network and primarily sells its products directly through mail order. But shop around — if your area has a GCC dealer, you may find the PLP II for less than $999.

The Personal LaserWriter LS may cost more than the PLP II, but it's a better printer. Although the LS holds less paper (unless you buy the optional 250-sheet tray), its engine is superior and the printer is easier to setup, thanks to its use of a serial cable instead of the SCSI connection scheme used in the PLP II series.

The LS's printer driver is also more smoothly integrated into the Mac environment. You can print in the background under MultiFinder and you'll never have to endure the two-step printing process that the PLP driver imposes on you when memory is tight. An LS tested by Macworld Lab was faster than the PLP II in text-oriented tasks, but slower when printing graphics.

Still, choosing an LS means living with some limitations. You can upgrade each PLP to a PostScript-based BLP Elite for $799; no such upgrade will be offered for the LS. And if your Mac's modem and printer ports are already connected to other devices, you'll need to buy a serial switch box in order to accommodate an LS. If you want to add PostScript down the road, the PLP II series may be a better choice.

If you'll be connecting a PostScript printer to more than a few computers, chances are that a 4- to 6-ppm printer will be too slow. Between $4,000 and $10,000 will buy a workhorse printer that combines a fast controller with a fast, heavy-duty engine capable of printing up to 16 to 22 pages per minute. The least expensive offering in this class is TI's 16-ppm microLaser XL. The 17-font version retails for $4,049; the 35-font version for $4,599. A 500-sheet feeder and 70-envelope feeder are also available.

Another recent entry in this class is Hewlett-Packard's LaserJet IIIsi, whose 17-ppm engine provides two paper trays and support for *duplex* printing — the ability to print on both sides of a sheet of paper. Equipped with PostScript and LocalTalk interface — a configuration HP says will be available in the fall of 1991 — the IIIsi will retail for approximately $8,000. The IIIsi also features HP's Resolution Enhancement Technology (RET) — a custom chip finely controls the print engine's laser to adjust the size and position of individual dots to smooth the jagged edges that plague diagonal lines and curves in both graphics and text (especially italics).

A step up in engine speed and page size is QMS's $9,995 PS 2210 which provides a 22-ppm engine that can print tabloid-sized (11 × 17-inch) pages. The PS 2210 provides a SCSI port for a font-storage hard disk and a 68020-based controller that provides 49 fonts and QMS's emulation-sensing features.

At the top of the laser printer spectrum is the QMS PS 2000, which can crank out 20 tabloid-sized pages per minute *and* supports duplex printing. The $15,995 PS 2000 sports a 25MHz RISC-based controller that provides 45 fonts, 8MB of memory, and emulation sensing. Internal and external hard disks are available as options (and can store incoming print jobs as well as fonts), as is a high-speed Ethernet network interface.

Then there's Kodak's 16-ppm Ektaplus 7016, which also does duty as a 6-ppm photocopier — even while accepting a print job from a Mac or PC. Retailing for $6,995 including a 4MB, 68020-based PostScript controller board, the Ektaplus 7016 uses an LED-based engine technology similar to that used in Kodak's Ektaprint copiers. A laser printer that's also a copier — it's a smart idea that lets you get more out of the printer's mechanism and more for your money. And when you spend several thousand dollars on a printer, you want to work it as hard as you can.

Color printers

Today's color Macs can display vivid images with photographic realism — it's this talent that has made the Mac the computer of choice for image processing, prepress, and color scanning jobs. But displaying an image is one thing, printing it is another. Printers capable of doing justice to the Mac's color capabilities have been slow in coming (some experts feel they have yet to arrive). The technology and the selection are improving, however, and prices are falling.

Low-end color ink-jet printers

The printers in this category are unsuitable for critical jobs such as prepress proofing, but are ideal for printing color overhead transparencies and presentation materials. Color ink-jet printers work much like the monochrome ink jets described earlier in this chapter. But where a monochrome ink jet's reservoir contains just one color (black), a color ink jet's contains four — cyan, magenta, yellow, and black. The printer can combine dot patterns of these colors to produce other colors, a technique called *dithering*. None of the printers described in this section use PostScript, but if you're patient, you can use a PostScript-emulation utility such as Freedom of Press to print color PostScript graphics.

> 66 *A laser printer that's also a copier — it's a smart idea that lets you get more out of the printer's mechanism, and more for your money.* 99

One of the best choices in low-end color ink-jet printers is Hewlett-Packard's PaintWriter, a faster successor to HP's now-discontinued PaintJet. Retailing for $1,395, the PaintWriter supports page sizes of up to 8½ × 11-inches and boasts a resolution of 180 dpi. The printer connects to the Mac via the modem or printer port, and includes a selection of outline fonts and a driver that supports background printing under MultiFinder or System 7 and is compatible with Adobe Type Manager. A wide-carriage model, the $2,595 PaintWriter XL, can print on 11 × 17-inch paper and provides a LocalTalk connector that allows the printer to be shared on a network.

A smaller and slightly sharper alternative to the PaintWriter is Kodak's Diconix color 4, which weighs just 13 pounds and prints on plain paper or ink-jet transparency film at a resolution of 192 dpi. Like HP's PaintWriter, the Diconix color 4 can print on cut sheets or continuous, pin-fed stock. The printer includes a cable, driver software, and serial interface for connection to the Mac's modem port. The Diconix color 4 retails for $1,595 in the United States and $2,195 in Canada.

Stepping up in resolution and price is the Textronix ColorQuick ink-jet printer, which prints at 216 dpi and retails for $2,495. The ColorQuick lives up to its name, in part because it attaches to the Mac's SCSI port rather than to the slower modem or printer ports. The printer supports page sizes of up to 12 × 18-inches.

Mid-range color printers

Color printers in this spectrum cost between $5,000 and $10,000, produce 300-dpi output, generally use Adobe PostScript or PostScript-clone controllers, and support popular color-matching systems such as Pantone. As with monochrome PostScript-based printers, the speed and type of processor used in a color printer's controller and the amount of memory in the controller directly affect the printer's performance at handling complex documents. Indeed, *complex* takes on new meaning in the color PostScript world, where a printer not only must generate font bitmaps and process PostScript graphics commands, it must also apply its coloring pigments in up to four passes — one each for cyan, magenta, yellow, and optionally, black. The extra memory and processing punch required for printing 300-dpi color contribute to the printers' hefty price tags.

The printers' engines aren't cheap, either. Among 300-dpi color printers, the most popular engine technology is *thermal wax-transfer.* A thermal wax-transfer printer uses wax-based pigments in each process color (cyan, yellow, magenta, and black), positioned one after another on a roll of film. A print head containing thousands of heating elements is sandwiched between the film ribbon and the paper. The print head's heating elements are turned on and off as needed to print individual dots in each of three or four passes.

Like ink-jet printers, thermal wax-transfer printers can produce other colors through combinations of cyan, magenta, and yellow. Thermal wax-transfer printers use dither patterns that simulate the color halftones produced by four-color printing presses. A 300-dpi printer's halftones aren't nearly as sharp, however — even the naked eye can easily discern the groups, or *rosettes,* of cyan, magenta, and yellow dots that the printer combines to create other colors.

Most thermal wax-transfer printers use individual cut sheets of paper, although Seiko's ColorPoint PS uses a roll of paper that's cut into individual sheets by a built-in cutter at the end of the printing job. Generally, thermal wax-transfer printers deliver poor results with plain paper, requiring special coated paper that can withstand the printhead's heat.

Seiko's ColorPoint PS is available in two models. The Model 4 retails for $6,999 and supports letter-sized pages; the Model 14 retails for $9,999 and prints tabloids. Both models use Intel 80960 RISC-based controllers running PhoenixPage, a Post-Script clone. The print quality is very good, but the printer's performance is a bit sluggish compared to that of its competitors.

One faster competitor is NEC's Colormate PS Model 80, which retails for $8,995 and prints on letter-sized sheets. The Colormate PS Model 80 uses an Adobe Atlas controller, wherein a 68020 processor running at 16MHz presides over 8MB of memory. Another good choice is Tektronix's $7,995 Phaser II PX, which also uses a 68020-based Adobe interpreter. QMS's $8,995 ColorScript 100 Model 10 delivers good performance too, but its output isn't quite as vivid as that of its competitors.

One interesting newcomer in this price range is Tektronix's $9,995 PhaserJet PXi. This printer uses a *phase change ink-jet* engine capable of printing on plain paper with excellent results. The PhaserJet PXi's inks are solid at room temperature; at printing time, the print engine melts the ink and then sprays them onto the paper, where they solidify so quickly that most of the ink sits on the paper's surface instead of soaking into its fibers. The PhaserJet PXi is also one of the first color printers to use Adobe's PostScript Level 2, which offers better support for color printing than does PostScript Level 1. The PhaserJet PXi supports page sizes of up to 12 × 18-inches.

High-end color printers

The most vivid color output currently comes from *dye sublimation* printers, which can produce near-photorealistic, continuous-tone images with smooth color gradations. Unlike the wax-based inks used in thermal ink-jet printers, sublimation dyes are transparent, and the printer is able to finely control the size of each dot. The results are remarkable — and remarkably expensive. Dupont's 4Cast sells for roughly $48,000, Kodak's XL 7700 goes for over $24,000, and Mitsubishi's S340-10 will set you back $13,995.

Equally promising are color laser printers such as ColorOcs' CP 4007, which offers PostScript compatibility and one-pass printing for $29,995. Canon USA is also finishing up a PostScript interface for its impressive $60,000 Color Laser Copier.

Summary

✔ Dot-matrix printers provide the poorest output quality, but they can print on carbon and carbon-less multipart forms and are ideal for mailing labels.

✔ Ink-jet printer output approaches laser output in quality, but can be smeared and requires careful paper selection. Ink-jet printers are also much slower than lasers.

✔ Laser printers provide excellent overall quality and performance. Factors to consider when choosing one include speed, paper handling features, and support for PostScript.

✔ Color printers are costly, but their prices are falling as quality improves. Low-end color ink-jet printers are suitable for presentation graphics and overheads; other, costlier color printers can be used for proofing desktop publications.

✔ If you don't mind a few minor incompatibilities now and then, you can use a printer designed to be used on an IBM PC with a Mac.

Where to buy

BLP Elite, $1,599
GCC Technologies, Inc.
580 Winter St.
Waltham, MA 02154
800-422-7777

Business LaserPrinter II, $1,999
GCC Technologies, Inc.
580 Winter St.
Waltham, MA 02154
800-422-7777

Business LaserPrinter IIs, $2,899
GCC Technologies, Inc.
580 Winter St.
Waltham, MA 02154
800-422-7777

CrystalPrint Publisher II, $3,795
QUME Corp.
500 Yosemite Dr.
Milpitas, CA 95035
408-942-4000
800-458-4549

Ektaplus 7016, $5,495
Eastman Kodak Company
901 Elmgrove Road
Rochester, NY 14653
800-344-0006

Ektaplus 7016 w/PostScript, $6,995
Eastman Kodak Company
901 Elmgrove Road
Rochester, NY 14653
800-344-0006

ELP-7500, $2,999
Epson America, Inc.
20770 Medrona Ave.
Torrance, CA 90503
213-782-2698
800-289-3776

Freedom of Press–light, $98 (15 fonts)
Custom Applications, Inc.
900 Technology Park Dr.
Billeriea, MA 01821
508-667-8585
800-873-4367

Freedom of Press–standard, $495 (35 fonts)
Custom Applications, Inc.
900 Technology Park Dr.
Billeriea, MA 01821
508-667-8585
800-873-4367

Freedom of Press–professional, $1495 (35 fonts)
Custom Applications, Inc.
900 Technology Park Dr.
Billeriea, MA 01821
508-667-8585
800-873-4367

ImageWriter II, $595
Apple Computer, Inc.
20525 Mariani Ave.
Cupertino, CA 95014
408-996-1010
800-776-2333

ImageWriter II/LQ LocalTalk Option, $139
Apple Computer, Inc.
20525 Mariani Ave.
Cupertino, CA 95014
408-996-1010
800-776-2333

JetLink Express, $159
GDT Softworks
4664 Lowughed Hwy.
Burnaby, BC
Canada B5C6B7
604-291-9121

LaserJet IIIsi, $5,495
Hewlett-Packard Co.
16399 W. Bernardo Dr.
San Diego, CA 92127
800-752-0900

LaserScript, $1,995
Abaton
48431 Milmont Dr., Bldg. 1
Fremont, CA 94538
415-683-2226
800-821-0806

LZR 960, $2,995
Dataproducts Corp.
6200 Canoga Ave.
Woodland Hills, CA 91367-2499
818-887-8000

MacPrint, $149
Insight Development Corp.
2200 Powell St., Ste. 500
Emeryville, CA 94608
415-652-4115
800-825-4115

microLaser PS17, $1,399
Texas Instruments
13500 N. Central Expwy.
Dallas, TX 75265
800-527-3500

microLaser PS35, $1,749
Texas Instruments
13500 N. Central Expwy.
Dallas, TX 75265
800-527-3500

OkiLaser 840, $2,599
Okidata
532 Fellowship Road
Mt. Laurel, NJ 08054
609-235-2600
800-654-3282

Personal LaserWriter NT, $2,599
Apple Computer, Inc.
20525 Mariani Ave.
Cupertino, CA 95014
408-996-1010
800-776-2333

Personal LaserWriter LS, $1,299
Apple Computer, Inc.
20525 Mariani Ave.
Cupertino, CA 95014
408-996-1010
800-776-2333

PLP II, $999
GCC Technologies, Inc.
580 Winter St.
Waltham, MA 02154
800-422-7777

PLP IIs, $1,499
GCC Technologies, Inc.
580 Winter St.
Waltham, MA 02154
800-422-7777

PS-410, $2,795
QMS
P.O. Box 81250
Mobile, AL 36689
800-631-2692 (ext. 906)

StyleWriter, $599
Apple Computer, Inc.
20525 Mariani Ave.
Cupertino, CA 95014
408-996-1010
800-776-2333

T-Script, $145
TeleTypesetting Co.
311 Harvard St.
Brookline, MA 02146
617-734-9700

TrueLaser, $2,695
Microtek Lab, Inc.
680 Knox
Torrance, CA 90502
213-321-2121 (ext.5)
800-654-4160 (outside CA)

UltraScript, $195
QMS, Inc.
P.O. Box 81250
Mobile, AL 36689
800-845-4843

UltraScript Plus, $445
QMS, Inc.
P.O. Box 81250
Mobile, AL 36689
800-845-4843

Chapter 7

Hard Disks and Other Storage Devices

by Cheryl England

In this chapter . . .

- ✔ Types of storage — hard drives, removable-cartridge drives, erasable optical drives — explained in detail.

- ✔ Determining the applications best suited for each type of storage device.

- ✔ A breakdown of the capacities and prices of storage types.

- ✔ Assessing the advantages and disadvantages of storage types.

- ✔ Shopping for a storage device — what to look for.

- ✔ A summary of the kind of service and support you can expect for each product.

Only a few years ago, everyone used floppy disks to store data and applications. But it didn't take long for people to get really tired of swapping floppy disks in and out of drives in order to use a new application or access a different file. So GCC Technologies and P.C.P.C. produced the first hard drives for the Mac so people could store all their applications and data in one place.

Floppy disks are still found in abundance in any Macintosh-based office. They are handy for copying small files that you need to take with you or give to another user. They are ideal for holding temporary copies of files that you are working on. (For instance, a floppy disk sits on my desk at this moment, holding the latest version of this chapter, just in case my Mac blows up or my hard drive crashes). But floppies have long outlived their usefulness as primary storage devices. Hard drives are now the most ubiquitous type of primary storage device, having become faster, bigger, and more reliable each year. Recently, however, users have had more choices than just hard drives. There are removable cartridge drives, removable hard drives, erasable optical drives, and WORM (write once, read many) optical drives. If you are confused by the options and want to make an informed buying decision, then read on to discover the secrets of storage.

About the author

Cheryl England started with *Macworld* October 1987 as Associate Editor in charge of planning/editing the Reviews section. She moved to Features nine months later to write and edit features. Currently she writes/edits/coordinates most of the Lab articles (hardware specialty) and also writes/edits/coordinates some productivity/business features. England's current title is Senior Associate Editor, Features.

Previous magazine experience includes Associate Feature Editor for Hayden's *Personal Computing Magazine* (one year) where she wrote and edited features/reviews.

England was also Associate Editor for M&T Publishing's *Business Software* (two years) and was in charge of the Database section (wrote and edited).

A quick overview

Hard drives provide the most versatile — and fastest — type of storage. They range in capacity from 20MB up to 1.2 gigabytes (GB). (You can get higher capacities but this entails putting two or more drives into a large case.) You can use hard drives to store the data and applications you use every day, or you can use them as a backup device. If you outgrow the capacity of a hard drive, you can attach a second one to your Mac or you can substitute a higher-capacity drive and give the old drive to someone else. Some external hard drives are even small enough that you can easily carry them in a briefcase, making them ideal for transporting data between Macs.

Nearly as versatile as hard drives, removable-cartridge drives have gained popularity over the last couple of years. These drives have a fixed mechanism that reads data from a cartridge that you insert. If you need more storage space, you simply buy more cartridges. Many people find it convenient to back up and archive data from a hard drive onto a cartridge. You can also swap cartridges between drives, making it easy to move data between Macs. And if the Mac is being shared by several people (say in a university setting), each user can have his or her own cartridge. The drawback to removable-cartridge drives, however, is that the cartridges currently hold either 45MB or 90MB of data. While 90MB of storage is sufficient for many users, those who do a lot of desktop publishing, animation, or 3-D modeling, or work with a large database, may find the 90MB cap limiting.

Don't confuse removable-cartridge drives with removable hard drives. Although rare these days, removable hard drives do still exist. Unlike removable-cartridge drives, where the mechanism that reads and writes data is in the drive case and the platters that hold data are in the cartridge, removable hard drives consist of a plastic chassis that does nothing more than connect to the Mac and act as a holder for a hard drive mechanism. Thus the chassis is relatively inexpensive — but you'll pay a premium for the hard drive mechanism. There's no reason to purchase one of these drives over a standard hard drive.

Erasable optical drives are appealing because you can store 600MB of data on an optical disc that is about the size of an audio compact disc. Unlike a compact disc, however, you can erase the data on the optical disc and rewrite new data onto it, just as you can with a floppy disk, hard drive, or removable cartridge. Erasable optical drives are excellent for archiving important data; the disks have a shelf life of up to 25 years. They are also handy for transporting large amounts of data (for instance, sending magazine pages to a printer) or distributing complex documentation or tutorials from a headquarters office to field offices. So why shouldn't you use these drives as primary storage? For two reasons: first, they are annoyingly slow when writing data to disk (say, when you save a file) and second, they are still very expensive.

> 66 *Erasable optical drives are excellent for archiving important data; the disks have a shelf life of up to 25 years.* 99

WORM drives are similar to erasable optical drives in that they use small optical discs to store data. But once the data is written to the disc, it's there for good — you can't erase it. You can, however, read the data as often as you like, and you can copy it to other media. The only time you'd want to opt for a WORM drive over a more versatile erasable optical drive is if you need to create permanent archives, such as ones containing legal, medical, or government records.

Hard drives

The first decision you'll face when purchasing a hard drive is what capacity you want. Hard drives range in capacity from 20MB to 1.2GB. The only reason to buy a 20MB drive is because of their small size — most 20MB drives today are 2½-inches wide and 1-inch (or less) high. Otherwise, you're better off buying a 40MB drive; you'll end up paying less per megabyte of storage capacity.

As you get into higher-capacity ranges — 300MB and up — hard drives start getting more expensive per megabyte of storage. That's because high-capacity drives are at a break-even point for manufacturers — they can include more advanced technology without bringing the overall drive price out of range for users. What you'll end up with is not only more storage capacity, but a faster drive as well (see Figure 7-1). These drives, however, are not any more or less reliable than lower-capacity drives.

How do you decide what capacity you need? Some people will tell you to buy all the capacity you can afford. But hard drives aren't like houses in California — they depreciate over time. There's no sense spending a few hundred dollars more for storage space you never use. Lower-capacity drives of 40MB to 80MB are perfect for people who only use word processors, spreadsheets, or small databases (such as a name and address file). Take a look at 100MB to 300MB drives if you use color graphics programs a lot or have a more complex database. If you perform storage-intensive tasks, such as color image editing, music creation, or 3-D modeling, or if you will be using the hard drive as a file server, then 300MB is the minimum capacity you should consider.

> **❝ ... hard drives aren't like houses in California — they depreciate over time. ❞**

Next, you need to decide whether the drive will be internal or external. If you are purchasing a new Mac, and Apple offers an internal drive with the capacity you want, you might as well order the Mac with a hard drive. Apple's prices for internal drives are fair, if not a bargain, and the drive will come already installed. All you'll need to do to start working is to plug in the Mac.

If you already have a Mac, or if you want a better deal than Apple offers, you still may want to consider an internal drive. Internal drives are cheaper than external ones since they don't need a case, a power supply, or a fan (the Mac provides these for the drive). In addition, an internal drive doesn't take up any extra desk space.

On the downside, if an internal drive crashes, you'll need to give up your Mac while it is being fixed (or at least while a technician is removing it). Even worse, you may not be able to get an internal drive in the capacity you want for your

Speed Secrets

High-capacity hard disk drives owe their speed to technology. These drives position the read-write heads with voice coil actuators, which are faster and more precise than the stepper motors used in smaller drives. Heads travel less on high-end disks, yielding faster access times because data is packed more densely than on low-end disks. The biggest speed boost, however, comes from the method used to position the heads over the data tracks. This method, called dedicated servo surface, uses one disk platter solely for aligning the heads over data tracks on other platters. In contrast, lower-capacity disks may use part of the data platters for positioning information (embedded servo method) or they may use no positioning information (open-loop method). With a dedicated servo surface, the drive positions its head over the right track with fewer retries.

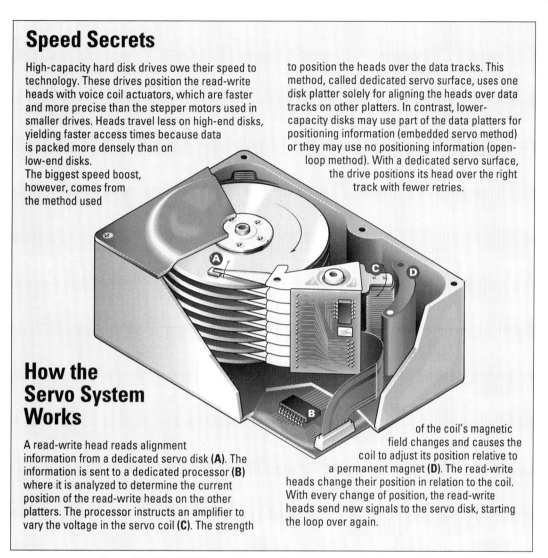

How the Servo System Works

A read-write head reads alignment information from a dedicated servo disk (**A**). The information is sent to a dedicated processor (**B**) where it is analyzed to determine the current position of the read-write heads on the other platters. The processor instructs an amplifier to vary the voltage in the servo coil (**C**). The strength of the coil's magnetic field changes and causes the coil to adjust its position relative to a permanent magnet (**D**). The read-write heads change their position in relation to the coil. With every change of position, the read-write heads send new signals to the servo disk, starting the loop over again.

Figure 7-1: A hard disk's speed is determined in large part by the metal platters which are stacked like records in a jukebox.

particular Mac. Drive mechanisms come in different physical sizes, and different models of Macs support different sizes of mechanisms. For instance, because of their small size, the Mac Classic, Mac LC, and Mac IIsi support only internal drive mechanisms that are 1-inch tall. (Vendors often refer to 1-inch tall mechanisms as third-height drives; half-height drives are 1.6-inches tall; full-height drives are 3¼-inches tall). Currently, third-height mechanisms can hold a maximum of 130MB of data.

On the other end, the Mac IIfx can support any mechanism available, although the largest — 5¼-inch wide, full-height mechanisms — will only fit internally if you use a special bracket that you get from the drive vendor. And even then there are some caveats you should be aware of; for instance, if you install more than two 4MB SIMMs in a IIfx and then add a hard drive, the IIfx will be running much hotter than Apple specifications state it should be. (Theoretically, too much heat can reduce the reliability of a drive or of the Mac's components.) You'll only need to use such a large mechanism if you are purchasing an internal drive that holds 600MB or more. As technology improves, mechanisms will get smaller, have higher capacities, and consume less power.

If you buy an external drive, you don't need to worry about the mechanism size. Instead, you need to consider the case that the drive comes in. A great many drives come packaged in what is frequently called a zero-footprint case. In everyday English, this means that the drive is designed to sit perfectly under a compact Mac such as the Classic or SE without taking up any additional desk space. These cases are just tall enough to house the hard drive mechanism.

Some zero-footprint drives can be set on their sides so that they run while sitting vertically next to a Mac. Some vendors, such as EMac, Optima, PLI, and Procom, include removable feet to help stabilize the drive in either position. Other drives, such as some models from Liberty, La Cie, and Optima, are specifically designed to sit vertically next to a Mac. These drives may be a better choice than zero-footprint drives if you own a modular Mac like the II or LC.

Several other vendors offer super-small drives that are designed to be portable. These drives are usually light-weight and fit nicely into a briefcase. Some vendors, such as La Cie and Liberty, offer optional carrying cases for their drives. The smallest of the portable drives, iDS's Wip, does not include a power supply in the case. Instead, these drives take their power from the Mac's floppy port. Mac IIs, however, don't have a floppy port — if you want to use one of these tiny drives on a Mac II, you'll need to purchase either an external power supply (thus negating the convenience of the drive's small size) or an adapter board that installs in a NuBus slot.

Once you've decided on capacity and style, you need to think about what's inside the drive. Most vendors purchase the actual mechanism from another company, usually Conner, Quantum, or Seagate. Vendors also get power supplies, fans, and cables from other companies. The vendors then assemble and test the drives.

As a general rule, *Macworld's* past testing has shown that drives under 300MB that are based on mechanisms from Quantum are 5 to 10 percent faster than other drives. For drives 300MB and above, Seagate's Wren series takes the performance lead. Overall, Conner mechanisms are the quietest.

But that doesn't mean that you should pick any, say, 40MB drive with a Quantum mechanism if you want speed, or any, say, 80MB drive with a Conner mechanism if you want silence. The driver software (the software that makes the drive work with the Mac) that a vendor uses can affect performance, ease-of-use, and reliability. And components such as the fan can make a huge difference in how quietly the drive runs. You'll also need to consider vendor reputation, service and support, warranty, quality of manuals, and software included.

In addition, before you jump to buy the fastest hard drive you can find, stop to consider which Mac you'll use it on. As technology has improved, drives have gotten faster — so fast, in fact, that today's crop of drives can generally send data faster than a Mac Plus's SCSI port can receive it. Therefore, if you have a Plus, you won't pay a penalty for buying a slower drive (and frequently you can get a better price on a slower drive). The Macintosh Classic and SE have a faster SCSI port than the Plus, and most drives equal or beat these Mac data transmission rates. Faster Macs such as the SE/30, Mac LC, and any member of the Mac II family can still generally outrun all but a few extremely fast drives (if you're looking for high-performance drives, check out products from FWB, Micronet, and Deltaic).

Removable-cartridge drives

Like hard drives, removable-cartridge drives make good primary storage devices. You can start the Mac up from them, and they are nearly as fast in reading and writing data as are lower-capacity hard drives. You can also use the cartridges to back up or archive data in lieu of a tape-backup drive. (See Chapter 13, "Backup — Defending Your Data," for a full discussion of backup options.)

The big decision in buying a removable-cartridge drive is whether to go with SyQuest, Ricoh, or Bernoulli technology. As with hard drives, many different vendors offer drives with mechanisms from SyQuest or Ricoh. Iomega makes Bernoulli drives, and currently only Iomega and Ocean Systems sell finished products to users.

SyQuest and Ricoh drives use plastic cartridges that house a hard disk platter — they more closely resemble a video or cassette tape than they do a hard drive or a floppy disk. You can write-protect these cartridges in the same way that you can a floppy — simply close a tab on the cartridge shell. This is handy for protecting a cartridge that holds, say, backup copies of your applications. See Figure 7-2 for more details on the mechanical variations of these cartridges. (To protect hard drives from being written to, you need to install security software that prevents anyone without a password from writing files.)

SyQuest

1) Drive head and arm assembly
2) Protective enclosure
3) Hub
4) Medium
5) Write-protect indicator
6) Dust cover

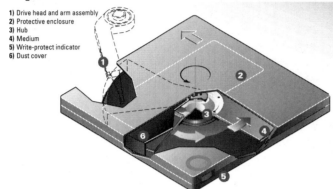

The SyQuest cartridge has the most basic design of the three types of removable cartridges. The rigid-medium platter is surrounded by a single plastic case and connected to a lightweight metal hub. A single, spring-loaded dust cover protects the medium from contamination while outside the drive, and opens to reveal the platter to the drive head when the cartridge is fully enclosed by the drive during operation. There are no air filters or seals to guard against incidental contamination while inside the drive. The head sweeps across the disk in the manner of a record player's tonearm and stylus, directly contacting both sides of the medium to read and write.

Ricoh

1) Drive head and arm assembly
2) Foam seals
3) Secondary circulation filter
4) Hub
5) Magnetic base
6) Primary circulation filter
7) Medium
8) Write-protect indicator
9) Dust shutter
10) Recirculated air

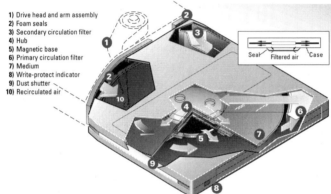

The more complex Ricoh cartridge uses multiple air filters and seals to prevent contamination that can cause disk or head crashes. An air-flow system clears dust away from the platter. As with the SyQuest cartridge, the read-write head directly contacts both sides of the rigid medium in a sweeping motion. The sturdier Ricoh cartridge features a heavy, balanced platter hub, positioned on a magnetic base. A seal prevents contaminated air from reaching the medium from below, via the hub assembly (see detail).

Bernoulli

1) Spicule ledge
2) Read-write heads
3) Dust shutter
4) Hub
5) Upper disk liner
6) Media
7) Lower disk liner
8) Write-protect indicator
9) Air-intake holes

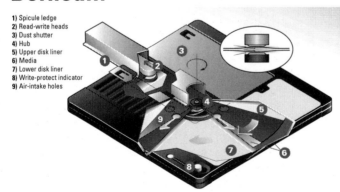

Bernoulli cartridges resemble standard floppy disks. Bernoulli technology uses two single-sided platters. The read-write heads move laterally, unlike in the other two drives. The Bernoulli does not filter dust particles, but circulates air to move dust away from the media. Unlike in the SyQuest and Ricoh units, the read-write heads do not actually contact the media, so head crashes cannot be caused by dust particles, and disk crashes are also rare. As seen in the detail, each platter flexes toward the head. An air cushion between the two floppy platters allows them to flex inward should a dust particle approach the head. The cartridge also locks in place while in use, preventing the loss of data that could result from accidentally removing the drive. This is necessary because unlike its competitors, the Bernoulli cartridge protrudes from the drive during operation.

Figure 7-2: The mechanical variations of the removable-cartridge drives available.

While cartridges from Ricoh and SyQuest use rigid platters, Bernoulli cartridges contain a flexible disk in a hard shell. These 5¼-inch cartridges look like over-weight floppy disks and can be write-protected. Iomega claims that a flexible disk prevents head crashes since the heads never need to touch the media and are thus undisturbed by dust particles. In addition, Bernoulli cartridges lock in place while in use, preventing someone from removing the cartridge and potentially causing you to lose all of the data on the cartridge. To back up its claim of better reliability, Iomega offers a five-year warranty on media.

In the past, SyQuest has been haunted by reliability problems. The cartridges were prone to contamination from dust and sometimes would "go bad" after only a couple months of use. That's because in a standard hard drive, the platter that holds the data and the heads that read and write the data are sealed in an airtight chassis. SyQuest cartridges, however, must open a metal shutter (like the one on a floppy disk) in order for the heads to read or write data. This exposes the media to contaminants in the air; dust can enter the cartridge and cause bad sectors, read and write errors, and even head crashes.

SyQuest has worked to eliminate reliability problems, and many vendors that sell SyQuest drives have learned to test the drives more thoroughly to weed out bad drives. Before purchasing a SyQuest drive, be sure to ask about a vendor's testing procedures. Even then, however, SyQuest dependability falls short of that of hard drives. Fortunately, a SyQuest cartridge will often give you some warning that it is going bad. When a SyQuest cartridge is about to fail, it tends to display a rapidly increasing number of errors — read and write errors when copying files, a high-pitched squeal, or trouble mounting the cartridge. Should you notice any of these signs, back up the cartridge's data to another cartridge or to a hard drive (or even to floppies), and reformat the suspect cartridge.

Although Ricoh's cartridges are similar to the SyQuest cartridges, Ricoh claims that they are more reliable than those from SyQuest. Ricoh's cartridges have a mechanism that locks the platter's hub and keeps it from turning when the cartridge is outside of the drive, a shutter that's more difficult to open than the one on the SyQuest, and an air filter to keep particles out. Ricoh drives and cartridges, however, are fairly new on the market, so these claims have not yet been fully tested.

What's it like to work with removable-cartridge drives? Most of the time you won't even know you are using a cartridge drive as opposed to a hard drive. SyQuest and Ricoh drives are about as fast as a lower-capacity hard drive. Bernoulli drives are faster, especially when copying files. The Bernoulli drives, however, are a bit noisier than the SyQuest drives, especially when starting up.

The Mac will recognize any cartridge that is inserted in the drive when you start up, and it will recognize a Ricoh or Bernoulli cartridge whenever it is inserted. With a SyQuest drive, however, the Mac won't recognize any cartridges inserted later. SyQuest drives also have the most complex eject sequence for cartridges. First you must drag the cartridge's icon to the Trash can, remove the cartridge by pressing a stop button on the drive, and then press a lever to release the cartridge. Ricoh and Bernoulli drives have a simpler eject sequence. You still need to drag the cartridge's icon to the Trash, but the drives then automatically spin to a stop. Pressing the Eject button pops the Ricoh cartridge out; a slight tug releases the Bernoulli cartridge.

You'll want to take great care in choosing one of the three technologies since you can't swap cartridges among the different types of drives — don't expect a Ricoh drive to read a SyQuest cartridge or vice versa. And Iomega and SyQuest's high-capacity drives can only read from — not write to — their respective 44MB cartridges. Because one of the clear advantages of using removable cartridges for data storage is the ability to send large files to other users easily, the question of compatibility becomes very important. In spite of some weak spots in its technology, and Ricoh's and Iomega's claims of better reliability, SyQuest has one important advantage: installed base. There are many more SyQuest drives running on Macs than there are Ricoh or Bernoulli drives. Chances are most Mac-ingrained organizations will have at least one SyQuest drive around.

Iomega is attempting to get around the installed base issue by making smaller, more portable drives. One version, the Bernoulli Transportable, comes with a carrying handle and a button on the back for setting termination on or off (the first and last devices hooked to a Mac's SCSI port must have termination on, while those in the middle must have termination off; thus, switchable termination is handy for moving a SCSI device between different Mac setups). But at 12 pounds, the Transportable is not as portable as it should be, especially when compared to some of the smaller 4-to-6 pound hard drives.

SyQuest and Bernoulli cartridges hold about 42MB or 43MB of data when formatted. SyQuest recently introduced a higher-capacity cartridge that holds 88MB of data, and Iomega has introduced a 90MB cartridge. Ricoh's cartridges hold about 46.7MB when formatted.

SyQuest drives and cartridges are the least expensive of the bunch. Currently, you can buy a SyQuest drive for as little as $450, although most fall in the $700 to $800 price range. Ricoh and Bernoulli drives cost more, ranging around $1,300. SyQuest cartridges cost about $70 for 42MB of capacity. Bernoulli cartridges are close, with the least expensive going for about $85. Ricoh cartridges, however, are a whopping $125 a pop — Ricoh drives, however, are still current to the Mac market and prices may come down as production volumes go up.

So which removable-cartridge drives are best? If you mainly want a removable-cartridge drive so that you can transport data to different Macs, you should opt for a SyQuest-based drive since this drive's larger installed base means you'll have an easier time finding a drive that can read your cartridge. For any other user, however, I recommend either a Ricoh or a Bernoulli drive. The Bernoulli drives have a more proven reliability record in the field, but the Ricoh drives are more likely to come down in price in the near future.

Erasable optical drives

Like removable-cartridge drives, magneto-optical drives (commonly called erasable optical drives) offer endless storage. These drives use erasable, removable 5¼-inch disks that store about 300MB of data per side, for a total of 600MB per disk. (Drives based on a mechanism from Maxtor have a higher capacity of 500MB per side or 1GB total.) As with hard drives, all erasable optical drive vendors buy a mechanism from one of a few manufacturers — Sony, Ricoh, Maxtor, or Canon — and add the extras you need to get the drive running. Sony- and Maxtor-based drives are generally faster — and more expensive — than the Ricoh- and Canon-based drives.

The disks for these drives look like audio compact discs and come packed in a hard plastic cartridge, much like the jewel box that protects audio compact disks. However, unlike compact discs, which you remove from the case to play, erasable optical discs always stay in their shell, even when you play them, and are often referred to as cartridges. The disks all use a format specified by the International Standards Organization (ISO), so you can swap them between drives that use the same mechanism. (There are a couple of exceptions — you'll want to check compatibility before you buy any particular drive.) Unlike removable cartridges, erasable optical discs can be ejected just like floppy disks. And, like floppy disks, optical discs have a metal shutter to protect the media, and a write-protect switch that you set to protect your data.

> ❝ *It's tempting to use an erasable optical for everyday work or as a file server, but the drives are still too slow, especially when writing data to disk, for this to be practical.* ❞

Because of their design, erasable opticals are highly reliable. Both hard drives and erasable opticals write and erase data using magnetization technology. But unlike hard drives, erasable opticals require heat to change the media's magnetization. Thus, erasable opticals are immune to damage by stray magnetic fields (such as those near the back of a monitor). Erasable optical drives don't suffer from head crashes either, since the read-write head is always relatively far from surface of the media. This reliability makes erasable opticals excellent choices for archiving data or holding libraries of, say, color images.

It's tempting to use an erasable optical for everyday work or as a file server, but the drives are still too slow, especially when writing data to disk, for this to be practical. Every time an erasable optical writes data, it must first erase the old data (a regular hard drive just writes over existing data). You can speed up an erasable optical with memory-caching software, such as PLI's Turbo Cache, or caching hardware, such as the NuBus board from Pinnacle Micro, but it will still be slower than a hard drive or a removable-cartridge drive. Another problem with using erasable opticals as your main storage is that they can only read one side of a disk at a time. To access the data on the other side, you must eject the disk and turn it over — a sometimes confusing and tiresome process. The problem exists because an erasable optical's read-write assembly is so large, heavy, and expensive that a drive can only contain one head. One lone read-write head can only access data on one side of one disk.

The only way around this is to buy a jukebox. Just like jukeboxes that play records (or these days, compact discs), optical jukeboxes store a stack of disks and use a simple mechanism to swap them in and out of the drive. Some companies such as Pinnacle, PLI, and Alphatronix offer stock systems, while other companies such as FWB will custom-design a jukebox. Be warned, however, that these systems aren't for everyone — prices range around $50,000 for a 36GB system with sixty disks. A smaller ten-disk system is more reasonably priced at $10,000.

One special drive is the REO-1300 from Pinnacle Micro. The Pinnacle REO-1300 uses 3½-inch disks that look almost exactly like floppy disks. These disks store 120MB of data on one side and cost about $130 each. At about $3,000, the drive itself is, on average, $1,000 less expensive than standard 5¼-inch erasable optical, and because the disks are smaller, the drive can access data more quickly. Because the disks for this drive are the same size as floppy disks, they are easy to store and mail.

Drive prices range from $3,000 to $6,500; 600MB disks are about $300 ($0.50 per megabyte); the Maxtor 1GB disks are $395 ($0.40 per megabyte). In comparison, SyQuest and Bernoulli drives are cheaper, but the media is more expensive per megabyte. SyQuest cartridges, for instance, cost about $1.50 per megabyte.

Erasable optical drives offer a trustworthy means of storing a lot of data in a small amount of space. (For everyday backup, you'll be better off with a less-expensive tape drive, however. See Chapter 13 on backup). Erasable opticals are also handy for transporting a lot of data — say, color pages for printing or a large database of accounting information. They are still too slow, however, for everyday use.

Deciding what extra features you want

So far, we've pointed out the main differences in the various storage options. When you actually get ready to purchase a drive — whether a standard hard drive, a removable-cartridge drive, or an erasable optical drive — you'll find that most vendors sell all types. You'll then need to consider each vendor's level of service and support, quality of components, type of software included, and pricing structure.

All types of drives include basic formatting and diagnostic software. If you're an experienced Macintosh user, you'll be able to get any of the drives up and running. But if you are new to the Mac, installing a hard drive for the first time, or just want a bit of elegance in the software you use, then you should check out a drive's formatting software to make sure it is logical and clear. The best formatting software prompts you through the formatting process step by step and includes informative dialog boxes. Some software is even downright fancy, sporting 3-D buttons and color — nice touches, but not necessities.

Numerous vendors include commercial software with their drives. Keep in mind, however, that as the price of the drive rises, the savings value of bundled software becomes less important. Of the various types of software, backup utilities such as DiskFit or Redux and hard drive-management and file-recovery utilities such as MacTools, Norton Utilities, SUM, and 911 Utilities are the most handy. Any serious Macintosh user should own at least one specialized backup package and one file-recovery package. (Apple's HD Backup doesn't count — although better than nothing, this backup utility is awkward to use, slow, and lacks many important features.)

If you are purchasing a hard drive of 150MB or more, or an erasable optical drive, you should make sure that the drive includes partitioning software. Partitioning software lets you divide a hard drive into volumes, each of which acts like a separate hard drive. Most users will want to partition a drive in order to keep data organized. For instance, one partition may hold data and applications for budgeting chores, while another partition may hold the data and applications you need for creating presentations. On a file server, each partition can hold data relevant to a specific group of workers, and each partition can be protected so that only authorized users can access it. If you are using a removable-cartridge drive you can partition each cartridge, but more realistically, people use individual cartridges to separate working files.

Most partitioning software works by creating separate physical areas on the platter. You won't notice any differences when working on a partitioned drive unless you try to change the size of a partition. To reconfigure disk space you'll have to back up your data, reformat the drive, and recreate the partitions.

Assessing the components of storage devices

Before buying a drive, you should also check out the components. Does the drive use 50-pin connectors for attaching the cable? These are more reliable than 25-pin connectors; most vendors use them today.

Does the drive use internal or external termination? (Terminators prevent signals from echoing down a cable, which can cause data errors; the first and last SCSI device hooked to a Mac should be terminated.) Some drives come with terminators installed inside the case — you can usually remove these easily, but it does require some extra work. Internally terminated drives are best suited for users who have just one peripheral attached to the Mac's SCSI port and who don't plan to move the drive to another Mac.

More and more vendors are supplying external terminators with their drives. These terminators are 50-pin adapters that attach between the drive's SCSI port and the SCSI cable. You'll want SCSI termination if you have (or plan to purchase) several SCSI peripherals, if you move the drive to another Mac frequently, or if you're working on the Mac IIfx (the IIfx includes a special terminator that you must use instead of the standard external terminator).

The best termination solutions, however, are those that let you flip a switch or move a button to turn termination on or off. Hard drives from La Cie, Procom, and PLI have this option, as do removable cartridge drives from Iomega, iDS, and PLI. Xyxis and Microtech offer switchable termination on their erasable optical drives. A switch is simple and elegant, and you don't have to worry about losing an external terminator or removing internal ones.

A question of price

Generally you can divide drive vendors into two groups — those who sell products for the lowest possible price and those who focus on the details that make a drive more elegant. Vendors who focus on price always sell products direct (mail-order vendors are included in this category). These companies offer the basic cables and formatting software you need to get the drive running, but they offer little in the way of extras. You won't get a fancy manual or the most elaborate software; you may or may not get backup or other utility software. And if you are purchasing a hard drive, you may not be able to get the mechanism you want, because these companies buy mechanisms in bulk from a variety of suppliers in order to keep their price to the consumer down. Thus, month to month, the mechanisms they have available may come from different makers — you may have to go with an unproven mechanism or one that is slower or louder than you want. (Companies in this category include Alliance Peripheral Systems, Club Mac, Ehman, Hard Drives International, MacAvenue, MacLand, MacProducts USA, Mirror, Relax, Third Wave, and Total Peripherals.)

The other group of vendors charges a bit more for their drives. They sell either direct or through a dealer. If they sell through a dealer, the list price can look astronomically high. In reality, however, dealers discount this price heavily — street prices for these drives are generally in line with similarly equipped drives that are sold direct. Generally, a slightly more expensive drive will include a professionally designed and bound manual, some sort of additional (and useful) commercial software, a sleek and sturdy external case, and a slightly better class of components. Some of these vendors, such as FWB, MicroNet, and Pinnacle, justify their higher prices by offering high-performance products. Others, such as Microtech, boast lengthy warranties. Frequently these companies have been in the hardware business longer than the discounters — they have an established base and less need to rely on price competition. (Other companies in this category include Apple, CMS, EMac, GCC, iDS, Jasmine, La Cie, Mass Microsystems, Microtech, Optima, PLI, Rodime, Ruby Systems, Storage Dimensions, and SuperMac.)

> 66 *Generally you can divide drive vendors into two groups — those who sell products for the lowest possible price and those who focus on the details that make a drive more elegant.* 99

Service and support

Good service and support begins with the drive's manual. Even an experienced user will appreciate a thorough manual. The best manuals clearly explain installation, using high-quality illustrations or photos. In addition, these manuals include hints on troubleshooting should installation not go smoothly the first time. And for owners of removable-cartridge drives and erasable optical drives, a good manual includes information on caring for cartridges.

Most helpful of all, any manual should include a telephone number for technical support in an obvious location (for example, the title page or the back cover of the manual). Technical support is something you don't think about until you need it. But when you do need it, you'd better hope it's good.

Most drive vendors offer at least a one-year warranty on their products. The longest warranty you can expect is five years, and very few vendors are willing to go that far yet. Some companies will sell you an extended warranty. If your drive breaks while under warranty, most vendors claim that they will repair or replace it within one or two days. If you bought your drive from a dealer, you can usually take it in and get an immediate replacement or a loaner until yours is fixed. (Some vendors will also send you a loaner via overnight mail when you call with a problem — sometimes this service is included in the purchase price of the drive, other times it is a service option you can purchase when you buy the drive.)

Several vendors will try to recover data from a crashed drive if you ask. Again, some vendors perform this service for free, while others charge either a fixed-rate fee or, in the case of standard hard drives, a fee based on the drive's capacity. For instance, Mirror Technologies will repair nearly any hard drive and recover the data from it. Charges vary based on the amount of data that must be recovered.

Summary

✔ Hard drives are the most versatile and fastest type of storage.

✔ Removable cartridge drives are best for people who need to move data between Macs, need to back up a hard drive, or need easily expandable storage.

✔ Erasable optical drives are best for people who need to archive a lot of data or transport large files.

✔ Before buying a storage device, check the quality of the components.

✔ Don't buy a storage device based solely on price, ask questions first.

✔ Because you are buying something that will store your most precious asset — data — be sure the vendor offers the level of service and support you need.

Where to buy

Alliance Peripheral Systems, Inc.
2900 S. 291 Hwy.
Independence, MO 64057-1722
816-478-8300
800-235-2752
816-478-4596 (FAX)

Alphatronix, Inc.
P.O. Box 13687
Research Triangle Park, NC 27709-3687
919-544-0001
800-229-8686

Apple Computer, Inc.
20525 Mariani Ave.
Cupertino, CA 95014
408-996-1010
800-776-2333

CD Technology, Inc.
766 San Aleso Ave.
Sunnyvale, CA 94086
408-752-8500

Club Mac
7 Musick
Irvine, CA 92718
714-768-1490
800-258-2622
714-768-7307 (FAX)

CMS Enhancements, Inc.
2722 Michelson Dr.
Irvine, CA 92715
714-222-6000
714-549-4004 (FAX)

Cutting Edge, Inc.
P.O. Box 1259
Evanston, WY 82931
307-789-0582
307-789-8516 (FAX)

Deltaic Systems
1701 Junction Ct. , Ste. 302B
San Jose, CA 95112
408-441-1240
800-745-1240
408-441-8343 (FAX)

DJK Development
32730 Cambridge
Warren, MI 48093
313-254-2632
313-254-1121 (FAX)

Ehman, Inc.
97 S. Red Willow Road
Evanston, WY 82931
307-789-3830
800-257-1666
307-789-4656 (FAX)

EMac
A Division of Everex Systems
48431 Milmont Dr.
Fremont, CA 94538
415-683-2222
800-821-0806
415-683-2151 (FAX)

FWB, Inc.
2040 Polk St., Ste. 215
San Francisco, CA 94109
415-474-8055
415-775-2125 (FAX)

GCC Technologies
580 Winter St.
Waltham, MA 02154
617-890-0880
800-422-7777

Hard Drives International
1912 W. 4th St.
Tempe, AZ 85281
602-967-5128
800-234-3475
602-829-9193 (FAX)

iDS Systems, Inc.
1225 Elko Dr.
Sunnyvale, CA 94089
408-752-2952
800-347-3228

Iomega Corp.
1821 W. 4000 South
Roy, UT 84067
801-778-3000
800-456-5522
801-778-3460 (FAX)

Jasmine Technologies, Inc.
1225 Elko Dr.
Sunnyvale, CA 94089
408-752-2900
800-347-3228

La Cie, Ltd.
19552 SW 90th Ct.
Tualatin, OR 97062
503-691-0917
800-999-0143

Liberty Systems, Inc.
160 Saratoga Ave., Ste. 38
Santa Clara, CA 95051
408-983-1127
408-243-2885 (FAX)

MacAvenue
12303 Technology Blvd.
Austin, TX 78727
512-331-9386
800-888-6221

MacLand
4685 S. Ash Ave., Ste. H5
Tempe, AZ 85282
602-820-5802
800-333-3353

MacProducts USA
608 West 22nd St.
Austin, TX 78705
512-472-8881
800-622-3475
512-343-6141 (FAX)

MacTel Technology Corp.
3007 North Lamar
Austin, TX 78705
512-451-2600
800-950-8411
512-451-3323 (FAX)

MacTown
1431 S. Cherryvale Road
Boulder, CO 80303
800-338-4273
303-442-7985 (FAX)

Mass Microsystems, Inc.
810 W. Maude Ave.
Sunnyvale, CA 94086
408-522-1200
800-522-7979
408-733-5499 (FAX)

MicroNet Technology, Inc.
20 Mason
Irvine, CA 92718
714-837-6033
714-837-1164 (FAX)

Microtech International, Inc.
158 Commerce St.
East Haven, CT 06512
203-468-6223
800-626-4276

Mirror Technologies, Inc.
2644 Patton Road
Roseville, MN 55113
612-633-4450
800-654-5294
612-633-3136 (FAX)

Ocean Microsystems, Inc.
246 E. Hacienda Ave.
Campbell, CA 95008
408-374-8300
800-262-3261
408-374-8309 (FAX)

Optima Technology
17526 Von Karman
Irvine, CA 92714
714-476-0515
714-476-0613 (FAX)

P.C.P.C.
4710 Eisenhower Blvd., Bldg. A4
Tampa, FL 33643
813-884-3092
800-622-2888
813-886-0520 (FAX)

Pinnacle Micro
15265 Alton Pkwy.
Irvine, CA 92718
714-727-3300
800-553-7070
714-727-1913 (FAX)

PLI
47421 Bayside Pkwy.
Fremont, CA 94538
415-657-2211
408-945-1850
800-288-8754
800-825-1850
415-683-9713 (FAX)

Procom Technology, Inc.
200 McCormick Ave.
Costa Mesa, CA 92626
714-549-9449
714-549-0527 (FAX)

Relax Technology
3101 Whipple Road
Union City, CA 94587
415-471-6112
415-471-6267 (FAX)

Rodime Systems, Inc.
7700 W. Camino Real, 2nd Fl.
Boca Raton, FL 33433
407-391-7333
800-277-4144
407-391-9958 (FAX)

Ruby Systems, Inc.
930 Thompson Place
Sunnyvale, CA 94086
408-735-8668
800-888-1668
408-735-8696 (FAX)

Storage Dimensions, Inc.
2145 Hamilton Ave.
San Jose, CA 95125
408-879-0300
408-377-4988 (FAX)

Sumo Systems
1580 Old Oakland Road, Ste. C103
San Jose, CA 95131
408-453-5744
408-453-5821 (FAX)

SuperMac Technology
485 Potrero Ave.
Sunnyvale, CA 94086
408-245-2202
408-735-7250 (FAX)

Tecmar
6225 Cochran Road
Solon, OH 44139
216-349-1009

Third Wave Computing
1826-B Kramer Lane
Austin, TX 78758
512-832-8282
800-284-0486

Toshiba America Information Systems, Inc.
750 City Dr. South, Ste. 250
Orange, CA 92668
714-587-6326

Total Peripherals
1 Brigham St.
Marlboro, MA 01752
508-480-9042

Univation
48521 Warm Springs, Blvd., Ste. 306
Fremont, CA 94539
415-226-0851
415-226-0501 (FAX)

Xyxis Corp.
14631 Martin Dr.
Eden Prairie, MN 55344
612-949-2388
612-949-2488 (FAX)

Chapter 8

Video and the Macintosh: A Developing Relationship

by Franklin Tessler, M.D., and Peter Marx

In this chapter...

- ✔ Importing still video images into your Mac.
- ✔ A look at image compression programs and techniques.
- ✔ Displaying video on the Mac.
- ✔ Combining Mac graphics with video.
- ✔ Editing video with the Mac.
- ✔ Guidelines for choosing hardware.
- ✔ A summary of what to look for in Mac video in the future.

From the television projector to the ubiquitous camcorder, video hardware is everywhere nowadays. Surrounded by all this technology, it's easy to forget that the simple notion of home videotaping seemed far fetched just 20 years ago. Spurred by the development of miniaturized electronic components, both home video and personal computing came of age in the 1980s. It seems a safe bet that the inevitable marriage of video and computer hardware and software will progress into the next century, leading to products that incorporate the best of both worlds. But before peering through the looking glass, let's examine how the Macintosh fits into the world of video today.

At first glance, the Mac appears to be ideally suited for video applications. After all, Macintosh display screens are just high-end television sets, so it should be easy to pipe video into the Mac and get high-quality graphics back out. Unfortunately, the Macintosh wasn't designed with video in mind: although Macintosh monitors and televisions use identical principles to produce images, they operate according to very different standards. For example, the NTSC (National Television System Committee) television standard found in North America and Japan uses an *interlaced* pattern to produce an image, whereas the Macintosh uses a *non-interlaced* scheme (see Figure 8-1). What all this means is that you can't plug a VCR or video camera directly into the Mac — separate hardware is necessary to convert television images into the Macintosh format and back.

Despite this limitation, third-party vendors have introduced a mind-boggling array of video hardware and software for the Mac. To make some sense out of the chaos, we'll discuss the various categories of Macintosh video applications and describe some of the best products available in the marketplace. We'll also give you some tips to help you decide how to configure a Macintosh for video work. Finally, we'll try to predict what advances you can expect to see over the next few years.

A guided tour of video applications

Although we're simplifying matters somewhat, it's helpful to divide video products into five main categories: import, display, overlay, output, and control. Let's examine them one by one.

About the authors

An avid television watcher at night, Dr. Tessler watches ultrasound images during the day and is a contributing editor to *Macworld*. He is currently developing video applications in ultrasound for the Macintosh using many of the techniques described here.

Peter Marx, an Apple Certified Developer, recently purchased his first television set. This was in order to have something to connect to the many different frame grabbers, scan converters, edit controllers, signal processors, graphics coprocessors, and Macintoshes within his reach. Having a background in biomedical research, he has spent the last several years developing diagnostic and research-oriented medical imaging software for the Macintosh.

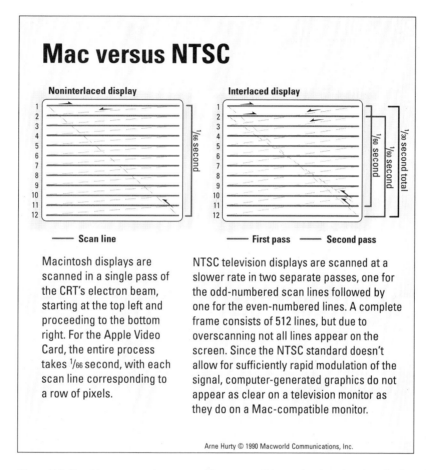

Mac versus NTSC

Noninterlaced display

Interlaced display

— Scan line

— First pass — Second pass

Macintosh displays are scanned in a single pass of the CRT's electron beam, starting at the top left and proceeding to the bottom right. For the Apple Video Card, the entire process takes $\frac{1}{66}$ second, with each scan line corresponding to a row of pixels.

NTSC television displays are scanned at a slower rate in two separate passes, one for the odd-numbered scan lines followed by one for the even-numbered lines. A complete frame consists of 512 lines, but due to overscanning not all lines appear on the screen. Since the NTSC standard doesn't allow for sufficiently rapid modulation of the signal, computer-generated graphics do not appear as clear on a television monitor as they do on a Mac-compatible monitor.

Arne Hurty © 1990 Macworld Communications, Inc.

Figure 8-1: Graphics appear clearer on a Mac-compatible monitor (non-interlaced scheme) than on a television monitor (interlaced scheme).

Video import

While TV cannot match the clarity of scanned slides and photographs, many images are available only in a video format. Copying television pictures was an early Macintosh application — the first video-input devices appeared not too long after the 128K Macintosh in 1984. Today, vendors offer a host of products that let you capture television pictures and convert them into Macintosh graphic files.

Video-import products typically fall into two classes: *digitizers*, which take several seconds to grab a single image, and *frame grabbers*, which accomplish the same task in a fraction of a second. Digitizers are slower because they process a number of video frames to capture an image, whereas frame grabbers contain circuitry to synchronize digitization with the frame rate of the video source.

Digitizers, like Digital Vision's ComputerEyes, are only suitable for working with stationary subjects or frozen TV images. However, they are relatively cheap, typically under $500. Like digitizers, frame grabbers can work with frozen images, but they're also capable of capturing video pictures on-the-fly. Since they usually come in the form of NuBus boards, they are only compatible with Macintosh II family CPUs.

As you might expect, frame grabbers are also more expensive than digitizers, with prices up to many thousands of dollars. Data Translation's QuickCapture and ColorCapture boards work with black-and-white and color video, respectively, and are fine for most work. A newer frame grabber called ColorSnap 32+ from Computer Friends comes with software that lets you take multiple snapshots from a videotape without having to save the images individually. This helps alleviate the problem of hunting to find the best frame in a video sequence.

Still more expensive systems are available from Truevision, which produces the NuVista line of frame grabbers for the Macintosh. Although they cost up to two or three times as much as other frame grabbers, they produce images of noticeably higher quality. We have used the NuVista to capture medical ultrasound images for processing on the Macintosh with excellent results.

Still video cameras — the portable alternative

As we've seen, digitizers and frame grabbers can be used to take snapshots from stationary video sources like cameras and VCRs. An alternative approach is to use a still video camera which offers the advantage of portability. Meant to replace traditional film-based cameras, still video cameras produce a video signal that can be fed into a frame grabber. The Sony Mavica was one of the first such systems on the market. The current version, the VC-5000, uses CCD (charge coupled device) technology to store images on a 3½-inch disk. Another still video camera is the Canon XapShot, which is available in a package along with the ComputerEyes digitizer. The Canon camera comes in both color and black-and-white versions. Still video images, once digitized, can be retouched using programs such as Adobe Photoshop. Although their resolution cannot match 35mm film, still video images do not have to be processed separately. A number of magazines and newspapers are already using still video cameras to cover fast-breaking news events.

Real-time video — motion video capture

The hardware we've discussed so far is fine for grabbing individual video frames. But capturing real-time video, which runs at 30 frames a second, poses a much bigger problem. Even extremely high-end systems like Truevision's can only digitize a few frames before running out of memory. The data transfer rates within the Macintosh also impede motion video capture because the NuBus data path built into every Macintosh II-series computer is only capable of transferring small frames in real time. To overcome this bottleneck, ingenious solutions have been tried by various companies. For example, Workstation Technologies's Moon-Raker (now being sold by E-Machines as QuickView Studio) takes over the NuBus in order to squeeze out the highest possible transfer rates. The board can handle two different video sources and comes with software for editing video images. Unfortunately, the system can only be used to record a few seconds of video in a format containing only about one-half of the video signal.

Saving disk space with image compression

To understand the challenge of motion video capture, consider that a frame-grabbed 24-bit color image takes about 900K to store. At this rate, a 30-second video sequence would occupy almost 800MB of disk space. Needless to say, even a Macintosh IIfx equipped with a fast, high-capacity hard drive would drown under such a data load. One answer to the problem lies in image compression, which reduces the amount of data in recorded images. The most common compression techniques are based upon the *JPEG* standard, named for the Joint Photographic Experts Group that devised it. JPEG is based on a mathematical technique called a cosine transform, which allows images to be compressed for storage or transmission and then decompressed for viewing. Because of errors introduced in the compression process, the original and decompressed images are not exact duplicates, although the differences may not be noticeable (this is referred to as lossy compression). One advantage of using a transform-based algorithm is the ability to vary the degree of compression, or compression ratio. The higher the compression ratio, the lower the quality of the decompressed image.

> 66 *To understand the challenge of motion video capture, consider that a frame-grabbed 24-bit color image takes about 900K to store.* 99

A typical JPEG-compressed image occupies only 1/10 the amount of storage as an uncompressed image. One system using this scheme, announced by VideoLogic, takes color motion video and records it onto a hard disk at 30 frames per second. This product relies on a chip from C-Cube Microsystems called the CL-550, which incorporates the JPEG standard.

Another image compression system on the market comes from Storm Technology, a company formed by one of C-Cube's founders. Storm produces a software solution called PicturePress and a hardware compression device called PicturePress Accelerator. In an extension to the JPEG standard, Storm's products implement a scheme called JPEG++, in which selected areas of an image can be more heavily compressed than other areas.

Although JPEG compression has been applied to video, it was originally designed to work with still images. A newer standard called *MPEG* (Motion Picture Experts

Group) has been proposed for video compression. Whereas JPEG compresses video on a frame-by-frame basis, the MPEG standard takes advantage of the similarity between successive frames in a typical video sequence. Only parts of the image that change between frames are encoded, resulting in much higher compression ratios. Still other compression schemes, such as ones based on the complex mathematics of fractal geometry, promise still better performance in the near future.

Viewing live images on the Mac with video display

Display products let you connect the Mac to a video source (such as a VCR or camera) and view the live image on a Macintosh monitor. There aren't many stand-alone applications for products like this, because all they do is convert the Mac into an expensive television set. As we'll see below, however, they become powerful tools when used with video overlay equipment. (Television display hardware shouldn't be confused with boards like Apple's Macintosh Display Card 8•24, which are not designed to work with television signals, although the two functions are sometimes combined.)

A number of products are available for viewing NTSC video. The RadiusTV, E-Machines's QuickView Studio, and the RasterOps ColorBoard 364 all provide high-quality video displays on a color Macintosh screen. They are designed for applications in which a videodisc or videotape needs to be combined with computer-generated graphics in an interactive presentation. As a side benefit, these boards double as frame grabbers, although they do not provide any sort of video output.

In addition to being compatible with standard video input signals, the ColorBoard 364 can also function as a 24-bit color display board in conjunction with an Apple 13-inch or other similar monitor. An optional tuner module which connects to an Apple Desktop Bus (ADB) port, lets you view standard television broadcasts from cable or an antenna.

Video overlay

Products in this category let you add Macintosh graphics to video images and are usually used in conjunction with video display boards. An application familiar to most television viewers is superimposing text or graphics (like a broadcaster's logo) over a television picture. The most sophisticated overlay products give the user complete control over how the video image and the Mac graphics flow together. So, for example, you can have live TV appear in the middle of a drawing, or you can add Macintosh-generated text to a video. With the Mac's inherent graphical prowess, the ability to mix a Macintosh display with video can be extremely useful.

The ColorSpace IIi and ColorSpace Plus/SE, both from Mass Micro, let you overlay Macintosh graphics on a video signal. The ColorSpace IIi can incorporate up to 256 different colors at once, and is compatible with either composite or RGB video inputs. Like the RasterOps ColorBoard 364, the ColorSpace IIi can capture images, but digitizing a single frame takes 20 seconds. Unlike the ColorBoard 364, the ColorSpace IIi is not designed to function as a Macintosh monitor display board since it only drives composite video monitors.

Mass Micro produces another board called the ColorSpace FX that works along with the ColorSpace IIi to produce live video on an AppleColor monitor. The two boards act together to combine a standard video signal with Macintosh graphics into a signal compatible with the Apple monitor. The ColorSpace FX also lets you add a number of special effects to a video sequence, including pan, zoom, shrink, mirror, and spin. Unlike the ColorSpace IIi, the IIi/IIfx combination can also perform true 24-frame grabbing in ⅓₀ of a second.

> 66 *If you plan to record Mac graphics on videotape, it is especially important to design your presentation with video in mind.* 99

A newer product, the Video Toaster from NewTek, incorporates a number of functions, including adding graphics to video, switching between four video sources, digital effects processing, character generation (for subtitles), frame grabbing, and color effects processing. The Video Toaster even includes built-in 3-D rendering to add 3-D computer graphics to video. If all this sounds like a Macintosh video amateur's dream, it is — almost. The Video Toaster was designed for the Commodore Amiga, the computer that Macintosh users love to hate. Fortunately, NewTek also offers a version of the Video Toaster that comes with an Amiga, and uses the Mac to control it.

Converting the Mac's video signal with video output

Once a video sequence has been embellished with Macintosh graphics, a video output device is needed to convert the Mac's video signal back into a form compatible with TV. These devices are known as encoders because they take the separate red, green, and blue signals used by the Macintosh and combine them into an NTSC composite signal.

Recent products for putting Macintosh graphics out to videotape include the NTSC Encoder, a low-cost solution from ComputerVideo, and the Mediator, a more expensive product from VideoLogic. The Mediator incorporates a number of special features, including adjustments for underscan and flicker.

If you plan to record Mac graphics on videotape, it is especially important to design your presentation with video in mind. Don't expect the same WYSIWYG (what you see is what you get) performance that you can get from a Macintosh and laser printer, though. For example, computer-generated text often looks terrible on television, largely because of flicker caused by high contrast between the characters and their background. To help improve the quality of your productions, here is a list of useful tips to remember when designing Macintosh graphics for video.

❖ Minimize fine details in your graphics: use thick lines and large type instead.

❖ Use sans serif typefaces (like Helvetica) in sizes larger than 18 points.

❖ Use only the central portion of the monitor for graphics. Most television systems rely on a technique called *overscanning* to ensure that the video picture will fill the screen. Computer monitors do the opposite: they underscan to ensure that the entire picture will fit on the computer's display. For NTSC-based systems, use only the middle 540 × 420 pixels (width by height). For PAL systems, use the middle 640 × 480 pixels. These areas correspond to the central two-thirds of the video image.

❖ Alleviate flicker by eliminating closely spaced horizontal lines (like the ones in the title bars of Macintosh windows). Avoid horizontal lines 1, 3, or 5 pixels wide.

❖ Avoid using bright colors such as pure white (use 80 percent instead) and saturated red. If your production will be broadcast, the TV station's equipment will modify your colors to make them broadcast-legal, to avoid letting their signal encroach on other stations. (A similar effect occurs when pure white letters on a dark background cause a humming sound in the audio channel of a television program.)

❖ Stay away from closely gridded patterns like the 50 percent gray of the Macintosh desktop — these patterns will cause color fringing and flickering.

To improve text display, techniques called *antialiasing* and *convoluting* can be used to soften the edges of characters by filling around them using colors in between text and background (see Figure 8-2). Specialized products like VideoQuill from Data Translation or general purpose programs like Adobe Photoshop can be used to create antialiased text. VideoQuill was specially designed for removing jagged edges and flicker from titles for video recording. Antialiasing capabilities can also be found in products from Digital F/X (see below), which use PostScript to produce extremely high-quality graphics for recording onto videotape.

Video output on a shoestring

There is a much less expensive way of recording the Macintosh screen on videotape — use a video camera. The resulting videotape will be of lower quality than one created using dedicated video output boards. Even worse, the recorded image will suffer because of the different frame rates employed by the Mac monitor and video recorder. In most cases the picture rolls with terrible-looking dark

Text without Jags

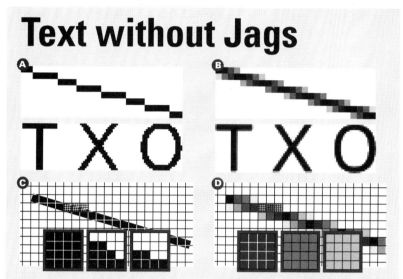

In Mac video, it's often useful to record images directly from the Mac screen. Unfortunately, Macintosh-generated text and lines can look terrible on videotape, due to flicker caused by the high contrast between the lines and letters and their background.

Diagonal lines and letters look jagged and have a characteristic stair-step pattern when moved to video (**A**). This is due to the differences in resolution between the Mac screen and the NTSC video standard; pixels that used to fall into place on a Mac screen don't fall accurately on a video screen.

Antialiasing alleviates jags and stairsteps by blending the colors of letter and line edges with the color of the background (**B**). To determine the blend for a diagonal black line on a white background, the antialiasing algorithm first makes the line four times larger than it really is, so that each pixel actually becomes a 4-by-4 grid (**C**). Then, the algorithm examines each of the 16 areas for each pixel and compares the color fill of each area to the edge of the diagonal line. The color and /or intensity of an individual pixel depends on the percentage of pixel areas on the ideal edge of the line. As a result, a pixel that falls only 10 percent on the ideal line becomes 10 percent of the line's color, a pixel 50 percent on the ideal line becomes 50 percent, and so on (**D**).

You can see the differences in antialiasing that occur with diagonal lines of varying angles (**E**). Notice that the horizontal line requires no antialiasing. You can also see the difference antialiasing makes in smoothing Mac-generated text in large type sizes (**F**).

VideoQuill from Data Translation is a specialized program designed for removing jagged edges and flicker from video-recorded titles. Or, you can turn to Adobe Photoshop or Time Arts' Oasis, general-purpose image processing applications, which provide smooth-looking text not only for video recording, but also for computer displays.

Figure 8-2: Antialiasing is one technique used to improve the quality of computer-generated text on a television monitor.

bands. (By the way, these are similar to the bands that appear when you try to photograph the Macintosh screen using a still camera — to eliminate them, use shutter speeds of ¹⁄₁₅ of a second or slower.)

Luckily for cost savers, Apple has produced a piece of software called VideoSync that eliminates most of the rolling effect. This cdev (control panel device), developed for producing Macintosh TV commercials, slows down the Apple 13-inch monitor's refresh rate to match standard video rates. In addition, it lets you alter the monitor's timing so that you can see when the rolling stops. The only drawback is that the software works only with Apple's video boards, and only with certain ones at that. The original 8-bit board is probably the best one for this type of work.

Video control — the Macintosh as editor

If you've ever been faced with the unpleasant task of having to assemble a series of video clips into a coherent sequence, then you understand why editing using manual techniques is such a headache. *Edit controllers* let you import sound and video from multiple sources and combine them into a seamless production, complete with titles, fade-ins, fade-outs, and special effects. Unfortunately, computerized editing systems have always been far beyond the means of most amateur video enthusiasts and many corporate video production departments.

High-quality work demands that an editor be able to locate individual frames within a video sequence, a capability known as *frame accuracy.* Although video is composed of a continuous electronic signal, frames in a video sequence can be numbered, much like the frames in a movie. Video professionals have devised a standardized numbering scheme for television, called *SMPTE timecode* (for the Society of Motion Picture and Television Engineers). All high-end video equipment (including Macintosh edit controllers) incorporates SMPTE or other similar timecode capabilities.

With such an impressive lineup of video input, output, and overlay products, the Macintosh should be a natural for video editing. It is therefore perhaps surprising that there are relatively few Macintosh products for controlling video editing equipment. However, the gap is quickly being filled by companies such as Digital F/X, Diaquest, Avid, and MacroMind.

Products fall into two categories — control products and edit systems. Video controllers like Diaquest's are used to record Macintosh animations (such as those produced with MacroMind Director) on videotape. They work by triggering the video recorder, recording the animation frame by frame. Editing systems, like Video F/X from Digital F/X, are designed to manage the entire editing process, from selecting individual audio and video clips, to adding graphics and special effects, to recording the final sequence on tape.

The Video F/X system is SMPTE-based and can produce so-called edit decision lists for use with still more sophisticated editing equipment employed by video professionals, like the CMX-6000. Video F/X includes a video controller box to manage source and destination recorders and a Macintosh II NuBus board. During the editing process, video clips are viewed on the Mac screen in digitized form. Once a video sequence has been laid out, Video F/X assembles the clips on tape. An option called Soft F/X offers the same editing functions in software, although the Video F/X hardware is still necessary for the final production. One major advantage of the Video F/X editing system is its support for antialiased PostScript text and graphics.

In order to use a video controller or editing system like Video F/X, you should have access to a frame-accurate controllable VCR like the Sony U-Matic. Costing around $5,000, these decks are designed for broadcast-quality video production. (For Betacam systems, expect to spend upwards of $40,000 each.) In order to use other video sources such as laser discs, you will need a similarly controllable player.

For those with more limited budgets, there are cheaper editing videocassette decks on the market. The NEC PC-VCR is an example of a computer-controllable VCR that is frame-accurate and relatively inexpensive. Software that allows users to control it from within HyperCard, SuperCard, and MacroMind Director is available as the Light Source Multimedia Toolkit.

Creating multimedia presentations with low-end video controllers
Still less-expensive solutions are available from MacroMind and Video Production Controls. MacroMind's MediaMaker lets you combine Macintosh graphics, animation, sound, and video into complete presentations. Unlike editing systems such as Video F/X, MediaMaker works with consumer-type equipment like VCRs and camcorders via Sony interfaces called *Control-L* and *Control-S*. SMPTE timecode is not supported, and the individual graphics or animations cannot be edited within the MediaMaker application.

MediaMaker's strength lies in its ability to take a variety of video and non-video sources such as CDs, laser discs, Macintosh sounds, and graphics, and interleave them to produce what Apple and others call multimedia. While multimedia is a fairly nebulous term, MediaMaker does provide a function that is well suited to the Mac — producing audiovisual presentations that incorporate a variety of media. In producing MediaMaker, MacroMind has taken its flagship Director product and upgraded it to include traditional video and sound. This is much the same goal that Apple intends with QuickTime, described in "Digital video and multimedia" of this chapter.

Other solutions for using inexpensive video equipment with the Mac are provided by Video Production Controls, The Voyager Company, and Apple. The VidClip VideoTape Control Toolkit from Video Production Controls lets you control many different types of Sony consumer VCRs from within HyperCard. A similar product for controlling laser disc players is produced by The Voyager Company. Voyager's VideoStack 2.0 is designed to control more than 20 types of players. Apple also provides a laser disc player control system called the Hyper-Card VideoDisc Toolkit. All three HyperCard-based products are available from the Apple Programmer's and Developer's Association (APDA).

Macintosh and video: guidelines for choosing equipment

Given the wide scope of Apple's product line, it may be hard to believe that there was once only one Macintosh: the 128K. Today, after more than seven years of product introductions, there are 12 varieties of Macintosh CPUs in users' hands, not counting variations with third-party upgrades. And although some models no longer appear on Apple's sales list, they're still being used productively.

Does having a low-end Mac prevent you from working with video? The answer depends, in large part, on what your goals are. If you only need to control a laser disc player or videocassette recorder at home, you can get by without Apple's hottest new CPU. On the other hand, if you want to combine several video sources while dubbing in an audio track, all while maintaining broadcast quality, you may find yourself wishing for at least a Macintosh II. A Mac II or higher is *required* if you wish to view video on the Mac's monitor, or if you want to record high-quality graphics from the Mac on videotape.

> 66 *If you only need to control a laser disc player or videocassette recorder at home, you can get by without Apple's hottest new CPU.* 99

To help you decide if your setup packs the horsepower to do what you need, we've compiled a list of the different models and their abilities.

Macintosh 128K and 512K

Although you might be able to find a video digitizer that will function with early model Macs, much of today's software requires at least 1MB of RAM to run. (Before you toss your computer into the trash, remember that upgrades are available from Apple and third-party vendors.)

Macintosh Plus, SE, Portable, and Classic

These Macintoshes can be used to digitize video, although you won't be able to view the captured images in gray scale or color. They can also be used to control video devices that can be connected to the Mac's serial port, such as laser disc players, Apple's CD ROM drive, and other devices with interfaces such as Control-S and Control-L (see "Creating multimedia presentations with low-end video controllers").

Macintosh SE/30 and LC

These Macs can provide video output via boards available from RasterOps and others. You can also use these computers with products such as ComputerEyes to digitize frames from video, though you will probably want to have a color monitor and adapter installed. View these computers as hybrids between the low-end and Macintosh II-series computers.

Macintosh II, IIx, IIcx, IIci, IIfx, IIsi, and beyond

In combination with the right hardware and software, these Macs can do almost everything — grab video frames, output video, overlay graphics on video, and control video equipment. In addition to having a hard drive and an 8-bit or better video board, most operations will require you to purchase circuit boards such as frame grabbers and overlay boards. Additionally, most video importing, overlaying, and viewing jobs will have you wishing for a color monitor. If you plan to author multimedia productions, you will need a large hard drive, a color monitor, and one of the faster CPUs. We also suggest installing as much RAM as your budget will allow (at least 8MB).

Digital video and multimedia

Unlike Macintosh text and graphics, which are handled digitally, television programs are transmitted and processed in analog form. However, video, like audio, may soon enter the digital domain. Digital video has already been a hot topic for several years now. Although industry experts don't expect digital video to be in wide use for several years, examples are already being shown. Apple Computer and Super-Mac Technologies have both shown prototypes of digital video on the Macintosh.

The Apple prototype has been extensively demonstrated at trade shows. This prototype demonstrated moving pictures with accompanying text and sound on Macintosh IIci and IIsi monitors. Video and sound were provided by CNN, while the text came from

> 66 *A Mac II or higher is required if you wish to view video on the Mac's monitor, or if you want to record high-quality graphics from the Mac on videotape.* 99

daily newspapers — the entire system was incorporated into an interactive newspaper that could be used by attendees at any one of 50 or so networked computers.

While Apple has not commented much on the technology, it has been reported that it is based upon a proprietary image compression scheme that can reduce storage needs by up to 10:1. The system will be a part of a larger package called QuickTime that will be released as an extension to System 7.0, although the EDUCOM demonstration used a version of System 6.0. The EDUCOM demonstration included video clips taken from CNN during the previous night, implying inherent real-time recording and editing capabilities. Also, the computers had no extra hardware — the video clips could be viewed using off-the-shelf Macintosh hardware.

> 66 *The trend toward multifunction products that combine video input, overlay, display, and output on a single board will continue, and prices will steadily drop.* 99

The major drawbacks of the Apple prototype were the relatively small picture (160 × 120 pixels) and low frame rate (15 to 20 frames per second). Two or more clips playing simultaneously slowed the display down to an unpleasant rate. It is safe to assume, though, that both of these problems will be remedied as the software becomes refined and the hardware gets more powerful.

The SuperMac Technologies digital video system, based on JPEG compression, has also been demonstrated extensively. Advantages of the SuperMac system include large images (640 × 480 pixels) and high frame rates (around 30 frames per second). This made it the rough equivalent of NTSC video, though the computer, hard drive, compression board, and display cost somewhat more than most NTSC television sets.

Through the looking glass — the future of Macintosh video

Although it's unlikely that video applications will achieve the phenomenal success that desktop publishing did in the 1980s, we think that the market for video products will increase steadily. The trend toward multifunction products that combine video input, overlay, display, and output on a single board will continue, and prices will steadily drop.

Another safe prediction is that compression technology, whether based on Apple's proprietary scheme or on a standard like JPEG or MPEG, will see more general use. Within a short time, we expect to see consumer-level products that let you digitize and compress video sequences and edit them on the Macintosh, just as easily as a word processor lets you edit text today.

Predicting what we can expect from desktop video in say, five years, is somewhat more difficult. The video industry is beginning to feel the effects of the digital video revolution, a transition that promises major changes in the way television is produced, recorded, transmitted, and viewed. Even more wide-ranging will be the effect of *high definition television*, or *HDTV*. Already available on a limited basis in Japan, HDTV vastly improves a television picture by approximately doubling the number of scanning lines that make up each video frame. HDTV pictures are also wider than standard television, with a shape better suited to movies than current TV receivers. As if to cement the relationship between digital video and HDTV, companies vying to develop an HDTV standard for the United States recently committed themselves to a digital format.

What does all this have to do with the Macintosh? For one thing, any video-related products for the Mac or its successors will have to cope with the larger, higher-resolution HDTV images. More important for Apple, consumer electronic giants like Japan's JVC are betting billions of dollars on "smart" television sets that could duplicate some of the functions of today's Macintosh. Apple and other computer vendors will have to develop innovative new hardware and software to stay ahead of the game. Stay tuned for more.

Summary

✔ Video import products fall into two classes: digitizers and frame grabbers. Digitizers, which allow you to take snapshots from stationary video sources like cameras and VCRs, are slower than frame grabbers because they process a number of video frames to capture an image; frame grabbers contain circuitry to synchronize digitization with the frame rate of the video source.

✔ Still video cameras are an alternative to digitizers and frame grabbers and offer the advantage of portability. These cameras produce a video signal that can be fed into a frame grabber.

✔ Reducing the amount of data in recorded images is called image compression. The most common compression techniques are based upon the JPEG (Joint Photographic Experts Group) standard which uses a mathematical technique called a cosine transform which allows images to be compressed and decompressed.

✔ Video overlay products such as Mass Micro's ColorSpace IIi, allow you to add Mac graphics to video images. For example, you can have live TV appear in the middle of a drawing or you can add Mac-generated text to a video.

✔ You can edit Mac-based video with Edit Controllers, which let you import sound and video from multiple sources and combine them into a seamless production, complete with titles, fade-ins, fade-outs, and special effects — all on the Mac.

✔ If you only need to control a laser disc player or videocassette recorder at home, you can get by without Apple's hottest new CPU. But if you want to combine several video sources while dubbing in an audio track, all while maintaining broadcast quality, you'll need at least a Macintosh II.

Where to buy

Computer Friends, Inc.
14250 NW Science Park Dr.
Portland, OR 97229
503-626-2291
503-643-5379 (FAX)

E-Machines, Inc.
9305 S.W. Gemini Dr.
Beaverton, OR 97005
503-646-6699

Radius, Inc.
1710 Fortune Dr.
San Jose, CA 95131-1744
408-434-1010
408-434-0770 (FAX–Gen'l.)
408-434-0127 (FAX–Int'l.)

RasterOps Corp.
2500 Walsh Ave.
Santa Clara, CA 95051
408-562-4200
408-562-4066 (FAX)

Storm Technology, Inc.
1101 San Antonio, Ste. 101
Mountain View, CA 94043
415-691-9825

SuperMac Technologies
485 Potrero Ave.
Sunnyvale, CA 94086
408-773-4489
408-735-7250 (FAX)

VideoLogic, Inc.
245 First St.
Cambridge, MA 02142
617-494-0530
617-494-0534 (FAX)

The Voyager Company
1351 Pacific Coast Hwy.
Santa Monica, CA 90401
213-451-1383

Chapter 9

Choosing a Monitor for Your Mac

by Robert C. Eckhardt

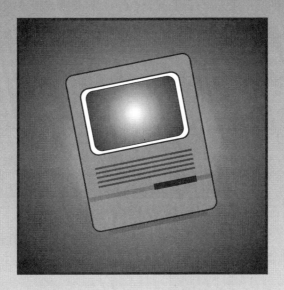

In this chapter...

- The pros and cons of black-and-white, gray-scale, and color displays.

- The four standard Macintosh display size classes, their pixel dimensions, and the uses to which each is best suited.

- What pixel density is, and why you should care.

- How to judge image quality in monochrome and color displays.

- Antiglare coatings: do you need them?

- Special issues regarding monitors for modular Macs.

Because you will have to stare at it day after day, year after year, selecting a monitor is one of the most important Macintosh decisions you'll ever make. If you choose a display merely because it's inexpensive, or buy one that turns out to be below par in some way, you may some day find yourself sitting opposite a monitor you can't stand to look at anymore. Eye strain, headaches, lost productivity, or worse may soon follow.

The bad news is that the number of variables involved in a monitor purchase is rather formidable; as a consumer conundrum, picking the right display ranks right up there with buying an automobile. The good news is that people buy automobiles — and Macintosh monitors — every day, and most are happy with the results. Armed with the information and advice on the following pages, you too can join the ranks of satisfied Macintosh monitor owners.

This chapter covers all types of Macintosh display systems — monochrome (black-and-white and gray-scale) and color — for the Macintosh II family as well as the Macintosh LC, SE/30, SE, Classic, and Plus. (Although it is possible to buy monitors and boards separately, I describe monitor and board combinations sold by a single vendor because the best price is usually obtained in a system purchase, and because most people prefer the simplicity and convenience of one-stop shopping.) In most cases, my comments apply equally to all types of display systems; in a few well-marked locations, however, I take special side trips that apply only to a particular type of monitor.

About the author

Before writing about the Macintosh full-time, Robert Eckhardt was a professor of Zoology at the University of Maine, a researcher in Tropical Ornithology at The American Museum of National History in New York, and the Editor-in-Chief and Publisher of Simon and Schuster's Computer Book Division. He is currently a Contributing Editor at *Publish* as well as *Macworld* and has written a number of Macworld Lab reports on monochrome and color monitors. He is the author of *The Fully Powered Mac, Inside Word for the Macintosh,* Publish *Book of Tips* and a soon-to-be-released power users' guide from IDG Books Worldwide.

What kind of monitor do you need?

Faced with dozens and dozens of monitors to choose from, your first task is to narrow the field to either black-and-white, gray-scale, or color displays. Everyone wants a color display, of course, because they're so, well, colorful. Two hundred and fifty-six colors at one time, in fact, with an 8-bit color system; millions of colors with a 24-bit system. The limited color palette of 8-bit systems is sufficient for most purposes; for the photorealistic colors required in graphic arts or multimedia, however, a 24-bit system is often a necessity.

But color systems — especially 24-bit systems — are considerably more expensive than their monochrome counterparts, they're usually bigger, bulkier and much heavier, and text is often not as sharp, clear, or easy on the eyes as it is on a monochrome monitor. In many cases, 24-bit systems also require an accelerator to bring performance up to a reasonable level. Consider color displays only if you really need to see and work with color on screen, have money to burn, or feel an irresistible urge to impress your friends.

Virtually all gray-scale monitors can display 256 shades of gray, while black-and-white monitors can display only two (black and white). Gray scale adds a fair amount to the cost of a monochrome display system, but is essential if you work with scanned photos or many kinds of PostScript art. It's also useful if you want to preview the color images created by others as gray-scale graphics. Black-and-white systems are less sexy; they're also less expensive and perfectly adequate for the tasks that occupy most of the workaday world: word processing, number-crunching, data processing, and bitmapped and object-oriented drawing. In addition, since they have to keep only two balls in the air at one time, rather than 256, black-and-white monitors are faster and more responsive.

> 66 *. . . as a consumer conundrum, picking the right display ranks right up there with buying an automobile.* 99

If you're uncertain about how to factor future needs into the equation, keep in mind that black and white can be considered just the first step toward gray scale, gray scale the first step toward color, and 8-bit color the first step toward 24-bit color. Since many monochrome monitors display gray-scale images as easily as black-and-white, you need only replace the board half of the system to upgrade from black-and-white to gray-scale. Similarly, many gray-scale systems use a board that can produce 256 colors as easily as 256 shades of gray; to upgrade from gray scale to color, you need only replace the monitor. Any color monitor can be used in either 8-bit or 24-bit color systems; to upgrade from 8-bit to 24-bit color, you need only replace the board or, in some cases, add more video RAM to your existing board.

Surveying the real estate

Next you'll want to decide how much terrain the monitor should be able to display. In general, monitors can be divided into four size classes: small (12- to 15-inch monitors); full-page or portrait (15-inch monitors oriented vertically); medium (16-inch monitors); and two-page (19-inch and larger monitors). Although these diagonal-dimension tube measurements are convenient for clumping monitors into groups, they don't tell you what you really need to know: how much page area the monitor can actually display. A better indicator of that is pixel dimensions (or, as the engineers call it, resolution). A pixel (short for picture element) is the smallest part of the picture — a dot — that a monitor can display; pixel dimensions are the height and width of the active area, the part of the screen that actually displays information, in pixels.

In comparison to a compact Mac's 9-inch, 512 × 342-pixel screen, most small displays aren't really all that small. Displays such as the 13-inch AppleColor High-Resolution RGB Monitor (Apple Computer; $1,647, 8-bit; $1,798, 24-bit), and the 12-inch Monochrome (Apple Computer; $947, gray scale), for example, have pixel dimensions of 640 × 480. These monitors can't display a full page all at once — either vertically or horizontally — but they're large enough for many people, myself included. The 15-inch Monochrome Pivot (Radius; $1,694-$1,840, gray scale) and Color Pivot (Radius; $2,790, 8-bit), both of which rotate on their axis to provide either a small horizontal or full-page vertical display, accommodate significantly larger pixel dimensions — about 870 × 640 — and page areas. And at 512 × 384 pixels, the 12-inch RGB Display (Apple Computer; $1,247, 8-bit; $1,398, 24-bit) is the only monitor in this size category that offers little improvement in displayed page area over a compact Mac.

Wordsmiths and others who think in 8½ × 11-inch chunks find full-page displays a nice compromise between the somewhat confined small monitors and the much more expensive two-page displays. Most monitors in this class, such as the Full-Page Monochrome Display (Ehman; $495, b&w) and the One-Page Display (Mobius Technologies; $795, b&w), have pixel dimensions of around 640 × 870. Because they are oriented vertically instead of horizontally, they can thus display a full, US letter-size page without scrolling. Almost all full-page displays are black-and-white. Exceptions are Radius's Monochrome Pivot (in its vertical orientation), the Portrait Display (Apple Computer; $1,747, gray scale), the QM885 (Qume Corporation, $1,149, gray scale) and Radius's Color Pivot (in its vertical orientation).

The third size class consists of a small but important group of color displays that bridge the gap between small horizontal monitors and two-page displays. This collection of 16-inch monitors covers a surprisingly broad spectrum of page areas, from pixel dimensions of 832 × 624 (close to full-page-display size, oriented horizontally) for the ColorPage T16 (E-Machines; $2,995, 8-bit; $3,995, 24-bit) to 1,024 × 808 (about the same as a small-dimension two-page display) for the TX (E-Machines; $3,795, 8-bit; $5,195, 24-bit). Many people who need a color display find monitors in this group ideal: they're high in quality, display a relatively large page area, and are smaller, lighter, and easier on the budget than two-page displays.

For the most part, two-page displays — the fourth and final size class — have either 19-inch or 21-inch screens and one of two pixel dimensions: approximately 1,024 × 768 or 1,152 × 870. (The smaller pixel dimensions don't necessarily corre-spond to the smaller tube size, by the way.) The Viking 3/2400 M (Moniterm; $2,090, b&w), with its 24-inch tube and 1,280 × 960 pixel dimensions, is an unusual excep-tion to both these generalizations.

Despite their name, most two-page monitors cannot display a full two pages without scrolling. Displays in the 1,024 × 768 range — such as the 19-inch Platinum Display (SuperMac; $1,898 b&w; $2,398 gray scale) and the PCPC II/19 (PCPC; $4,995, 8-bit; $5,995, 24-bit) — chop about one inch top and bottom and two inches right and left from a full two pages. Displays in the 1152 × 870 range — such as the SilverView (Sigma Designs; $1,999, b&w; $2,399, gray scale) and the Radius Color Display (Radius; $5,290, 8-bit; $7,690, 24-bit) — lose about one inch right and left. Only the 1,280 × 960-pixel dimensions of the Viking 3/2400 M can display two full pages. But whether they live up to their name or not, two-page monitors are prized by Mac owners who produce newsletters and other periodicals, work on very large spreadsheets, or create large or complex graphics. As with real estate, however, the greater acreage demands a premium price, especially if it's in color.

Note that a few monitors — including the L-View Multi-Mode (Sigma Designs; $1,999, b&w) and PageView Multi-Mode (Sigma Designs; $1,199, b&w) on the monochrome side and the Color Pivot and 19-inch Trinitron Color Display (SuperMac; $5,199, 8-bit; $7,199, 24-bit) on the color side — offer several pixel dimensions and can quickly switch from one to another. The two-page L-View Multi-Mode, for example, can display six different pixel dimensions from 512 × 384 to 1,664 × 1,200, while the full-page PageView Multi-Mode offers three (from 576 × 768 to 704 × 940) and the Color Pivot two (760 × 564 and 870 × 640). Monitors such as these can be useful in situations where one Macintosh serves several functions with radically different display requirements.

Pixel density

In monochrome monitors, each dot on the screen is a pixel, and pixel density is the number of pixels per linear inch. (In Macintosh monitors, the pixel density is — or should be — the same both horizontally and vertically.) Because pixels and dots are one and the same, pixels per inch (ppi) and dots per inch (dpi) are both used to define pixel density in monochrome monitors. In color monitors, the situation is a little more complex. That's because three electron guns — one each for red, green, and blue — shoot beams of color onto the screen. Each beam produces a dot in a given location, and each cluster of red, green, and blue dots creates a full-color pixel. Since dots and pixels are not equivalent on color monitors, color monitor pixel densities should always be given in pixels per inch.

Most monitors have a fixed pixel density and, as a result, fixed pixel dimensions. Monitors that offer two or more pixel dimensions — such as the four mentioned above — can change their pixel density in much the same way my old IBM Selectric typewriter could alternate between 10- and 12-pitch type. The L-View Multi-Mode, for example, offers six densities from a low of 36 ppi to a high of 120 ppi. As it increases the pixel density, more pixels are squeezed onto the screen and larger pixel dimensions are the result.

Compared to the L-View Multi-Mode, the range of pixel densities displayed by fixed-density monitors as a group is actually rather small. Monitors with pixel densities lower than 72 ppi are quite rare; at 64 ppi, Apple's 12-inch RGB Display is one of the few. At this density (and even smaller ones, such as the L-View Multi-Mode's 36 ppi), everything on screen appears larger than life, much like the pages of the large-type edition of *Reader's Digest*. Some people, especially those with visual impairments, will find this useful; others, however, will regret the concomitant decrease in displayed page area.

Many displays — including the ClearVue/II (RasterOps; $1,795, b&w; $2,195, gray scale) and SuperMac's 19-inch Trinitron Color Display — have the same pixel density as a compact Mac screen (72 ppi) and for good reason. This density is the de facto Macintosh standard and, as a result, most applications and all screen fonts are built around it. At 72 ppi, what is displayed on the screen most closely approximates the dimensions of the actual printed page. Pixel densities between 73 and 77 ppi are also common — they're found in Apple's 12-inch Monochrome (76 ppi) and Radius' Color Pivot (75 ppi), for example — and produce images only slightly smaller than actual size. For most people, the difference between these densities and 72 ppi is negligible. If what-you-see-is-what-you-get (WYSIWYG) is what you want, most any monitor in the 72 to 77 ppi range ought to make you happy.

> **❝ Choosing black-and-white, gray scale, or color and determining the optimum pixel density and pixel dimensions for your work is equivalent to selecting the right tool for the job. ❞**

At pixel densities of about 78 ppi and above, the difference between the size of printed and on-screen pages is more noticeable. On the other hand, at these pixel densities, a display can accommodate a larger page area without scrolling, and text, though slightly smaller, is sharper and thus easier to read. Beyond moderate increases in pixel density, however, everyday type sizes can be too small for comfort. Type at pixel densities such as the 87 ppi of E-Machines' TX is already too small for some, and the tiny type of the L-View Multi-Mode in its 120 dpi mode is, for almost everyone except CAD specialists (for whom the monitor was designed), just too much of a good thing. Displays in the 78 to 84 ppi range are thus good choices for those who work primarily with text; consider pixel densities above 85 ppi or so, however, only if you have good eyesight and need to see as much page area as possible.

What to look for in a monitor

Choosing black-and-white, gray scale, or color and determining the optimum pixel density and pixel dimensions for your work is equivalent to selecting the right tool for the job. Now comes the hard part: determining which brand of tool feels right in your hand. The quality of the screen image is the essential part of that feeling. Image quality is an elusive beast, however, depending on many different elements including distortion, focus, contrast, brightness, flicker, phosphor color, and more.

Distortion

Perfection is theoretically possible in a Macintosh monitor, but only the Pentagon would be willing or able to pay the price. Thus almost every monitor has some sort of visual flaw. Since no Mac vendor makes the perfect monitor, you shouldn't waste time looking for one. Rather, you should search for the monitor with the fewest flaws (and most flaws these days are relatively minor), and make sure that the flaws that do exist aren't the type you find especially irritating. Because they're rather high on most people's irritation scales, you'll want to pay special attention to problems of distortion and focus.

Distortion manifests itself in a variety of ways — as kinks in straight lines, squares that look like rectangles, circles that look like ovals, squashed menu bars, bowed or pinched borders of the active area — and is usually most pronounced in the corners, especially (for reasons best known to video engineers) the upper-left corner. Generally speaking, larger monitors tend to have more distortion problems than smaller monitors. Among color monitors, for example, distortion in the 16-inch models, such as E-Machines' TX and the 16-inch Color 2008 Hi-Res System (MegaGraphics; $3,595, 8-bit; $6,795, 24-bit), is much less of a problem than it is in almost any of the two-page color displays.

> **Perfection is theoretically possible in a Macintosh monitor, but only the Pentagon would be willing or able to pay the price.**

Compared to only a few years ago, however, even the worst offenders are rarely so bad nowadays that I would rule them out because of distortion alone. A relative of distortion that does rule out some full-page displays for me, though, is the curvature of the long axis of the video tube itself. The Index Portrait Monitor (MacTel Technology; $579, b&w), the PixelView I (Mirror Technologies; $477, b&w), and Ehman's Full-Page Monochrome Display use a relatively convex tube which makes the screen appear as if it were bending over backward. Qume's QM885, Sigma Designs' PageView, Apple's Portrait Display, Mobius's One-Page Display, and Radius's Monochrome Pivot, on the other hand, all use superflat tubes that largely avoid the problem. If you're considering buying a full-page display, check the curve of the screen itself and make sure it doesn't irritate you.

Focus

Because focus is the product of many different factors, a pair of human eyes is probably the most sensitive instrument you can use to measure it. Focus often varies from one part of the screen to another; it's most often a problem in the corners and along the edges of the screen, so that's where I always look first and most carefully. And don't forget the menu bar at the top of the screen; although some people consider it merely a cosmetic distraction, an out-of-focus menu bar is, to me at least, a major visual irritant.

Among color monitors, the E-Machines TX and ColorPage T16 and Mega-Graphics's 16-inch Color 2008 Hi-Res System have the best focus. A number of the larger color displays — the Radius Color Display, SuperMac's 19-inch Trinitron Color Display, the 19-inch SuperMatch Color Display (SuperMac; $3,799, 8-bit; $5,799, 24-bit), and the 19-inch Color 2008 Hi-Res System (MegaGraphics; $5,948, 8-bit; $9,148, 24-bit) — have excellent focus as well.

Among two-page monochrome monitors, those with the best focus include Sigma Designs's L-View Multi-Mode and SilverView, the TPD/21 (Radius; $2,390 b&w; $3,190, gray-scale), SuperMac's 19-inch Platinum Display, the Ranger Dual Page Monitor (Ranger Technologies; $1,395, b&w), and RasterOps', ClearVue/II. Almost all the full-page displays have very good focus — a cut above most two-page displays, in fact. Best of the lot are Mobius's One Page and Ehman's Full-Page Monochrome Displays. Also quite sharp is the Apple 12-inch Monochrome Display.

At the other extreme, a small number of two-page displays — the Nutmeg 19 (Nutmeg Systems; $1,299, b&w; $1,499, gray scale), the Viking 3/72 (Moniterm; $1,295 b&w; $1,990, gray-scale), the Platinum Two-Page Display (SuperMac Technology; $2,298, b&w; $2,798, gray scale), and the Gray-Vision Two-Page Display (CalComp; $2,995, gray scale) — one full-page display, Mirror's PixelView I, and one small display, Qume's QM880, have focus problems significant enough to cast doubt on their suitability for text-intensive work.

Moiré patterns and convergence on color monitors

A moiré is a ripple pattern in what should be a uniform color or texture. Like focus, the moiré patterns that sometimes appear on a color display are caused by a complexity of factors. As with focus, moiré problems are best judged by eye. Most color monitors display noticeable moiré patterns in the standard desktop background of alternating light and dark pixels. You should be concerned only if moiré patterns crop up frequently elsewhere, such as in solid colors or in complex color images, as sometimes happens on the MegaGraphics' 19-inch Color 2008 Hi-Res System.

When convergence in a color monitor is out of whack (the three electron beams fail to hit their phosphor targets accurately), the image goes out of focus and objects acquire red or blue shadows. All monitors have good convergence somewhere on the screen, usually in the center; the real test is whether or not convergence is equally good everywhere. If convergence varies markedly from one area to the next, you may need to adjust and readjust the convergence controls (if there are any) to see different parts of the screen clearly.

Color monitors with the best convergence include the AppleColor High-Resolution RGB Display, E-Machines' TX and ColorPage T16, MegaGraphics' 16-inch Color 2008 Hi-Res System, Radius' Color Display, the XLI Trinitron System (RasterOps; $1,999, 8-bit; $3,999, 24-bit) and SuperMac's 19-inch Trinitron Color Display. The Sigma ColorMax 8/24 (Sigma Designs; $6,095, 8-bit; $6,695, 24-bit) has the poorest convergence.

Antiglare, brightness, and contrast

The color of your office, the location of windows, the level of ambient light—these and other aspects of your work environment need to be factored into your choice of a monitor as well. For example, consider antiglare treatment, which is standard on some monitors and not on others. If you habitually wear white shirts and work in a brightly lit room, even the best antiglare treatment may not help much. On the other hand, if you usually wear dark colors and have some control over the lighting and physical arrangement of your work area, you may not need any antiglare treatment at all.

In favorable conditions such as low light, antiglare treatment can actually enhance contrast. In unfavorable conditions (lots of light, lots of glare), antiglare treatment can reduce contrast as well as glare. Under all conditions, antiglare treatment reduces brightness and often makes the screen image appear slightly unfocused. (Turning up the brightness to compensate can put the image even more out of focus.) If your work environment permits, I recommend that you avoid antiglare treatment, or at least heavy-duty treatment such as that found on the Two-Page Monochrome Display (Apple; $2,797, gray scale).

Most people prefer a bright monitor — the colors are more vivid on a bright monitor, and bright monitors are easier on the eyes in a high light level environment. Good contrast works with brightness to prevent that washed-out look, producing whiter whites, blacker blacks, and richer colors. Keep in mind, however, that the right brightness and contrast for one situation may be much more or far less than is needed in another. In general, if your workplace has low light levels, you won't need to crank the brightness and contrast up very high. If you use your monitor for, say, public demonstrations in brightly lit areas, you'll need all the brightness and contrast you can get.

Among monochrome and color monitors, contrast and brightness vary considerably. On the monochrome side, the displays with the greatest usable brightness level — the level above which the image goes out of focus — include SuperMac's Platinum Two-Page and 19-inch Platinum Displays, the Nutmeg 19, CalComp's Gray-Vision Two-Page Display, the MegaScreen 19-inch (Dotronix; $1,499, b&w; $2,065, gray scale), Apple's Portrait Display, Mobius's One-Page Display, Qume's QM880, and Apple's 12-inch Monochrome Display. The best of the brightest color displays include E-Machines's TX and ColorPage T16, MegaGraphics's 16-inch Color 2008 Hi-Res System, the Mac II Color System (Generation Systems; $4,395, 8-bit; $5,690, 24-bit), the Relax/Ikegami Trinitron System (Relax; $1,099, 8-bit), SuperMac's 19-inch SuperMatch, and the PCPC II/21 (PCPC; $3,658, 8-bit; $4,858, 24-bit).

If you work in a bright office or use a monitor for public demonstrations, avoid monitors at the low end of the brightness scale, such as Sigma Designs's L-View Multi-Mode, Moniterm's Viking 3/72, the Monochrome Display (Generation Systems; $995, b&w), Radius's TPD/21 and Color Display, Apple's Two-Page Monochrome Display, and Mirror's PixelView I.

One final point about brightness: Monitors tend to decrease in brightness as time passes and the display's phosphor loses its youthful glow. If you buy a monitor whose brightness control can be turned up higher than you currently need, you'll be able to compensate for the monitor's inevitable senescence later on. If the monitor needs to be set at full brightness from the very beginning, however, there's no way you'll be able to adjust it bright enough a year or two down the road.

Phosphor color

A phosphor coating on the inside of the tube's face is what creates the image you see on the screen. When pure white pixels are called for, the phosphors used in most Macintosh monitors don't actually glow a pure white. Instead, in monochrome monitors, they tend to be one of three different shades: light blue (as in Apple's Two-Page Monochrome and Portrait Displays), light amber (as in Sigma Designs's L-View Multi-Mode), or a paper white that's close to but not quite pure white (as in SuperMac's 19-inch Platinum Display). In color monitors, the color temperature (as video engineers term it) is usually slightly blue; a few color displays (such as the Relax/Ikegami Trinitron System) have a decided green cast which some find unappealing.

Many Macintosh owners prefer displays with a blue cast to them, since that's what they're accustomed to on a compact Mac. First-time monitor buyers, however, should know that people usually find an amber tint more comfortable to look at in incandescent light, and a blue tint more comfortable under fluorescent light. Regardless of lighting conditions, if you are buying a second monitor, it's usually a good idea to stick with more or less the same phosphor color as your original monitor. Blue and amber yellow monitors never look so jarringly different as when sitting side-by-side.

Purity and gray-scale uniformity in color monitors

Ideally, a blank, white screen on a color monitor should be uniform across the whole display, and gray-scale images should be free of blushes of color. In reality, however, purity problems sometimes add color where it's not wanted. Purity is the consistency of a given color across the entire screen. For example, on a pure white field, there should be no red, green, or blue blemishes. If there are, and if demagnetizing the display by pressing the degauss button doesn't eliminate them, the display has purity problems that can muddy colors in the problem areas. Color monitors with excellent purity include E-Machines' TX and ColorPage T16, MegaGraphics's 16-inch and 19-inch Color 2008 Hi-Res Systems, the Radius Color Display, and the PCPC II/19. Monitors with noticeable purity problems include the Relax/Ikegami Trinitron System, the PCPC II/21, and the ChromaVision 2-Page Display (CalComp; $5,995, 8-bit; $6,995, 24-bit).

When it comes to gray-scale images on color monitors — and most color display owners have to deal with gray scale as well as color images — purity isn't the only issue. Also important is gray-scale uniformity, the monitor's ability to display clearly the different gray levels in a gray-scale sequence. In this regard, RasterOps's XLI Trinitron System, the PCPC II/19 and II/21, and E-Machines's TX come out on top.

Flicker and text quality

What you see on a monitor's screen is in some ways comparable to a movie; a sequence of dozens of images per second gives the impression of a rock-solid picture. The rate at which those images are flashed on the screen is called the vertical refresh rate; a rate of 74 Hz, for example, means that 74 images per second are painted on the screen. If the refresh rate is below 60 Hz, the screen will seem to flicker, like an old-time movie. Above 65 Hz, most people will see a steady, flicker-free image. What you see at rates between 60 Hz and 65 Hz depends on the acuity of your vision.

Screen flicker is at best a strain on the eyes and, at worst, a form of information-age torture. It may not give you a migraine today, but it will sooner or later (probably sooner). Nowadays, most monitors have flicker-free refresh rates above 70 Hz. But low-refresh-rate monitors do still exist and you should strike them from consideration if you detect flicker. Sigma Designs's L-View Multi-Mode and the Relax/Ikegami Trinitron System both have refresh rates in the low 60s, for example, and I can detect flicker in both of them. If you are thinking of purchasing either of these monitors, or any monitor with a low vertical refresh rate, be sure to give it your own personal flicker test.

> **66 It's a little-known fact that individual pixels vary in size and shape from one brand of monitor to the next. 99**

If you work primarily with words, you'll also want to look closely at the text quality of the monitors you're considering. It's a little-known fact that individual pixels vary in size and shape from one brand of monitor to the next. Because body-text type is often composed of one- and two-pixel-wide strokes, this variation can have a significant effect on the appearance of type on the screen. Text that's bold and easy to read on some monitors can appear fuzzy or anemic on others.

Different people have different tastes and opinions when it comes to on-screen text. Among color monitors, my favorites include the AppleColor High-Resolution RGB Monitor, E-Machines's TX and ColorPage T16, MegaGraphics's 16-inch and 19-inch Color 2008 Hi-Res Systems, and RasterOps's XLI Trinitron System. Among monochrome monitors, I prefer Apple's 12-inch Monochrome and Portrait Displays, Ehman's Full-Page Monochrome Display, Mobius's One-Page Display, Radius's TPD/21, SuperMac's 19-inch Platinum Display, and Sigma Designs's SilverView and L-View Multi-Mode. You may have different preferences, and should compare monitors first-hand to determine your own favorites.

Utility software

Display systems differ significantly in the amount and quality of utility software they provide. Many monitors, such as those from Apple, are sold without software of any kind. Others, such as those from Radius and E-Machines, include screen savers and utilities for tear-off menus, larger menu bars, automatic dialog-box centering, and more. Since utility software is not essential to the operation of the monitor and can even conflict with your existing collection of startup documents, it should figure little, if at all, in your buying decision. If the monitor you like best lacks utility software, you can always obtain a screen saver, a tear-off menu utility, or whatever elsewhere.

Special considerations for modular Macs

All the display systems mentioned above work with members of the Mac II family. Some of the color systems also work with an SE/30 or an LC, and many of the black-and-white monitors can be used as a second monitor for the SE, SE/30, Plus, LC, and Classic. In general, a monitor's attributes are largely independent of the board that runs it and the computer it is hooked up to. The only notable exception to this rule is brightness — some boards are tuned to drive a monitor more brightly than others are — although the differences are usually relatively minor (about 5 to 10 percent). Thus the comments in previous paragraphs apply equally well to Mac II, LC, and compact Mac systems.

When purchasing a second screen for a compact Mac, however, one other item — the software that makes it function properly — can be an important consideration. Most such software allows you to use both screens at the same time (software for Sigma Designs's L-View is an unusual exception), while in only a few systems, such as the MegaGraphics Rival (MegaGraphics; $1,698-$1,848, b&w) and the ClearVue/SE (RasterOps; $1,795, b&w), can you display the same view on both screens at the same time (for a live demonstration, say). All allow you to specify whether the Mac screen is to the left or the right; only in some, you can adjust the cursor crossover point so that it matches the actual vertical relationship of the two monitors.

Keep in mind, too, that large screens attached to an SE or a Classic are usually sluggish due to the slower overall speed of these two compact Macs. In most instances, you'll have to purchase a compatible accelerator if you want to pep things up. Exceptions to this include RasterOps's ClearVue/SE and Mobius's One-Page Display, both of which include acceleration — at no extra charge — as part of the standard SE system.

Intangibles

There will always be some aspects of a monitor purchase decision which are somewhat nebulous; aspects for which it's hard to determine just what the facts are and even harder to know how much they should influence your decision. For example, some manufacturers, usually those with higher retail prices (such as Radius), claim to test and tweak their units repeatedly to eliminate problems before they leave the factory. Some manufacturers (again, usually those with higher retail prices) claim better and/or faster service if problems do crop up. And some manufacturers (sometimes, but not always, those with higher retail prices) have a healthier financial outlook and are more likely to still be in business when and if you do need help.

Unfortunately, it's well-nigh impossible to rate manufacturers on testing, service, support, or longevity, and difficult to know how much weight to give these issues in your deliberations. But there are some things you can do to minimize potential problems. Once you've decided on one or two models, ask your colleagues or fellow user group members about their experiences with these displays. Keep your eyes peeled for relevant tales of valor or woe in the "Conspicuous Consumer" column in *Macworld*. If possible, buy your monitor from a local, authorized dealer with a good service record, and take the monitor you'll actually be purchasing out of the box and test it at the store before any money changes hands.

One other point to consider is street price vs. retail price. The prices listed in this chapter are all suggested retail prices. For the less-expensive systems in each category, that's the price you'll probably end up paying. For the more-expensive systems, however, discounts (sometimes deep discounts) are more the rule than the exception. As a result, the price spread within any group of similar display systems is probably less than what's indicated here. Keep in mind, too, that some full-page and small monitors can use the built-in video circuitry of the Macintosh LC, IIsi, or IIci; this obviates the need for a separate video board and, not surprisingly, significantly reduces the price of the display system.

The right tool for the job

It wasn't that long ago that you had to pay top dollar for a monitor that didn't give you a headache. It is thus a welcome sign that there are excellent choices in every price category, and some of my favorites are among the least expensive. Overall, in fact, the quality of Macintosh monochrome and color display systems is higher than ever — so high that it is often necessary to make fine distinctions to choose among them. But choose among them I have. Keep in mind, however, that the Macintosh display universe is, like the real universe, constantly expanding. You'll need to judge new models using the criteria described above, and compare them against my recommendations to decide for yourself which are best.

If you're looking for a two-page, black-and-white monitor, Ehman's Two-Page Monochrome Display is a remarkable bargain. The Genius Dual Page Monitor (Ranger Technologies; $1,395, b&w), which is slightly more expensive, comes in a close second in the budget category. For economical gray-scale, two-page displays, I recommend either PCPC's ShadowGraph or the Ikegami Gray-scale Package (Relax; $799, gray scale); both offer reasonable quality and rock-bottom prices. In the highest quality, money-is-no-object division, my favorite two-page displays, for both black-and-white and gray scale, are Sigma Designs's SilverView and Radius's 19-inch Platinum Display.

If you've decided on a full-page display, I recommend Ehman's Full-Page Monochrome Display — it's rare to find such high quality and low price in one package — or the slightly more expensive One-Page Display from Mobius. If you want both a full-page display and a small landscape monitor, the Radius Monochrome Pivot has no peer. And if you need only a relatively small monochrome monitor, Apple's 12-inch Monochrome Display is both an excellent choice and, if your Macintosh has on-board video, an unbeatable bargain.

Of the two-page color monitors, I especially like the PCPC II/19, MegaGraphics's 19-inch Color 2008 Hi-Res System, RasterOps's XLI Trinitron System, the T19 (E-Machines; $5,495, 8-bit; $7,395, 24-bit), SuperMac's 19-inch Trinitron Color Display, and the Radius Color Display. Of the medium-sized color displays, I recommend MegaGraphics's 16-inch Color 2008 Hi-Res System and E-Machines's TX and ColorPage T16. I give the TX slightly higher marks than the other two, but its 87-ppi pixel density may rule it out for some people. Of the smaller color displays, Radius's Color Pivot is a good, versatile choice, but the AppleColor High-Resolution RGB Monitor remains my favorite. It is the best color bargain in town, and is an easy and obvious winner if color and cost, but not size or ability to rotate, are of primary concern.

Although *Macworld* believes that there may be a health hazard involved with the use of monitors — especially color ones, which have more electronic circuitry than do monochrome monitors — it seems premature to suggest that we dump all our display systems in the garbage. Certainly, we all should push our monitors farther back on our desks in order to keep the screen the recommended arm's length (with fingers extended) away. As long as you take such precautions, you should be relatively safe from electromagnetic emissions and still be able to see what you're doing. With most monitors available today — and especially with the ones recommended above — you should be able to see what you're doing more clearly than ever before.

Summary

✔ Color monitors are essential for color graphics, but they're overkill for most other tasks. Gray scale is less expensive, and black-and-white, cheapest of all, is quite adequate for word processing, number crunching, and data processing.

✔ Choose a monitor that can display the minimum page area you need to see at one time (a half page, a full page, or two facing pages); use pixel dimensions, not tube size, as a barometer of displayed page area.

✔ Pixel densities of or close to 72 ppi are best for work that requires a true WYSIWYG display. At pixel densities above 78 ppi, the screen image is noticeably smaller than the printed page; at between 78 and 84 ppi, however, text is often sharper and easier to read.

✔ Most displays, especially large ones, have some sort of visual flaw, but most flaws these days are relatively minor. The important thing is that the flaws that do exist shouldn't irritate you. A bent upper-left corner is not that difficult to live with, for example, while poor focus or significant distortion definitely are.

✔ Antiglare coatings can reduce brightness and contrast and blur the screen image. If your work environment permits, choose a monitor with minimal antiglare treatment or none at all.

✔ If possible, pick a monitor whose brightness control can be turned up higher than you currently need; as the display ages, you'll be able to compensate for the inevitable dimming of the display's phosphor coating.

✔ Unless you're buying a monitor for a compact Mac, don't base your decision on the kind of software (if any) that comes with the monitor. If your first pick monitor doesn't come with the utilities you want, you can always buy comparable programs separately.

Where to buy

AppleColor High-Resolution RGB Monitor
($1,647, 8-bit; $1,798, 24-bit)
12" RGB Display
($1,247, 8-bit; $1398, 24-bit)
12" Monochrome
($947, gray scale)
Portrait Display
($1747, gray scale)
Two-Page Monochrome Display
($2,797, gray scale)
Apple Computer, Inc.
20525 Mariani Ave.
Cupertino, CA 95014
408-996-1010
800-776-2333

Gray-Vision Two-Page Display
($2,995, gray scale)
ChromaVision 2-Page Display
($5,995, 8-bit; $6,995, 24-bit)
CalComp
65 River Road
Hudson, NH 03051
603-885-8031
800-696-3741

MegaScreen 19" ($1,499, b&w;
$2,065, gray scale)
Dotronix
160 First St., SE
New Brighton, MN 55112
612-633-1742

Full-Page Monochrome
Display ($495, b&w)
Two Page Monochrome
System ($895, b&w)
Ehman
P.O. Box 2126
Evanston, WY 82931
307-789-3830
800-257-1666

ColorPage T16
($2,995, 8-bit; $3,995, 24-bit)
TX ($3,795, 8-bit; $5,195, 24-bit)
T19 ($5,495, 8-bit; $7,395, 24-bit)
E-Machines
9305 SW Gemini Dr.
Beaverton, OR 97005
503-646-6699
800-344-7274

Mac II Color System
($4,395, 8-bit; $5,690, 24-bit)
Monochrome Display
($995, b&w)
Generation Systems
2648 Patton Road
St. Paul, MN 55113
612-633-5222
800-325-5811

Index Portrait Monitor
($579, b&w)
MacTel Technology
3007 N. Lamar
Austin, TX 78705
512-451-2600
800-950-8411

MegaGraphics Rival
($1,698-$1,848, b&w)
16" Color 2008 Hi-Res System
($3,595, 8-bit; $6,795, 24-bit)
19" Color 2008 Hi-Res System
($5,948, 8-bit; $9,148, 24-bit)
MegaGraphics
805-484-3799
800-487-6342

PixelView I ($477, b&w)
Mirror Technologies
2644 Patton Road
Roseville, MN 55113
612-633-4450
800-654-5294

One-Page Display ($795, b&w)
Mobius Technologies
5835 Doyle
Emeryville, CA 94608
415-654-0556
800-669-0556

Viking 3/72 ($1,295 b&w;
$1,990, gray scale),
Viking 3/2400 M ($2,090, b&w)
Moniterm
5740 Green Circle
Minnetonka, MN 55343
612-935-4151
800-933-5740

Nutmeg 19 ($1,299, b&w;
$1,499, gray scale)
Nutmeg Systems
25 South Ave.
New Canaan, CT 06084
203-966-3226
800-777-8439

PCPC II/19
($4,995, 8-bit; $5,995, 24-bit)
PCPC II/21
($3,658, 8-bit; $4,858, 24-bit)
ShadowGraph
($1,595, gray scale)
P.C.P.C.
4710 Eisenhower Blvd., Bldg. A4
Tampa, FL 33643
813-884-3092
800-622-2888

QM880 ($1,099, gray scale)
QM885 ($1,069, gray scale)
Qume Corporation
500 Yosemite Dr.
Milpitas, CA 95035
408-942-4000
800-457-4447

Monochrome Pivot
($1,694-$1,840, gray scale)
Color Pivot ($2,790, 8-bit)
Radius Color Display
($5,290, 8-bit; $7,690, 24-bit)
TPD/21 ($2,390 b&w;
$3,190, gray scale)
Radius
P.O. Box 201960
Austin, TX 78720
408-434-1010
800-227-2795

Genius Dual Page Monitor
($1,395, b&w)
Ranger Technologies, Inc.
313 East Second St.
Hastings, MN 55033
612-437-2233

ClearVue/II ($1,795, b&w;
$2,195, gray scale)
ClearVue/SE
($1,795, b&w)
XLI Trinitron System
($1,999, 8-bit; $3,999, 24-bit)
RasterOps
2500 Walsh Ave.
Santa Clara, CA 95051
408-562-4200
800-468-7600

Relax/Ikegami Trinitron
System ($3,689, 8-bit)
Ikegami Gray-scale Package
($1,659, gray scale)
Relax Technology
3101 Whipple Road
Union City, CA 94587
415-471-6112
415-471-6267 (FAX)

SilverView ($1,999, b&w;
$2,399, gray scale)
L-View Multi-Mode
($1,999, b&w)
PageView Multi-Mode
($1,199, b&w)
Sigma ColorMax 8/24
($6,095, 8-bit; $6,695, 24-bit)
Sigma Designs
46501 Landing Pkwy.
Fremont, CA 94538
415-770-0100
800-845-8086

19" Platinum Display
($1,898 b&w; $2,398 gray
scale)
Platinum Two-Page Display
($2,298, b&w;
$2,798, gray scale)
19" Trinitron Color Display
($5,199, 8-bit; $7,199, 24-bit)
19" SuperMatch Color Display
($3,799, 8-bit; $5,799, 24-bit)
SuperMac Technology
485 Potrero Ave.
Sunnyvale, CA 94086
408-245-2202

Chapter 10
Understanding System Software

by Lon Poole

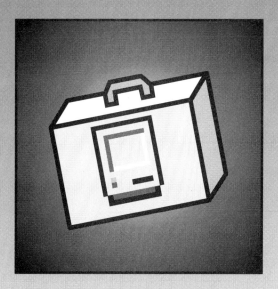

In this chapter...

- ✔ What system software is and what it does.
- ✔ Compared: System 7 and older versions of system software.
- ✔ Which system version is best for you.
- ✔ Mixing versions of system software.
- ✔ Capabilities System 7 has that older system software lacks.
- ✔ Where to get system software.

The application programs and desk accessories with which you get work done on a Macintosh depend on an underlying foundation of system software. For example, the application program tells the system software the titles of its menus and their contents, and the system software displays the titles in the menu bar, notices when you click in the menu bar, shows the appropriate menu, and tells the application program which item you chose. Similarly, the system software manages windows, dialog boxes, keyboard entry, transferring information to and from disks, and a host of other basic operations. By handling basic operations, the system software effects a consistent look and method of operation among all application programs.

About the author

Lon Poole, a *Macworld* contributing editor since 1983, answers readers' questions every month in his column "Quick Tips." He also writes feature articles regularly, including "Installing Memory," which won a 1988 Maggie award for Best How-To Article in a Consumer Publication. He helped found *Macworld* in 1983, and every issue ever published has carried at least one of his columns or articles.

In addition, Lon Poole has authored five Mac books. Four of these, published by Microsoft Press, include: *MacWork, MacPlay* (1984), *Mac Insights* (1986), *HyperTalk* (1988), and *Amazing Mac Facts* (1991). He also wrote the now-classic *Apple II User's Guide,* which has sold over half a million copies worldwide. He has been writing books about personal computers and their applications since 1976.

Lon Poole has reported on System 7 since Apple announced it in May 1989. He has used System 7 on a variety of large and small Macs in preparation for this chapter and for his complete book on the subject, *Macworld Guide to System 7* (IDG Books Worldwide, 1991).

Much of the system software is located in the computer's permanent memory, which is called *ROM* (read-only memory). The System file contains additional system software, and so do other items in the System Folder (or in special folders inside the System Folder). One of those items, the Finder, is a special component of system software that lets you manage your disks and their contents. Portions of the System file, Finder, and other items in the System Folder are transferred to the computer's memory at start-up time, and other portions are transferred as needed.

Picking a version

Because part of the system software resides on disk in the System Folder, you can easily replace it with a new, improved version. Apple revises the system software periodically to add new capabilities, improve performance, and fix problems that turn up. There are two versions of Macintosh system software in widespread use today. The most recent, System 7, has many more capabilities than the various versions of System 6 that some people still use. Those people stick with the older system software because it requires less RAM (random-access memory), doesn't need a hard drive, and works with all older application programs and utility software. Also, System 7 doesn't work with the oldest Macintosh models — the Mac 128K, 512K, 512KE, and XL — so those systems must use older system software.

System 7 requires at least 2MB of RAM. You'll need more than the minimum 2MB if you use large or complex application programs or if you want to open several programs at once. As a rule of thumb, figure you'll need 1MB more than you need with older system software. You'll enjoy System 7 more if your Macintosh has at least 4MB of RAM. See "Where to get system software" for details on obtaining System 7.

A standard installation of System 7 uses about 3MB of disk space. You'll need more space if you install additional fonts, printer software, or other software that extends the standard system-software capabilities.

For Macintosh users whose machines have enough RAM and a hard disk, System 7 is the best version of system software. You might want to continue using older system software if your Macintosh doesn't have enough memory for System 7 and you can't install any more memory in your computer (it won't hold any more or you can't afford more). You might have to continue using older system software if someone else in your company has decided you may not move up to System 7 yet.

Where to get system software

Apple ships System 7 with all new Macintosh models except those few with less than 2MB of RAM and no hard disk. If you already own a Macintosh and want to upgrade it, you can obtain System 7 from a variety of sources:

❖ Buy the System 7 package from an Apple authorized dealer, VAR (value-added reseller), or other reseller. The $99 price includes the installation disks, the complete set of Apple manuals and training disks, and 90 days of phone support direct from Apple. A $349 group upgrade kit includes the software on CD-ROM, a set of user manuals, and a special upgrade book for group support personnel. Individuals in the group can upgrade over the network from the CD-ROM.

❖ Buy a set of installation disks from a user group that has a license to distribute system software. These usually cost $30 to $40 per set. Try BMUG at 415-549-2684 or BCS•Mac at 617-625-7080. Or contact the Apple User Group Clearinghouse at 800-538-9696 for the name and number of the user group nearest you.

❖ Copy the System 7 installation disks from a person, group, or business. Unless your source has a license from Apple to distribute system software, such copying is technically illegal. Apple has not yet sued anyone for copying system software, however. **M**

> 66 *You might want to continue using older system software if your Macintosh doesn't have enough memory for System 7 and you can't install any more memory in your computer.* 99

You might need to continue using older system software until you can upgrade all your application programs and utility software to versions compatible with System 7. (For more information on compatibility, see "System 7 compatibility" in this chapter.) If you must use older system software, version 6.0.5 is the best bet for most Macintosh models; later versions are OK. If you have a Classic, LC, IIsi, or backlit Portable, you must use System 6.0.7 or later. A Macintosh 512KE should use version 2.0.1; a Macintosh 512K or XL should use version 1.1; and a Macintosh 128 should use System 2.0/Finder 4.1.

Mixing systems

Like many Macintosh users, you may have access to more than one Macintosh. Or your Macintosh may be connected to a network with others. In either scenario, some computers may use System 7 while others use older system software, such as System 6. All computers on a network must use compatible versions of LaserWriter software. Otherwise the printer must be reinitialized whenever someone uses it with a version of LaserWriter software different than the previous user's version.

System 7 and System 6 can coexist on the same network if System 6 users install LaserWriter software version 6.1 or the version that comes with System 7. To install LaserWriter 7, they must use the Installer program on the System 7 "Printing" disk; dragging the LaserWriter icon from that disk to their System Folders will not work.

When using disks with System 6 after using them with System 7, you see two automatically created folders. The Desktop Folder contains icons that were on the System 7 desktop. The Trash folder contains items you dragged to the Trash and left there in System 7. When you restart your Macintosh with System 7 after using older system software, the Finder may automatically rebuild its desktop database on the start-up hard disk. You lose all info window comments in the process.

System 7 boiled down

The system software that ships with today's Macintosh — System 7 — is far more capable and sophisticated than older system software. The new system software's improvements let you:

❖ Access and organize files on your disks faster and easier with a greatly improved and omnipresent Finder.

❖ Open several programs concurrently (memory permitting) and have unattended tasks done in the background while you continue working.

❖ Use disk space as if it were memory for opening programs and documents (though not on a Mac Plus, SE, Classic, LC, or Portable).

❖ Share files with other computers networked to your Macintosh.

❖ See sharp text at any size on any screen, printer, or other output device.

❖ Be cool with color windows and icons (requires a color monitor).

All these capabilities are available with the programs you have now. With many new or upgraded programs since System 7 became available in May 1991, you can also:

❖ Remain proficient in a wider variety of programs and learn new ones more easily by using interactive help.

❖ Have copied material in a document automatically updated when the original material in another document (which can be on another Mac in your network) is changed.

❖ Link programs to merge their capabilities.

❖ Get data from large databases on other computers with one simple menu command.

With all these improvements, you might expect System 7 to be overly complex, but it looks and feels amazingly like older system software. If you're used to older system software, you could upgrade your Macintosh to System 7 and barely know its new capabilities exist. As the days and weeks pass, you could explore the new system software at your own pace. The remainder of this chapter describes the new capabilities as you might first encounter them.

Balloon help

One of the most noticeable changes in System 7 is in the menu bar. It has two new permanent menus at its right end, the Help menu and the Application menu. The Help menu gives the Macintosh the means to explain itself. You use its Show Balloons command to turn on System 7's optional balloon help, which gives you a description of objects you see on screen (see Figure 10-1). Aside from balloons appearing and disappearing, everything works normally when balloon help is on. You may perceive a slight delay as help balloons come and go, especially if you use a slower Macintosh.

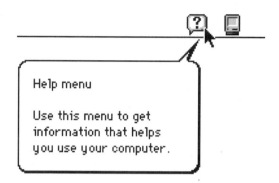

Figure 10-1: Choosing Show Balloons from the Help menu (permanently located near the right end of the menu bar) turns on balloon help. With balloon help on, you place the pointer over an object and a concise description of it appears in a cartoon-style balloon. It's like having someone stand over your shoulder and describe objects on the screen to you.

Balloon help knows about all standard objects in the Macintosh interface. However, it cannot describe a specific program's menu commands, window contents, dialog boxes, and so forth unless the program has been revised to include the necessary help balloons.

Each program can add items to the Help menu for accessing other types of help, such as how-to help. For example, the Finder adds a Finder Shortcuts item that displays a list of tricks for using the Finder.

Multitasking

You will need balloon help, and your wits about you, to get used to System 7's multitasking capabilities unless you already use MultiFinder with System 6. With System 7, multitasking is no longer optional. The Finder is always available without quitting the program you're using, and you can have as many programs open simultaneously as will fit in your computer's memory.

Multitasking's valuable benefits can have disorienting side effects. For instance, you may think the program you're using has unexpectedly quit, when actually you switched to another open program by clicking one of its windows. You must condition yourself to look at the menu bar when you need to know which open program is currently active. The active program's icon appears at the right end of the menu bar as the placeholder for the new Application menu. That menu lists the programs that are open; choosing a program makes it the active program. The Application menu also lets you hide program windows without closing them

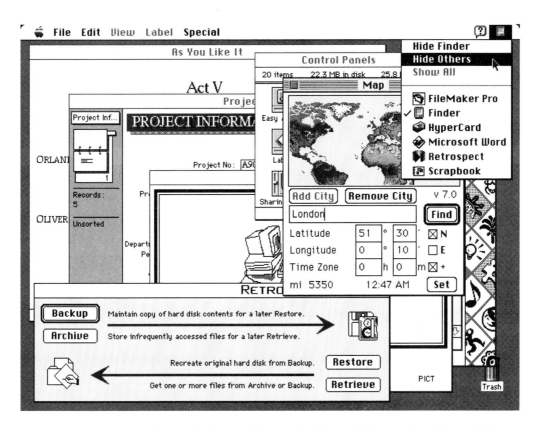

Figure 10-2: The Application menu's icon at the right end of the menu bar tells you which program is active. The menu itself lists all currently open programs below the gray dividing line. Choosing a program makes it the active program. The first command hides (but doesn't quit) the active program and switches to another open program. The Hide Others command hides the windows of all open programs except the active program.

or quitting programs, thereby reducing window clutter. Figure 10-2 shows the Application menu with several programs open.

Programs that know how can operate in the background by using System 7's multitasking capabilities. Background programs operate during the intervals — often only split seconds long — when the active program isn't using the computer. Background programs can't use the menu bar or interact directly with you in any other way. They can, however, recalculate spreadsheets, back up disks, print documents, sort databases, copy documents and folders, send and receive electronic mail, and more.

The Apple menu's new role

The Application menu takes over listing open programs from the Apple menu (which does that with MultiFinder active in older system software). Now the Apple menu has a new role. It expedites opening anything you use frequently. Any item you can open using the Finder you can put in the Apple menu and open it by choosing it there. This includes documents, application programs, desk accessories, folders, control panels, and even fonts and sounds.

You put an item in the Apple menu by dragging it into the Apple Menu Items folder, which is inside the System Folder. The item becomes instantly available in the Apple menu. (No need to restart your Macintosh.)

Desk accessories no longer have to be in the Apple menu. You now open them like regular application programs, for example by double-clicking their icons. You can still install desk accessories in the Apple menu by dragging them to the Apple Menu Items folder. You do not use the Font/DA Mover utility program.

Color windows and icons

Aside from the new system-wide menus (Apple, Help, and Application), the most pervasive change in System 7 is its use of color. Trendy three-dimensional shading modernizes all types of standard windows and dialog boxes — on monitors displaying at least 16 grays or 256 colors, that is. This doesn't do much to improve your productivity, but it sure makes you feel better when you see a NeXT computer.

You choose one shading tint for all windows from nine tints listed in a pop-up menu in the Color control panel. The window tint you choose will not apply to tool palettes and special-purpose windows created by some application programs until those programs have been upgraded for System 7.

> 66 *Aside from the new system-wide menus (Apple, Help, and Application), the most pervasive change in System 7 is its use of color.* 99

Additionally, standard Apple icons have three-dimensional shading on monitors displaying at least 16 colors or grays. Most other icons are black and white, though software developers will probably add color when they upgrade their products for System 7. You can customize any icon by pasting a picture from a painting or drawing program into the icon's Get Info window.

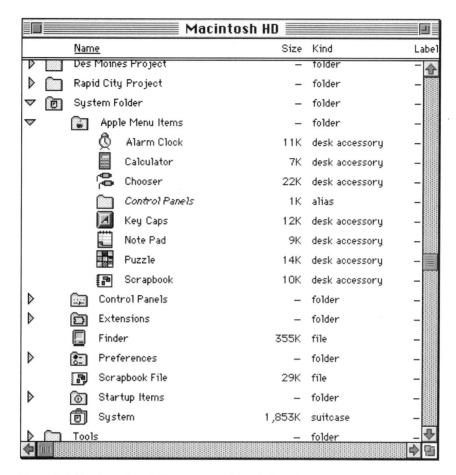

Macintosh HD			
<u>Name</u>	Size	Kind	Label
▷ ▨ Des Moines Project	—	folder	—
▷ ▢ Rapid City Project	—	folder	—
▽ ▣ System Folder	—	folder	—
▽ ▣ Apple Menu Items	—	folder	—
◔ Alarm Clock	11K	desk accessory	—
▤ Calculator	7K	desk accessory	—
⌨ Chooser	22K	desk accessory	—
▢ *Control Panels*	1K	alias	—
◹ Key Caps	12K	desk accessory	—
▤ Note Pad	9K	desk accessory	—
▦ Puzzle	14K	desk accessory	—
▣ Scrapbook	10K	desk accessory	—
▷ ▣ Control Panels	—	folder	—
▷ ▣ Extensions	—	folder	—
▢ Finder	355K	file	—
▷ ▣ Preferences	—	folder	—
▣ Scrapbook File	29K	file	—
▷ ▣ Startup Items	—	folder	—
▣ System	1,853K	suitcase	—
▷ ▢ Tools	—	folder	—

Figure 10-3: List views show folder structure with an indented outline. To expand a folder and list its contents, click the triangle next to the folder's icon. To collapse a folder and hide its contents, click the triangle again.

New views

As soon as you start using System 7 you notice the myriad improvements in the Finder. For instance, now you can see, select, and reorganize items from different folders in the same window. All list views (name, size, kind, and so forth) display folders and their contents in an indented outline format. The levels of indentation in the outline clearly diagram the structure of your nested folders. You expand or collapse any level in the outline to show or hide the corresponding folder's contents by clicking a triangle next to the folder's icon (see Figure 10-3).

The new Finder gives you control over the format and content of its windows. You select options using the Views control panel, and your settings immediately affect all windows. You set the font and size of item names and window headings for all views. You also set an alignment method for icon and small icon views. For list views (name, size, kind, and so forth), you select the icon size (tiny, small, or standard) and pick which of six columns of information you want to see: size, kind, label, date, version, and comments. In addition, you decide whether list views show folder sizes and whether the disk information that formerly appeared only in icon views appears at the top of list views.

Finding items

No more hunting through folders and disks for lost items — a chore even with the new outline views — nor waiting for the old, slow Find File desk accessory to turn them up. Finder 7's Find command finds and fetches lost items for you quickly. In its simplest form, the Find command looks through all disks whose icons are on the desktop for an item whose name contains the text you specify. It displays the first item it finds, opening the folder that contains the item to show the item in its native surroundings. You can find additional matching items with the Find Again command (File menu).

The Find command has an exotic form as well. It lets you specify the type of search: by name, size, kind, label, date created, date modified, version, comments, or lock status. You also specify exactly what you want matched (for example, you enter a date) and how you want it matched (for example, look for items modified before the date you specify). You can restrict the search to a single disk or to the active window. If you want, the Find command will select all the items it finds at once in an outline view.

Aliases

Although the new Find command is very fast, it doesn't take the place of well-organized disks. Finder 7's aliases aid your organizing efforts immensely. Aliases act like real items when you open them or drag items to them, but they are only small (1K to 3K) stand-ins. An alias looks exactly like the original item except its name is in italics and has the word *alias* as a suffix.

Aliases have a variety of uses, some of which are:

❖ Opening frequently used programs, documents, and folders from the desktop while the real items remain buried in nested folders.

❖ Adding items to the Apple menu without moving them from the folders they are in.

Figure 10-4: To select an item name for editing, you either click the icon and then press Return or Enter, or you click the name itself. A box around the name confirms that the name (not the icon) is selected.

❖ Organizing documents and folders according to multiple filing schemes without duplicating items.

❖ Simplifying access to file servers and individual items on servers.

❖ Getting nearly automatic access to your Mac's hard drive(s) using a floppy disk in any other Mac on the same network.

Editing icon names

Before you can edit the name of an alias, a folder, a document, or another item in Finder 7, you must carefully select the name. Clicking an icon no longer also selects the name for editing (see Figure 10-4). On the good side, you can no longer accidentally, and perhaps unknowingly, rename a selected document or folder by bumping the keyboard. On the bad side, you have to relearn how to change icon names.

Experienced Macintosh users will probably find the new method of editing icon names one of the toughest changes to get used to because old editing habits suddenly cause unexpected behavior.

System Folder renovation

Nothing mentioned so far helps you organize the king of clutter, your System Folder. Control panel documents here, start-up documents there, preference files everywhere — Finder 7 keeps such items in special new folders inside the System Folder. Other new folders provide new features. All the new folders have distinctive folder icons which you can see in Figure 10-5.

Moreover, Finder 7 puts many items in their proper places when you drag them to the System Folder icon. However, some items from old System Folders don't work right when they're put in the new Extensions, Control Panel, or Preferences folders. You have to put stubborn old preference files, control panels, and system extensions loose in the System Folder by dragging them to its window (not to its icon).

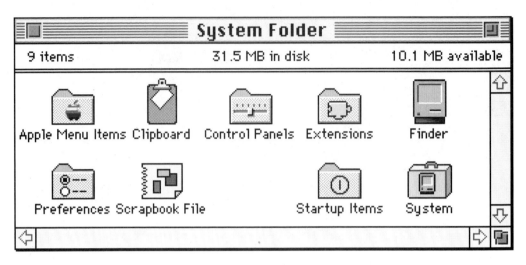

Figure 10-5: Special folders relieve System Folder overcrowding. The Control Panel folder, for example, contains individual control panels.

You also install fonts by dragging their icons to the System Folder. You don't use the Font/DA Mover utility program any more. Finder 7 puts fixed-size bitmap fonts and TrueType outline fonts in the System file for you. To remove or inspect fonts, you open the System file as if it were a folder. Each installed font has an icon in the System file window, and opening a font icon displays some sample text using that font. You remove a font by dragging its icon to a folder or the desktop. You install, inspect, and remove three other kinds of items like fonts. They include system alert sounds (for use with the Sound control panel), keyboard layouts, and language system scripts.

Divided Control Panel

The Control Panel desk accessory, like the System Folder, can become overcrowded and hard to use with older system software. In System 7, the sections of the Control Panel desk accessory are separate control panels, each of which you open like an ordinary application program (see Figure 10-6). They are kept in a special Control Panel folder within the System Folder. For convenience, an alias of the Control Panel folder appears in the Apple menu so you can open the folder easily.

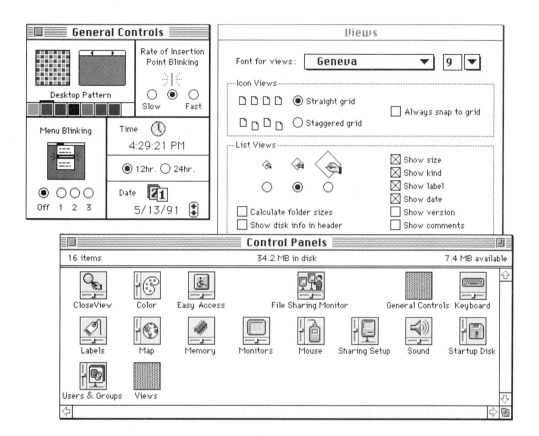

Figure 10-6: In System 7, control panels are kept in a special folder instead of a desk accessory. With the Control Panel folder open, you can rearrange the individual control panels in it by using the View menu or by dragging icons. You open one or more control panels as you would any ordinary documents and each open control panel appears in its own window.

More Finder improvements

A number of improvements to the Finder give you more control over its windows. You can scroll automatically by dragging an item or a group of selected items past the active area of the window. Dragging into a window corner scrolls diagonally. Clicking the zoom box makes the window just large enough to show all items in it. You can also select multiple items by dragging over them in any view, not just in icon and small-icon views. Items are highlighted one-by-one as you drag over them, not en masse when you stop dragging. In addition, you can change the order of items in a list view by clicking a column heading instead of using the View menu.

A pop-up menu in the title bar of the active Finder window reveals the path through your folder structure from the active window to the disk containing it. The menu pops up when you press Command while clicking the window title. You can open any folder along the path by choosing the folder from the pop-up menu.

You can select an item in a Finder window or on the desktop without using the mouse. Typing an item's name or the first part of it selects the item. Other keystrokes select an item near the currently selected item, open the item, and more. The details are spelled out by the Finder Shortcuts command in Finder 7's Help menu.

When you drag an item from one Finder window to a folder in an overlapping window, Finder 7 keeps the destination folder in view. Older Finders bring the source window in front of an overlapping target window as soon as you begin dragging, possibly covering the destination folder. This feature only works when you drag a single item. Selecting multiple items in an inactive window brings that window to the front.

Windows have become smarter and the Trash has become dumber (and safer). Now the Trash is emptied only on your command. Unlike older Finders, Finder 7 does not fuss if you delete application programs and system files. It also lets you drag locked items to the Trash, but won't delete them until you unlock them.

Finder 7 lets you classify folders, programs, and documents by labeling them with a word or phrase. On systems able to display colors or gray shades, labeling an item also colorizes it. You label items using the Label menu, which replaces the Color menu that older Finders have on color systems. Then you can view Finder window contents arranged by label. You can also search for items by label with the Find command. You change the seven label names and colors with the new Labels control panel.

Directory dialog improvements

The directory dialog boxes you get when you use Open and Save As commands from any program work more than ever like a one-window Finder. As always, a single directory window lists the contents of one folder or disk at a time, alphabetically by name. The directory window now uses compressed-style text for names longer than 25 characters.

For the first time, directory dialog boxes provide a view of the desktop and let you open disks and other items on it. In fact, opening a disk at the desktop level is the new method of switching disks. Figure 10-7 illustrates the new method.

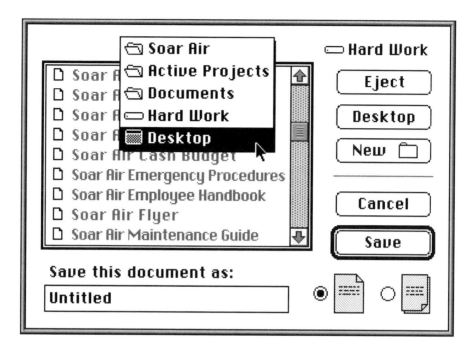

Figure 10-7: In Open, Save As, and other directory dialog boxes, you get to the desktop level by choosing Desktop from the pop-up menu or by clicking the Desktop button.

You can now open items and move through folders in any directory dialog box using the keyboard as well as the mouse. For example, typing *k* selects the first item that begins with the letter *K* or *k*. Older system software doesn't allow this keyboard navigation in Save or Save As dialog boxes, where you must use the keyboard to edit the name of the item you're saving. In System 7, a heavy black border around a Save or Save As dialog's directory window tells you that your typing will select an item in the window. The Save or Save As dialog boxes of some programs also include a new button that you can click to create a new folder. In addition, you can use the Edit menu to cut, copy, and paste while editing the name of an item you're saving.

TrueType

Almost all programs display and print smooth text at any size using System 7's TrueType fonts, which are variable-size outline fonts similar to the PostScript fonts that look so sharp on LaserWriters. (Programs that restrict your selection of text sizes can't take full advantage of TrueType fonts.) Old-style fonts still work.

Figure 10-8: Text looks lumpy when displayed or printed with fixed-size fonts unless you stick to installed sizes (top). Apple's TrueType font technology, a standard part of System 7, makes all sizes look good on any screen or printer (bottom). TrueType's spacing doesn't always match fixed-font spacing (compare the 11-point and 16-point samples here) because it's designed to better match the PostScript equivalents in a LaserWriter.

They look good at their fixed sizes and look lumpy when scaled to other sizes. Figure 10-8 illustrates the difference between TrueType and fixed-size fonts.

TrueType fonts save disk space if you use large sizes or if you have a printing device that uses screen fonts. ImageWriters, fax modems, ink-jet printers, and laser printers without PostScript no longer need the double, triple, or quadruple fixed sizes that take up lots of disk space.

LaserWriters and other PostScript devices use PostScript fonts instead of equivalent TrueType fonts. If a document contains a TrueType font that has no PostScript equivalent, System 7 smoothly scales the TrueType font to the resolution of the output device.

Extending memory

Less flashy than TrueType fonts but probably more important to your productivity are System 7's two means of letting you use more memory. Some Macintosh models can access more RAM (random-access memory) by using System 7's 32-bit addressing feature. To turn it on and off, you use the new Memory control panel. With 4MB RAM SIMMs installed, for example, turning on 32-bit addressing lets you use 10MB of RAM on an LC, 17MB on a IIsi, and 32MB on a IIci or IIfx. If 32-bit addressing is off, you can only use 8MB of RAM regardless of the amount installed.

Your old programs may not all be compatible with 32-bit addressing. Apple has been exhorting developers to make their products "32-bit clean" since 1987, but not all have. Mac II, IIx, IIcx, and SE/30 models cannot use 32-bit addressing because their ROMs (permanent read-only memory) are incompatible with it. Mac Classic, SE, Plus, and Portable models can't use 32-bit addressing because their 68000 central processing units don't support it.

You may be able to increase the amount of memory available on your Macintosh without installing more RAM. System 7 can transparently use part of a hard disk as additional memory. This extra memory, called virtual memory, lets you open more programs at once and increase the amount of memory each program gets when you open it. Virtual memory lets you get by with less RAM. You buy only as much as you need for average use, not for peak use.

To use virtual memory, you need a block of hard drive space as large as the total amount of memory you want available (RAM plus virtual memory). You use the Memory control panel to set up virtual memory.

Virtual memory only works on a Macintosh equipped with a paged memory management unit (PMMU). The SE/30, IIcx, IIx, IIsi, IIci, and IIfx models all have PMMUs, and a Mac II can be retrofitted with one. An LC can be upgraded with an accelerator board containing a PMMU. However, a Mac Plus, SE, Classic, or Portable with such an accelerator can't use virtual memory because its ROM lacks some necessary information.

File sharing

If your Macintosh is connected to others in a network, System 7 lets you share hard drives, folders, and the files in them with other network users. You can access folders and disks others have made available to you. You can also make your folders and disks available to others on the network (including those using System 6 with AppleShare client software). Before you can share your disks or folders, you must configure your Macintosh as an AppleShare file server with the new Sharing Setup control panel. To share one of your disks or folders with others, you select it and use the Finder's new Sharing command to display the item's sharing information window. There you specify who can see the item's folders, see its files, and make changes to it. You can grant these access privileges differently to the owner of the item (usually you), to one other registered user or group of registered users you designate, and to everyone else. You identify registered users, set their passwords, and create groups of users with the new Users & Groups control panel. Another new control panel, File Sharing Monitor, lets you see who is sharing what and how busy they're keeping your Macintosh. You can also use that control panel to disconnect individual users who are sharing your folders and disks.

To share another Mac's folder or disk, you use the Chooser desk accessory. It lists as AppleShare file servers the names of all computers that are sharing their folders and disks. After you choose one, the Chooser asks you to connect as a guest or a registered user and then presents a list of items you may share. Accessing someone else's folders or disks is considerably slower than accessing your own. Also, your computer's performance de-grades markedly while others share your folders or disks. For best performance, especially in networks with more than ten active users, everyone can put folders to be shared on the hard drive of a Macintosh dedicated to sharing its files (a dedicated file server).

> 66 *Your Macintosh should have at least 2.5MB of RAM if you want to open more than a single midsize program (and maybe a desk accessory or two as well) while sharing your folders or disks.* 99

Your Macintosh should have at least 2.5MB of RAM if you want to open more than a single midsize program (and maybe a desk accessory or two as well) while sharing your folders or disks. Sharing items with others increases your system's memory usage by at least 250K. That leaves only about 600K for opening programs on a 2MB Mac.

Live copy/paste

Some programs use System 7 to let you share information dynamically among documents. Because the sharing is dynamic, changing the original information automatically updates copies of it wherever they are. Think of it as live copy-and-paste. The automatic updating extends to computers interconnected on a network, so a document on your computer can dynamically share information from a document on another networked Macintosh. By contrast, copying and pasting shares information statically and on one Macintosh only.

You make a live copy of material you have selected by publishing an edition of it. You include copies of the material in a document by subscribing to the edition. Figure 10-9 diagrams the procedure. Information can only be shared dynamically among documents created by programs that include Edit menu commands for publishing and subscribing. You won't find these commands in the programs made before May 1991, because developers must upgrade those older programs to include publishing and subscribing commands.

Accessing data

The programs made before May 1991 must also be upgraded to take advantage of System 7's Data Access Manager (DAM). It provides a common, simple method for getting data from a variety of large databases resident on host computers of all brands and sizes. You can usually recognize a program that supports the DAM by the Open Query command in its File menu.

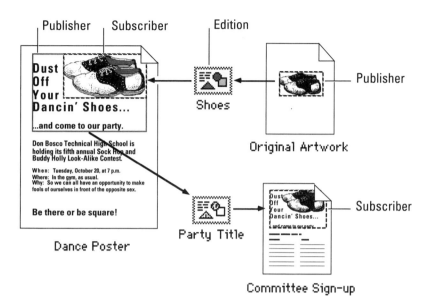

Figure 10-9: Publishing material from a document creates a live copy of the material in an edition file on disk. Any number of other documents (on your Mac or other networked Macs) include live copies of the material by subscribing to the edition. When you change the original material and save the document it's in, the edition is automatically updated. Every subscribing document learns of the update right away, or if it's closed, the next time it is opened.

To get data, you use the Open Query command to open a query document that describes the type of data you want. A dialog box describes what you will get if you enter the information it requests and click a button to start the query. For example, it may ask you to enter your name and password and select a type of report. Then behind the scenes the query document and the DAM connect to the host computer, request the information using the arcane commands of the host database, obtain the information, and paste it into your document.

Program linking

System 7 paves the way for programs to work together. While you work in one program, you will be able to use the commands and tools of other programs made by different software vendors. For example, a word processing program could get spell-checking services from a second program, thesaurus services from a third program, outlining services from a fourth, indexing services from a fifth, and so on. You could combine program modules à la carte instead of settling for a packaged TV dinner. You might pick an elaborate outlining module, a thesaurus, and no drawing module, whereas the next person might want an elaborate drawing module, no thesaurus, and basic outlining. Not only would you get a word processor you really like, you could also use the same spelling checker (and the same spelling dictionary) with other programs.

Program linking relies on System 7's framework for information interchange, called AppleEvents. It lets any program send messages to other programs. System 7 stores AppleEvents messages sent to a closed program and forwards the messages when the program is next opened. It also dispatches messages across a network to programs on another Macintosh.

Getting used to System 7

So many new features and capabilities may sound intimidating. Remember, though, that you can learn how to use most of them at your own pace. Take your time exploring the many Finder improvements. Wait on file sharing, virtual

System 7 compatibility

Almost all application programs, desk accessories, control panels, system extensions (startup documents), and other software works with the various versions of System 6, and a great deal of it works with System 7. Some older programs have minor cosmetic flaws that won't affect their operation. Some lose minor capabilities but are still able to function. A number of older programs don't work with 32-bit addressing turned on or with virtual memory active. Several important System 7 capabilities — balloon help, publish and subscribe, program linking, and data access — don't work in a program until its developer updates it to take advantage of them. Lesser improvements such as separate large and small icon designs, color icons, and the New Folder button in the Save As dialog box may also require software revision. Although System 7 itself is quite rugged,

you should expect more system crashes using it than System 6.0.5 or 6.0.7 until you upgrade your other software to versions made for System 7.

So that you don't have to crash-test all your software, Apple includes with System 7 a utility program called Compatibility Checker. It checks your application programs, desk accessories, system extensions, and control panels against information that Apple compiled from software developers. Compatibility Checker reports each item on your disks known not to work with System 7 along with a phone number to call for an upgrade. The utility also lists older version items that work as well as newer version items. The older and more obscure the software, the more likely it is to have serious problems until it has been upgraded for System 7. **M**

memory, and 32-bit addressing until you need them. Turn on balloon help only when you find it beneficial. Figure out publishing and subscribing (live copy/paste) and data access when you get programs that include them.

System 7 brings only a few changes you must face from the moment you begin using it. You can't dodge multitasking; you must get used to having multiple programs open at once. Also, you have to relearn a few basic skills like editing icon names and using the standard directory dialog boxes for opening and saving items. You upgrade to System 7 not for the changes it forces on you immediately, but for the possibilities it offers.

Summary

- The Finder, which is always available with System 7, lets you access and organize files on your disks.
- System 7's multitasking allows several programs to be open concurrently (memory permitting) and allows tasks to continue unattended in the background while you work in the foreground.
- Virtual memory lets you use disk space as if it were RAM for opening programs and documents (though not on a Mac Plus, SE, Classic, standard LC, or Portable). File sharing lets you share folders, disks, and files with others on the same network.
- Variable-size TrueType fonts let you see sharp text at any size on any screen, printer, or other output device.
- Color windows and icons jazz up a Mac with a color or gray-scale monitor.

Where to buy

System 7 ($99, single; $349 group)
Apple Computer, Inc.
20525 Mariani Ave.
Cupertino, CA 95014
408-996-1010
800-776-2333
(Customer service)

Chapter 11
Utilities for the Macintosh

by David Pogue

In this chapter...

- Defining utilities and understanding how they affect your computing environment.
- Learning which ones you really need, and what you'll have to pay.
- Mini-reviews of dozens of competitors.
- Unequivocal recommendation of utilities in each category.

O ther than the company whose monthly bills go up when you use your Mac, what's a *utility*?

In the Macintosh world, a utility is a program that makes your work easier or more efficient. For the purposes of this chapter, let's refine the definition even further: utilities affect your actual *computing environment* but don't help you process the work itself. A utility usually doesn't need a Print command, because you don't use it to generate actual output, as you would with a spreadsheet or word processor; instead, a utility affects what you see on the screen, how your hard disk handles data, and other aspects of the computer itself.

There are hundreds of utilities for the Mac. Many are sold by established software companies; many more are *shareware,* written by individuals and distributed informally — either made available to the public through the online networks like CompuServe and America Online, or distributed through Mac user groups. As a general rule, you pay more for commercial software and you get better service — technical help, for example, and upgrades.

So what kinds of utilities are there? *Hard disk utilities* protect and manage your hard drive, including letting you rescue data you might have assumed was erased or corrupted. *Defragmenters/optimizers* comb the disk surface for files that, for want of space, have had to be stored in pieces, and reassemble them, making your disk faster. Technically, backup programs are utilities, too, but you'll find them described in Chapter 13. *Virus protection software* watches out for, and helps cure infections by, computer viruses — malignant, self-cloning programs that spread from disk to disk. *Macro software* lets you automate repetitive tasks on the Mac — typing your return address, fetching a logo from the Scrapbook, or downloading your e-mail and printing it unattended, for example.

Screen savers automatically darken the Mac screen after a few idle minutes, to prevent whatever's on the screen from permanently burning into the phosphor of your monitor. *File management* utilities help you find (or delete, copy, or rename) files or launch programs, without returning to the Finder. *Compression* programs encode (shrink) files, making them easier to store on disk or transmit by modem. *Font and desk accessory* utilities let you install typefaces and DAs without having to use Apple's somewhat unfriendly Font/DA Mover program.

And in the miscellaneous category, there are *screen-capture programs, colorizer/customizers, MultiFinder enhancements, partitioning software,*

About the author

David Pogue is a *Macworld* contributing editor, a theater composer, and author of the play *HARD DRIVE,* the first Macintosh thriller. He lives in New York City where he is also a magician, computer instructor, and Broadway conductor.

and dozens more; in fact, once you've installed even a few of these utilities, you'll probably need an *INIT manager* just to help you switch them all on and off.

The point is that there are hundreds of programs available that aren't even work processors — they're *Mac* processors. Most are heavily advertised, and they all clamor for your software dollars. Not only would it be prohibitively expensive to buy all of them, but utilities often conflict with each other . . . so it's best to be selective. In this chapter, you'll get a glimpse of most of these products, find out whether or not you really need them, and get some advice on picking the best from each category.

Hard disk recovery software

What they do: Help recover data from a crashed disk; restore trashed files.

Who needs them: Anyone with a hard drive who uses the Mac more than once a month.

Least you'll pay: $80.

Examples: SUM II, Norton Utilities, 911 Utilities, Mac Tools Deluxe.

There is no lousier experience than having something go wrong with your hard disk, and losing a lifetime of data. You turn on your Mac as usual, but only the blinking question-mark disk icon appears. You sit there, panicked, denial welling, as one revelation after another dawns on you: You didn't back up. It's Friday at 7 p.m., and no dealer will be open till Monday. You could call your consultant, but the phone number is on the dead disk.

Nowadays, you're often not entirely sunk. Hard drive failures fall into several categories; only if the disk's platters won't even spin do you have to take the thing to a dealer and even then your data's not necessarily gone. If the problem is anything else — a corrupted directory, accidental erasure, bad sectors — then hard disk utility programs give you a fighting chance of recovering your files. The four major hard disk protection kits are 911 Utilities, Symantec Utilities for the Macintosh, Mac Tools Deluxe, and Norton Utilities; any of them can usually rescue at least some of the data on the disk.

SUM, Mac Tools Deluxe, and Norton Utilities work in much the same way. The first portion of each manual has the hysterical reader in mind, featuring huge type, shaded pages, and arrow-driven flow charts. The program and manual carefully walk you through a series of evaluative questions: Are we fixing a hard disk or floppy? Did the disk crash, or did you erase it by mistake? If I can recover some files, what disk should I copy them to? (It helps to have a second hard disk, or a pile of floppies, for this purpose.)

Good news, bad news

Once you answer the questions, you're offered three methods for recovering data from the ailing disk. All four packages include a preventive INIT program that, if you were smart, you installed when you got the program — that is, before the crash. If this INIT watchdog was installed at the time of the crash, recovering files is a cinch; assuming this directory-tracking file is itself intact, you have a very good chance of getting most of your data back by clicking a single button.

If you didn't install the INIT — for example, if you bought the program *because* your hard disk crashed — then you can try recovering files by their *file headers* (using SUM, Mac Tools, or Norton Utilities). In this method, the program scours the disk looking for specific programs' "footprints." Unfortunately, each program only recognizes a couple dozen file types — Word and Excel, of course, plus a bunch of miscellaneous others — and only Mac Tools Deluxe provides a way to teach it new ones.

Since the file-header method only recognizes a few file types, you usually wind up using Method Number Three: a complete scan of the hard disk surface in search of anything that looks like a file. After a long time (SUM) or a few minutes (Norton or Mac Tools), you see a list of hundreds of files.

But now another emotional rollercoaster ride begins, because not every listed file is marked "recoverable." Sometimes unimportant files are recoverable, but your vital ones aren't. Worse, sometimes you recover a "recoverable" file — but when you open it, you get a screenful of gibberish or a system crash.

Norton Utilities is the best of these programs. It's faster than SUM and shows much more information about each recovered file than SUM or Mac Tools: name, size, date modified, type, creator, and — most important — Recoverability. This last piece of information (such as Poor, Very Good, Excellent, and so on) is priceless, because it means you don't waste time trying to recover files that are actually long gone. Even better, you can actually view any text contained within any file Norton Utilities thinks it can recover. Viewing the text in a file gives you something to go on when you have to decide whether or not to spend the time and disk space to recover it. Mac Tools Deluxe also lets you view text in the recovered files, and its manual is excellent.

Dial 911

The core program of 911 Utilities, 1st Aid (not to be confused with Apple's Disk First Aid), is considered ancillary to its manual, the impressive *Troubleshooting Guide*. This book explains hundreds of typical Mac error messages and glitches, and tells you what to do in every single case. In its pages, you can find out why "Some files were skipped" when copying them; what to do when you're told "This is not a Macintosh disk"; and even why "The Trash couldn't be emptied." The 1st Aid program itself is much more of a hard-core data-recovery toolkit, without the flashy graphics and self-guiding screen-by-screen procedures of Mac Tools or Norton Utilities. But it's mind-bogglingly good at rescuing data from disks that the Mac insists it can't read. Other pluses: 911 Utilities includes the excellent Virex virus-protection software, as well as its own file-recovery INIT, called Complete Undelete. This cdev, also sold separately, is especially handy because it lets you recover deleted files instantly from within the Control Panel.

For a total hard disk security blanket, get Norton Utilities or Mac Tools, depending on which of the included extra utilities appeal to you (see the end of the chapter for lists).

Defragmenters/optimizers

What they do:	Place file data into contiguous sectors on the hard disk surface, resulting in faster overall operation.
Who needs them:	Nobody, really — you can defragment manually. But these do a better job, and they're automatic.
Least you'll pay:	$60, or nothing if you get a utility package.
Examples:	DiskExpress II, Speed Disk (Norton Utilities), SUM Tune-Up, SilverLining.

After you've used your hard drive a lot — creating files, erasing files — the data on it begins to get *fragmented*. As the Norton Utilities manual puts it:

> *Files are written to physically contiguous [segments of your hard disk].... Suppose you have a 5K file on your hard disk, immediately followed by a 15K file. If you modify the first file so that it grows from 5K to 12K, the extra part of that file must be placed after the 15K file. In other words, the file becomes fragmented, and reading it from disk takes longer.*

> *As your hard disk's files become fragmented, the entire operation of your Mac slows down. That's because the hard disk head has to move faster and farther around the disk surface to read a particular file — which isn't good for hard disk longevity, either.*

So how do you defragment a disk? Actually, you can do it without any utility software at all: just copy the entire disk's contents to another disk (or even to floppy disks) — in other words, back up. Then erase the original hard disk and copy the files back onto it. The result: every file will once again be whole and unfragmented.

That method strikes some as being a little low-tech, however. With a defragmenter program, you can sit back and relax while the computer does the work for you, carefully copying bits and pieces of files all over the disk surface, laying them end-to-end so that, by the time it's finished, there are no fragmented files left. The other advantage of defragmenters is that some of them can *optimize* the placement of the files. Instead of just putting your files back together again, it also tries to position them on the hard disk so that they'll be less likely to refragment. For example, the program might decide to put applications at the end of the disk, since they can be counted upon not to change size from day to day.

Disk defragmenters and defragmenter/optimizers are included in many hard disk utility packages — the same ones that contain file-recovery utilities, for example. SUM II, Norton Utilities, the SilverLining hard disk formatting software, and Mac Tools Deluxe all include disk-optimizing software. Of these, the best is Speed Disk, included with Norton Utilities. It's not only very fast, but its graphic display of the files on your hard drive is astonishing: documents, programs, System files, and other items are all color-coded (see Figure 11-1). As the optimization proceeds, you can actually see the data shift position, gradually consolidating until they're neatly organized (and all the free space on the disk is in one contiguous chunk, in case you plan to use System 7's virtual memory feature). And Speed Disk has one incredible, mind-expanding feature: a cursor that, when dragged over the graphic "map" of your hard drive, identifies by name every file whose graphic sector it touches. In other words, you get to see *where* your files are really kept on the physical disk surface, and precisely *how* they've had to be fragmented.

Take the express

There's one other important possibility for people who want their hard drives to be especially neat: DiskExpress II. This unique program is a cdev — a program that you put in your System Folder and forget. It runs all the time, in the background, continually and gradually defragmenting and optimizing your hard drive. It not only tries to put things on the disk surface where they'll be least likely to refragment, but it even studies your files, your work habits, and your disk usage over a period of five days; then it *really* knows where to put things. (The recent 2.04 version has cured the instability problems you may have read about in earlier versions.)

What could possibly be the disadvantage of DiskExpress II's automatic, in-the-background approach? Not much, really; some people are alarmed by the fact that it makes their disk-access lights blink and their hard drives whir even when nothing else is happening on the Mac. (That's just the point, really — DiskExpress waits for 30 seconds of inactivity before continuing its job.) Of course, it's a stand-alone program with its own modest cost, and it's probably a little overkill

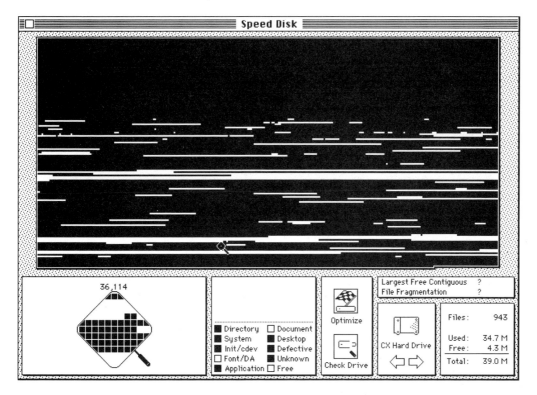

Figure 11-1: Part of the Norton Utilities, Speed Disk is an excellent disk defragmenter. Before you begin, you can see a map of your disk surface; here, white parts are empty. In color, the effect is amazing, since each color corresponds to a different type of file: application, System file, and so on.

when measured in terms of actual necessity — most people only need to defragment their drives once a month at most. But DiskExpress is the perfectionist's only choice.

The rub

Here we arrive at the Catch-22 of Mac utilities. Remember those deleted-file protection INITs that come with the hard disk recovery programs? They work by remembering where everything was on your disk. Unfortunately, a disk defragmenter's purpose is to move files around, swapping pieces, shifting things — a process at utterly cross-purposes with a file-undeletion program. In other words, it's pointless to use DiskExpress II and a file-undeletion INIT — the former will render the latter useless.

If you plan to use any of the hard disk recovery programs (and their file-protection INITs), then don't get DiskExpress. Get Speed Disk, and only use it to defragment your drive once a month; only just afterward will your trashed-file protection be trashed.

Get Norton Utilities, which contains the terrific Speed Disk optimizer. If (1) you're pretty fastidious about your hard drive — you want it optimized at every moment — and (2) you don't plan to use Complete Undelete or another file-recovery INIT . . . then get DiskExpress II.

Virus protectors

What they do: Prevent, diagnose, and eradicate computer-virus infections.

Who needs them: Anyone who regularly exchanges disks with others, uses the modem to transfer files, or shares a network with somebody who does.

Least you'll pay: Nothing.

Examples: Virex, SAM, Disinfectant, VirusDetective, Rival.

Viruses sound awfully scary. They're malignant little mini-programs, designed, written, debugged, and released by vindictive programmers. A virus is designed to reproduce as fast as it can, infecting one file after another. Sometimes it just clones itself and then sits still forever. Sometimes a virus is programmed to do other deeds, like displaying a sarcastic message on your screen, playing a sound, or even deleting files behind your back.

In fact, however, few people have lost data to viruses on the Mac. There have been about ten Mac viruses; according to a *Macworld* poll, only about 8 percent of Mac users have ever had an infection. Almost all of these have been harmless, just gumming up the works without destroying data. Therefore, viruses really aren't nearly as real a threat as they may seem.

For those who worry, virus protection software is state-of-the-art on the Mac. There are numerous commercial packages, such as Virex and Symantec Anti-Virus for Macintosh (SAM), which have three functions. First, they can tell if your disk is infected by any known virus and, if you type in the correct numbers (available by phone hotline), they can detect any *new* viruses that appear. Second, they can cure your disk of most of these viruses, putting you back in business with no side effects. And third, Virex and SAM can be told to scan every floppy disk you insert, so you're essentially inoculated against getting viruses through the floppy drive.

In general, the two packages differ only in tone. SAM's approach is slightly paranoid, almost fierce. Its SAM Intercept feature continually monitors your Mac system against viral infections as you work; unfortunately, it interprets any attempt to make any changes to any program on your disk as an attempted virus attack. The result: dozens of false alarms during the first few weeks of using SAM. With each cry of 'wolf,' you teach SAM: "No, that was the Font/DA Mover. Don't worry about that next time." Eventually, SAM's ratio of false-to-true alarms improves. In general, however, Virex strikes a better balance between paranoia and practicality. It's very thorough, simpler to use, and has almost all of the same features.

Sharewareland

Most of the Mac anti-virus utilities aren't commercial products at all. Instead, they're written as shareware by individual authors and distributed freely via user groups and online services (like America Online or CompuServe). VirusDetective is a desk accessory that's extremely good at telling you whether or not you have a virus. It was the first anti-virus utility to be programmable — that is, the first to let you enter codes for any new viruses that should appear. With its INIT, Virus Blockade II, it's every bit as good at alerting you as the commercial packages. Virus Detective is not designed, however, to cure virus infections.

For that purpose, you should probably get the superlative Disinfectant. It's free. It has a virus-watchdog INIT and a seek-and-destroy application, just like Virex or SAM. Disinfectant doesn't have the "type-in-a-new-virus" feature — the whole package is re-released each time a new virus is discovered — but otherwise it's a terrific piece of protection.

Get Disinfectant. It's free, elegant, and works very well. If the ability to protect yourself instantly against new viruses without having to update your program appeals to you, get Virex. Get SAM if you want SAM's trial-by-error learning feature.

Macro software programs

What they do:	Automate repetitive or tedious tasks.
Who needs them:	Power users, data crunchers, or even slight control freaks.
Least you'll pay:	Nothing (MacroMaker).
Examples:	QuicKeys 2, Tempo II Plus, MacroMaker, AutoMac III.

Every time you type your return address, back up your hard drive, or open a desk accessory, you're doing work the computer could be doing for you. After all, it's a computer — handling repetitive tasks should be its favorite work!

Using a macro program, you can train the Mac to perform these tasks automatically at your cue with the press of a particular key. You might make Command-T empty the Trash, define Control-M to launch MacWrite, or enable the Esc key to click the Cancel button whenever it appears. Once you've gone to the trouble of training the Mac, you'll be overjoyed by the efficiency you'll gain.

MacroMaker came on your Mac System disks (up until System 7). It's the easiest to use of all the programs, by far: all the macros you record appear in a menu, so you never forget what trigger keystroke you've given each one (if any). You create a macro by performing the task once while MacroMaker watches. The only drawback to this free macro utility is that it can only perform three kinds of tasks: menu selections, typing, and mouse clicks (and combinations of these).

QuicKeys 2 is a more ambitious and more capable program. It lets you do every task MacroMaker can do, plus dozens more. With one keystroke, you can switch your monitor to color, change printers without opening the Chooser, paste some boilerplate text, automatically log onto and dial a BBS, launch any document or program, shut the Mac down safely from within any program, and so on. It's by far the most popular macro program, and it generally works beautifully.

In tempo

Tempo II Plus does almost everything QuicKeys 2 does, with one dramatic difference: it has *conditional branching* capabilities. That means you can teach it to choose between two courses of action, depending on the circumstances: make some text boldface if it's preceded by an asterisk — otherwise, italicize it. If it's past midnight, automatically sign onto CompuServe — otherwise, wait another half hour, and so on. You can make Tempo II do absolutely incredible things: Reformat databases containing thousands of records. Download, format, save and print your e-mail in the middle of the night. Take a set of data through an exhaustive conversion process involving several programs and lots of copying and pasting.

The price you pay for this brilliance is a somewhat technical interface. Tempo II is not nearly as beautiful as QuicKeys. And when you're editing a multi-step macro, QuicKeys shows you a list of all the steps in the macro — in Tempo, each component of the macro appears on its own screen, so you can't see the overall effect.

Try MacroMaker. If you crave more flexibility, get QuicKeys 2. If you really need heavy-duty macros with either/or decision-making features, get Tempo II, but be prepared to do a little bit of programming. And note that at this writing, QuicKeys 2.1 is the only one that works with System 7.

Screen savers

What they do:	Dim your screen after a few minutes of idleness.
Who needs them:	Honestly? Nobody. But they're fun.
Least you'll pay:	$10.
Examples:	After Dark, Pyro, Protector Shark, Moire, FlowFazer.

If you've ever seen the ghost of an automated teller machine's welcoming screen permanently etched in the display, you'll understand the reason for *screen savers*. These programs ensure that your Mac monitor won't suffer the same burn-in syndrome if left on for a long time, because they automatically blank the screen after a few minutes of disuse. To signal you that the computer is still on, however, a screen saver must bounce some moving image around the screen. That's where the fun comes in.

The programmers of these utilities figure: if you've got to display some "I'm still on!" signal on the monitor, might as well make it entertaining. That's why the shareware Moire bounces around a mind-bending, swirling pattern of lines. FlowFazer displays wild, psychedelic lava-lampish images. Protector Shark, the first screen saver/game, shows a shark and a diver swimming back and forth; you control the diver with the mouse, shooting spears at the shark. After Dark and Pyro let you choose from dozens of different displays: fireworks, random patterns, swirling lines, and in After Dark, you can have the now-famous Flying Toasters or colorful, bubbling underwater Fish (see Figure 11-2). Both of these commercial programs also have sound effects to match: thunder with the lightning display, the soft flap of wings for Flying Toasters, and so on.

Do you really need one of these? Nah. You'd have to leave your Mac sitting idle for days to get screen burn-in. On the one-piece Macs, you can just turn down the screen brightness.

But screen savers are really, really neat. Protector Shark gives you something to do while you're on the phone with someone boring (hunt sharks), and After Dark helps you justify the purchase of a color monitor.

And while we're on the topic of screen display: If you have an Apple 13-inch color monitor with a standard Mac II video card, you just have to get an amazing shareware utility called MaxAppleZoom. It eliminates that ¾-inch black band of darkness around the perimeter of your monitor, filling every single pixel behind the glass with usable image, right up to the plastic collar. Suddenly you've got 17 percent more screen area — as though you traded in your 13-inch monitor for a 14-incher. The author points out that at Apple's price for screen real estate, you've just gained $375 worth of extra space!

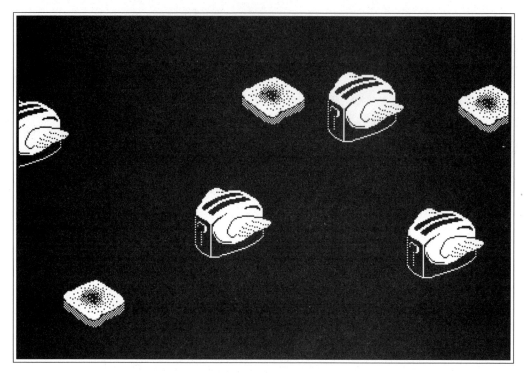

Figure 11-2: After Dark 2.0 has the one and only Flying Toasters module. Unfortunately, from this close-up you can neither see the glistening brown and silver colors nor hear the soft fluttering of the toasters' wings. Suffice it to say that the effect is lulling, absurdist, and profound — and it appears whenever your Mac is idle for a few minutes.

Get After Dark 2.0. If you're interested in saving money, get the shareware Moire. And if you're interested in interactivity, Protector Shark is the one.

File management utilities

What they do: Let you launch programs and manipulate files even when you're not in the Finder.

Who needs them: Almost everyone except System 7 users.

Least you'll pay: $35.

Examples: DiskTop, MasterFinder, OnCue, Hand-Off II, MultiMaster.

Especially when compared to the IBM-PC equivalent, the Finder is an amazing piece of software. It lets you easily and simply rename files, copy them, trash them, and move them among folders. By double-clicking a file, you open it; couldn't be simpler.

Trouble is, to get any work done, you've got to leave the Finder. And once you're in Word (or whatever), you can no longer perform those file management tasks. That's why file management utilities are so useful: they let you do your housekeeping without having to return to the Finder.

There are four different kinds of file management utilities: Finder replacements, file finders, file launchers, and — for want of a better term — boomerangers.

DiskTop is a Finder replacement utility. It's a desk accessory whose main window shows every folder and file on your hard drive. Click any file and use the Copy, Rename, or Delete buttons (see Figure 11-3). And DiskTop has a feature the real Finder doesn't have: a Move command that puts a file in another folder, or on another disk, without leaving a copy behind.

Find it fast

As hard disks cost less and less for more and more capacity, the tendency to forget where you put a file increases. For this reason, Apple gives you a desk accessory called Find File that lets you search for any file by its name (in System 7, this command is in the File menu). But plenty of programmers have tried to improve on Find File — by making equivalents that are faster or more powerful. DiskTop, for example, has a flexible — but, by today's standards, slow — Find command that lets you locate a misfiled file by searching for any characteristic: its name, creation date, file type, and so on. You could ask DiskTop, for example, to find any Excel document created last week that's between 2K and 5K in size.

> **❝ As hard disks cost less and less for more and more capacity, the tendency to forget where you put a file increases. ❞**

Norton Utilities includes the Fast Find desk accessory. It can only search by name, but it's much faster than either DiskTop or Apple's Find File. And once you've located a file, you can not only view the text within it — by double-clicking its name — you can even launch it. Mac Tools Deluxe has a similar DA called Locate; like the separately sold Gofer it's slower, but adds the nifty ability to search for text *within* any file, in the not uncommon event that you can't even remember what you called some file.

| ≡□□ | DiskTop | □≡ |

Name	Type	Creator	Data	Resource	Modified
Copy	Move				
Delete	Rename	HFS 34910K Used 89% 4455K Free 11% 18 items		○ CH Hard Drive ▢ Drive(s)	
Find	Sizes	○ CH Hard Drive		Eject	Unmount

○ **Name**	**Type**	**Creator**	**Data**	**Resource**	**Modified**
🗋 Desktop DF	DTFL	DMGR	348K		6/23/91
🗀 Desktop Folder	1 files/folders		---	---	6/23/91
🗀 Disk 2	2 files/folders		---	---	3/20/91
🗀 DWP stuff	26 files/folders		---	---	6/23/91
🗀 FONTS	11 files/folders		---	---	6/23/91
🗋 Leslie pages	WDBN	MSWD	2K		6/20/91
🗋 Picture 1	PICT	ttxt	77K		6/23/91
🗀 Program Disk	3 files/folders		---	---	6/10/91
🗀 System Folder	34 files/folders		---	---	6/23/91
🗀 Trash	30 files/folders		---	---	6/23/91
🗋 [DiskExpress Activity Lo...	DLog	DExp	40K		5/2/91

| CE Software | #21536 |

Figure 11-3: In DiskTop all the functions of the Finder are available under the Apple menu. Your files appear in an alphabetical list; just highlight one, then click Copy, Rename, Move, Delete, or whatever. DiskTop's Find command is very powerful, but not as quick as some of its more recent rivals.

If that ability interests you, consider ON Location. This remarkable DA is fastest of all — it searches for filenames *and* for text within files practically instantaneously. How could it be so many times faster than the other programs? ON Location takes five or ten minutes when you first install it to *index* every single file on your drive, storing this internal table of contents in your System Folder. ON Location's nonstandard interface is a little silly-looking and the indexing is a pain — but brother, it sure is nice to have instantaneous search results for any text in any file on your drive. (Version 1.0 is not completely compatible with System 7.)

Launch pads

File launchers add a new menu to your menu bar, containing a list of programs and documents you use often. It's a sensational idea: now the things you work on most frequently are immediately accessible, instead of being buried somewhere in a folder-within-a-folder.

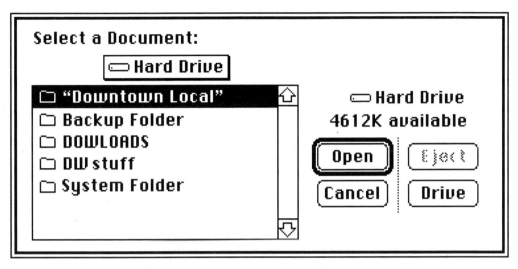

Figure 11-4: The normal, inconvenient file-selection box you get when you use a program's Open command.

Note, first of all, that the need for dedicated file launchers will probably disappear with System 7 which lets you add applications and documents directly into your Apple menu.

In the meantime: DiskTop comes with its own file launcher, as do the Now Utilities. Of the stand-alones, Hand-Off is better than On Cue, because it also offers "application substitution" — if you double-click a MacWrite document but don't have MacWrite, Hand-Off will open it with, say, Word. Without Hand-Off, you'd get the dreaded "Application not found" message.

Boomerangers

The third category of file-manipulation utilities is the hardest to explain, but one of the most useful. When you use a program's Open command, you normally see something like Figure 11-4.

This file-selection box has several inconvenient aspects. First, you have to root around in your folders until you find the file you want. Second, there's no direct way to locate a file whose folder you don't remember. Third, the Mac always highlights the first file name in the list, which can be a pain if you have to open several files in a row at the bottom of the list of a folder's contents.

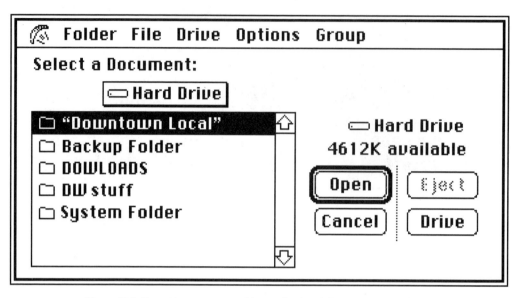

Figure 11-5: Super Boomerang provides navigational shortcuts to your file-selection boxes by adding a menu bar to an Open File box, for example.

Super Boomerang is a sensational solution to these problems you never knew you had. It's part of Now Utilities. It adds a menu bar to your Open File box, as shown in Figure 11-5.

Super Boomerang's File menu is a list of the last 30 files you've opened — a navigational shortcut that cuts down drastically on the time you spend foraging through folders. What's more, Super Boomerang doesn't automatically highlight the first file in the list, as the Mac does; instead, it highlights the file you opened most recently. This feature, too, helps you figure out where you are and what you're doing. The utility includes an unbelievably fast Find command, capable of searching an 80MB hard drive in three seconds. Since you're using the Find command from within the Open File box, opening the file (once you've found it) is a matter of simply pressing Enter. Finally, Super Boomerang gives every program's Open menu command a pop-up menu, listing the most recently-opened files, as shown in Figure 11-6. By opening a file from this submenu, you don't encounter the Open File dialog box at all.

File		
New	⌘N	
Open...	**⌘O**	Open...
Close		Consumer Reports
Save	⌘S	IRS 1040 ES letter
Save As...	⇧F7	Valentine
Delete...		**Flank steak recipe**
		Dialog agreement
Print Preview...	⌥F13	CY INVOICE
Page Setup...	⇧F8	Song List
Print...	⌘P	1/28 Song Order
Quit	⌘Q	

Figure 11-6: One of Super Boomerang's nicest features is that it remembers the last few files you opened within each program. Here, you can see the submenu it adds to Word's Open command; you can open your most frequently-used files without even having to encounter a dialog box.

Aladdin Systems's Shortcut also modifies the Open File box, adding a Find command and jumping to the most recently-opened file, and it can also open StuffIt archives (files compressed with Aladdin Systems's StuffIt compression program) from within the Open File dialog box. But its interface isn't as clear, and it doesn't offer the Open command submenu. (Both products, incidentally, add a noticeable lag time opening and closing files.) Directory Assistance (part of Norton Utilities) has some Boomerang-like features, too — you can duplicate, find, or delete files from within the Open File and Save As dialog boxes. Directory Assistance, as well as the shareware programs Rebound and ScrollInit, emulates Boomerang's highlight-the-last-file-opened feature.

Get DiskTop if you want a Finder replacement, file launcher, and file finder all in one. Get Now Utilities too, or instead, for its file launcher and the indispensable Boomerang.

Compression programs

What they do: Encode files to take up less disk space.

Who needs them: Modem users, anyone running out of disk space.

Least you'll pay: $25.

Examples: StuffIt Deluxe, Compact Pro, DiskDoubler, SuperDisk, PakWorks.

It could have been a piece of Confucian wisdom: no matter how big your hard drive, eventually it gets full.

When that happens, you can either transfer stuff onto floppies, get another hard drive, or get a compression utility. Such a program encodes any file into a format that's roughly half its original size, so you can store more on a particular hard drive. When you need the file, the same utility expands it to its normal state. The other dramatic advantage to smaller files is for telecommunications: modem users would just as soon download smaller files from the online services, which bill by the hour for the time it takes. That's why nearly every Macintosh file on any BBS or online service is in a compressed format.

> 66 *It could have been a piece of Confucian wisdom: no matter how big your hard drive, eventually it gets full.* 99

In the beginning, there was StuffIt. Almost 100 percent of downloadable files on these dial-up services have the familiar .sit suffix, indicating that they've been stuffed using the original shareware StuffIt. The program has recently been upgraded to a new file format, and re-released in two versions: a commercial one, StuffIt Deluxe, and another shareware one, StuffIt Classic. The new programs can read the old file format — but not vice versa! The new Deluxe/Classic compression format is somewhat faster than the old, results in smaller files, and makes viewing the contents of a compressed file easier.

StuffIt rivals

Compact Pro is a new shareware program that's faster, more efficient, and easier to use than any StuffIt version. Its only drawback: almost no online service files are compressed using its file format, making it suitable primarily for archiving your own files.

But if that's your aim, there's a still better bet: the amazing DiskDoubler. This incredible INIT compresses and expands files faster than those other programs and produces the smallest files of all. Better yet, you don't have to launch a program to compress a file, because DiskDoubler adds the Compress and Expand commands to your Finder menu bar — just select any icons and choose Compress. And you don't have to explicitly decompress one of these crunched files before using it: Disk-Doubler files automatically re-expand when double-clicked. DiskDoubler can even decompress old-format StuffIt files (the ones posted on the online services by the thousand).

SuperDisk is similar to DiskDoubler in many ways; it compresses files or folders right in the Finder when you append .s to a file's name. It compresses faster, but the resulting files aren't as small. Furthermore, it's not as safe to use as DiskDoubler, because Version 1.07's speed gains come at the expense of error checking. It's handy, but don't entrust any critical files to it until an improved version is released.

Finally, note that all of these programs can create self-extracting files — in other words, files that you can send to friends who don't own a compression program; by double-clicking the compressed file, they can make it expand. But SuperDisk only increases the compressed file's size by 5K to make it self-extracting; DiskDoubler adds 7K, Compact Pro adds 11K, and StuffIt adds 20K to the file's size.

Get DiskDoubler. It's the most convenient compression utility you can find, it's inexpensive, and it even reads StuffIt files. If you want to be able to create new-format StuffIt files, get the shareware StuffIt Classic.

Font and desk accessory utilities

What they do:	Install fonts and DAs without using the Font/DA Mover.
Who needs them:	Anybody without System 7.
Least you'll pay:	$50.
Examples:	SuitCase II, MasterJuggler.

These INITs let you install a font into your system, or a desk accessory into your Apple menu, without having to use Apple's Font/DA Mover program. They're incredibly convenient, they let you have more than 15 DAs, and they also install Fkeys and sounds.

Suitcase is easier to figure out (but that doesn't mean it's easy) and MasterJuggler has more features. In their current incarnations, both will be largely obsolete if you use System 7. (To install a font or DA in System 7, you just drag its icon to the System file or the Apple Menu Items folder, respectively.) Otherwise, these two programs are identical, and nearly indispensable. Both will, no doubt, be upgraded so that they don't duplicate System 7 features.

If you don't plan to install System 7, get either Suitcase II or MasterJuggler.

Miscellany

What they do:	Colorize your icons or scroll bars, capture the screen image, make MultiFinder easier to manage, make your font menus neater, enhance System 7 features, and so on.
Who needs them:	No one. But creative people and power users will get a kick out of them.
Least you'll pay:	Nothing.
Examples:	Personality, SunDesk, Icon Colorizer, ScreenShot, Capture, ImageGrabber.

Customizers: These programs include Personality, Kolor, SunDesk, Icon Colorizer, and SoundMaster. They let you add color to the windows, icons, and menus of your Mac environment, and let you change the sounds the Mac plays when different events occur: shutting down, ejecting a disk, and so on. The novelty wears off pretty quickly, actually, but hey — you gotta live a little, right? A turquoise File menu could be just the thing.

Screen capture utilities: You've always been able to take a MacPaint picture of any black-and-white Mac screen by pressing Command-Shift-3 — a trick that requires no utility software at all. But if you're a writer, manual author, or trainer, you might wish for something more flexible. You might want to capture only a menu or a window, for example, instead of the entire screen. You might need the snapshot to be in color.

A screen-capture utility like Capture or ScreenShot lets you specify what portion of the screen you want captured. You can also specify what format you want the resultant image saved in: MacPaint, PICT, the Clipboard, and so on. Of the INIT-type screen grabbers, ScreenShot is by far the best (see Figure 11-7). Its options are creative and useful: it can automatically give your screen shot a light-blue tint, as you often see in Mac magazines; it can automatically title the resultant files using the name of the program being illustrated ("HyperCard Shot 1," for example); and it has special features for capturing menus and dialog boxes with a single click. (Other programs make you manually erase unwanted portions of screen shots, even when all you wanted to illustrate was a menu.)

The alternative is ImageGrabber 3.0, a desk accessory. Its desk-accessory format has some advantages — it won't conflict with INITs, it works in a few rare situations when an INIT doesn't, and (using Suitcase or MasterJuggler) you can load it instantly without restarting the Mac. The only drawback: Image-Grabber isn't quite as smart as ScreenShot in capturing menus, and doesn't have as many options.

Figure 11-7: Fast, slick, and simple: Screen-Shot's interface makes capturing screens a joy. Press the key combo of your choice and this windoid appears; select a destination for the shot — Printer, Clipboard, PICT file, or Scrapbook — from the pop-up menu. Then click one of the four big square buttons to tell Screen-Shot what to capture: Window, Menu, the whole Screen, or just a Selection.

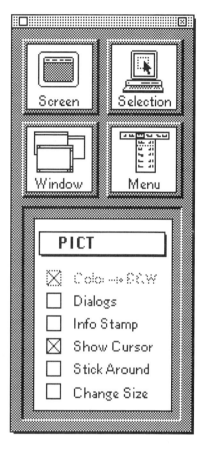

Font menu helpers: Another category of Mac utilities is devoted to cleaning up your Font menu. Adobe Type Reunion is for people who have purchased Adobe type families, which usually have odd names like "BI Helvetica BoldOblique." As a result of that naming convention, related font styles (such as Italic and Bold of the same font) are scattered all over the alphabetical Font menu. Type Reunion reunites all styles under the family name (like "Helvetica") in your Font menus; a hierarchical menu pops out, listing the various styles for that family. Unfortunately, you can't access a font *at all* unless you use this submenu. That is, if you choose the family name from the main menu ("Helvetica"), you might expect your text's font to change to plain Helvetica. It doesn't. You have to use the pop-up menu to select the Roman style.

Other font menu helpers include Suitcase (performing another useful function), WYSIWYG Menus (one of the Now Utilities), and MenuFonts, all three of which display every font name in its actual typeface.

And speaking of fonts: Adobe Type Manager (ATM) is a must for non-System 7 users with non-PostScript printers, especially ImageWriters. It lets you display and print smooth type at any point size — especially large sizes — even if it's not 10, 12, 14, 18 or 24 point. It only works for laser fonts and it's a memory hog. But it sure does make headlines look gorgeous. (Apple's TrueType, included as part of System 7, works much the same way — but only with fonts in its own special format, which are still rare at this writing.)

Get ScreenShot if you need a screen grabber. Get ATM if you do design or desktop publishing work, or if you have an ImageWriter. Get everything else if you're a utility junky.

INIT/cdev managers

What they do: Give you control over which INITs and cdevs load when you turn on the Mac.

Who needs them: Primarily power users, or anyone with more than a handful of INITs.

Least you'll pay: Nothing.

Examples: Aask, INITpicker, INIT CDEV, Init-Kit, Startup Manager, INIT Manager.

So now you've got your hard drive utilities, virus protectors, macro software, screen saver, file launcher, file compression utilities, font/DA manager, and customization software installed. Terrific. Now you need one more: a utility to manage those utilities! Enter the INIT/cdev manager.

First, the standard definitions: an *INIT* is a program that, when placed in your System Folder, automatically loads and lurks in the background the next time you turn on the Mac. An INIT (or, in System 7 parlance, an Extension) can be anything that has to be available at all times while you're working: a file launcher utility, a macro utility, a font/DA manager, and so on. A *cdev,* or Control Panel device, is almost exactly the same — the only difference is that a cdev has a corresponding control panel where you can change its settings.

So why do you need a manager for these things? Because, as is often the case with utilities, INITs and cdevs can conflict — they may argue over the same piece of memory real estate, for example, and the result is almost always a system crash. So you need a way to turn your various start-up programs on and off.

One or two INIT managers are commercial — Init Kit, for example, or Startup Manager (one of the Now Utilities). Most are shareware, however, and are excellent. The best of them let you specify sets of INITs — you might have a bare-minimum set for when memory is at a premium, and a full-fledged set for normal use. Of the shareware, something called INIT CDEV is fast, efficient, and lets you request your minimum configuration when you press the Tab key as the Mac is starting up. That's a less bothersome approach than Aask's, for example, which interrupts the boot process to present a list of INITs for you to manually switch on or off. Of the commercial versions, Startup Manager is as good as they come; it lets you create INIT sets,

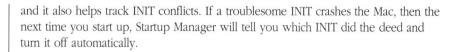

and it also helps track INIT conflicts. If a troublesome INIT crashes the Mac, then the next time you start up, Startup Manager will tell you which INIT did the deed and turn it off automatically.

If you're getting Now Utilities, use Startup Manager. Otherwise, get INIT CDEV from a user group or online service. (Not all of these utilities work with System 7, however.)

Utilities in space

Would you believe all this is only the tip of the iceberg? There are great utilities that affect the way scroll bars work (Scroll Init); put a clock in your menu bar (SuperClock!); hide unused program windows in MultiFinder (TableCloth); password-protect your data (Sentinel); change the cursor shape (Cursors!); keep track of the programs you use (MacInUse); report on the status of your Mac's innards (MacEnvy); give you virtual memory even without System 7 (Virtual) — the list would exhaust a mile-long scroll bar.

If you've tried a few of these gizmos and decide you like them, here are three low-cost, high-quality ideas for you:

❖ *Packaged utilities*. These sets are amazingly good and amazingly inexpensive. The table in Figure 11-8 shows what you get in each of the major packages.

❖ *Online services*. America Online, CompuServe, GEnie, and so on. They're loaded with good shareware stuff; use the download count as an indication of how popular (and, therefore, how useful) they are. All you need is a modem and a telecommunications program (America Online provides its own software).

❖ *Mac user groups*. Most have disk libraries crammed with the same shareware you find on the modem services. User-group software disks usually cost about $5 per disk, and the major ones (BMUG, Boston Computer Society, NYMUG) keep their collections current and well cataloged.

Finally, remember that under System 7 the whole utilities ballgame changes drastically. Many existing utilities don't work with System 7, and dozens of others have been made obsolete by System 7's new features. Have no doubt, however — thousands of *new* utilities will be born to fill in the gaps. Keep your eyes out for them: little programs that make the Mac more efficient, nicer to look at, and more fun to work with.

Utility packages

Norton Utilities	What it's for
Disk Doctor	Hard disk recovery, like SUM
UnErase	Instant trashed-file recovery
Speed Disk	Defragmenter/optimizer
Disk Editor	Hard-disk sector reader: shows the actual raw data
Layout Plus	Finder editor: change font, icon spacing, etc.
Fast Find	Fast DA file-finder, with text viewing and file launching
KeyFinder	Improved version of Key Caps DA
Directory Assistance	Adds Find and View commands to the Open File/Save As box, something like Boomerang
DiskLight	Adds on-screen signal when your hard drive is accessed
911 Utilities	**What it's for**
1st Aid	Disk and file recovery package w/*Troubleshooting Guide*
Virex	Complete virus protection kit
Complete Undelete	Instant trashed-file recovery cdev
Sector Collector	Finds and locks out bad spots on hard disk
MacTools Deluxe	**What it's for**
Mirror	Instant trashed-file recovery cdev
Rescue	Hard disk recovery, like SUM
Locate	DA file and text-in-file finder, with text viewing
Secure	DA to password-protect individual files
Partition	INIT/DA to divide hard disk into multiple "volumes"
Backup	Backup program with selective-file backup
Optimizer	Defragmenter/optimizer
FastCopy	Floppy-disk copier/initializer
FileEdit	Hard-disk sector reader: shows the actual raw data

Figure 11-8: Buying utilities in a package is a good and inexpensive way to try the various types of utilities available.

Utility packages *(continued)*

SUM II	What it's for
Shield	Instant trashed-file recovery
Recover	Hard disk recovery
TuneUp	Defragmenter/optimizer
BackUp	Backup program with selective-file backup
Partition	INIT/DA to divide hard disk into multiple "volumes"
QuickCopy	Floppy-disk copier/initializer
Encrypt	Application to password-protect folders or files
Tools	Hard-disk sector reader: shows the actual raw data
Now Utilities	**What it's for**
Alarm Clock	Menu-bar alarm clock with reminders
Customizer	Finder editor: change font, icon spacing, etc.
DeskPicture	Replaces desktop background with a PICT picture
FinderKeys	Lets you select files in Finder by typing their names
MultiMaster	File launcher, like On Cue
NowMenus	Makes DA menu hierarchical
Print Previewer	Adds Print Preview to every program
Screen Locker	Password-protected screen saver
Startup Manager	INIT/cdev manager
Super Boomerang	Adds Find command to the Open File/Save As boxes, remembers most recently opened files

Figure 11-8: continued.

Summary

✔ Some Mac utilities are definite must-haves. These include: a hard disk utility program, a file-management tool, and a font/DA installer. (System 7 users can do without the last two.) And power users aren't power users if they don't use a macro program.

✔ In Mac software terms, a utility is a program designed to make operating your Mac more efficient or more fun. Some make up for features that seem to be missing from Apple's own System software; others add shortcuts and speed enhancements. In almost every category of utility software, home-grown programs called shareware often offer tremendous features at a fraction of the cost of shrink-wrapped commercial programs.

✔ Utilities that are not vital but are recommended include: an anti-virus program, a file-compression gizmo, a hard-drive defragmenter, and an INIT manager. Most of them cost next to nothing, especially if you go with shareware.

✔ You can add an element of wackiness to the Mac by getting screen-capture programs, screen-saving programs, sound and music programs, and anything else that adds spice to your Mac life.

Where to buy

911 Utilities
Microcom, Inc.
500 River Ridge Dr.
Norwood, MA 02062
617-551-1000
800-822-8224

Adobe Type Manager
Adobe Systems
1585 Charleston Road
P.O. Box 7900
Mountain View, CA 94039-7900
415-961-4400
800-833-6687

After Dark
Berkeley System Design, Inc.
1700 Shattuck Ave.
Berkeley, CA 94709
415-540-5536

Capture
Mainstay
5311-B Derry Ave.
Agoura Hills, CA 91301
818-991-6540

Complete Undelete
Microcom, Inc.
500 River Ridge Dr.
Norwood, MA 02062
617-551-1000
800-822-8224

DiskDoubler
Salient Software, Inc.
124 University Ave., Ste. 300
Palo Alto, CA 94301
415-321-5375

DiskExpress II
ALSoft, Inc.
22557 Aldine Westfield Road, #122
Spring, TX 77373
713-353-4090

DiskTop
CE Software
1801 Industrial Circle
P.O. Box 65580
West Des Moines, IA 50265
515-224-1995
800-523-7638

FlowFazer
Utopia Grokware Ltd.
300 Valley St., #302
Sausalito, CA 94965
415-331-0714
415-331-9361 (FAX)

GOfer
Selectronics & Microlytics, Inc.
#2 Tobey Village Office Park
Pittsford, NY 14534
716-248-9150
800-828-6293

Handoff II
Connectix Corp.
125 Constitution Dr.
Menlo Park, CA 94025
415-324-0727
800-950-5880

ImageGrabber
Sabastian Software
P.O. Box 70278
Bellevue, WA 98007
206-861-0602

MacInUse 3.0
SoftView, Inc.
6330 Nancy Ridge Road, Ste. 103
San Diego, CA 92121-2246
619-453-8722

MacTools Deluxe 1.2
Central Point Software, Inc.
15220 NW Greenbrier Pkwy, #200
Beaverton, OR 97006
503-690-8090
800-888-8199

MasterFinder
Tactic Software
11925 SW 128th St.
Miami, FL 33186
305-378-4110
800-344-4818

MasterJuggler
ALSoft, Inc.
22557 Aldine Westfield Road, #122
Spring, TX 77373
713-353-4090

Norton Utilities
Symantec Corp.
10201 Torre Ave.
Cupertino, CA 95014
408-253-9600
800-441-7234

Now Utilities
Now Software, Inc.
520 SW Harrison St., #435
Portland, OR 97201
503-274-2800
800-237-3611

On Cue
ICOM Simulations, Inc.
648 S. Wheeling Road
Wheeling, IL 60090
708-520-4440
800-877-ICOM

ON Location
ON Technologies
155 Second St.
Cambridge, MA 02141
617-876-0900

Personality
Baseline Publishing, Inc.
1770 Moriah Woods Blvd., Ste. 14
Memphis, TN 38117-7118
901-682-9676
800-926-9677

Protector Shark
Ibis Software
625 Second St., Ste. 308
San Francisco, CA 94107
415-546-1917

Pyro
Fifth Generation Systems, Inc.
10049 N. Reiger Road
Baton Rouge, LA 70809
504-291-7221
800-225-2775

QuicKeys
CE Software
1801 Industrial Circle
P.O. Box 65580
West Des Moines, IA 50265
515-224-1995
800-523-7638

QuickTools/ScreenShot
Advanced Software, Inc.
1095 E. Duane Ave., #103
Sunnyvale, CA 94086
408-733-0745
800-346-5392

Redux
Microseeds Publishing, Inc.
5801 Benjamin Center Dr. Ste. 103
Tampa, FL 33634
813-882-8635

Rival
Microseeds Publishing, Inc.
5801 Benjamin Center Dr.
Ste. 103
Tampa, FL 33634
813-882-8635

SAM
Symantec Corp.
10201 Torre Ave.
Cupertino, CA 95014
408-253-9600
800-441-7234

Sentinel
SuperMac Technology
485 Potrero Ave.
Sunnyvale, CA 94086
408-245-2202

Shortcut
Aladdin Systems, Inc.
165 Westridge Dr.
Watsonville, CA 95076
408-761-6200
408-761-6206 (FAX)

SilverLining
La Cie, Ltd.
19522 SW 90th Ct.
Tualatin, OR 97062
503-691-0771
800-999-0143

StuffIt
Aladdin Systems, Inc.
165 Westridge Dr.
Watsonville, CA 95076
408-761-6200
408-761-6206 (FAX)

Suitcase II
Fifth Generation Systems, Inc.
10049 N. Reiger Road
Baton Rouge, LA 70809
504-291-7221
800-225-2775

SUM
Symantec Corp.
10201 Torre Ave.
Cupertino, CA 95014
408-253-9600
800-441-7234

Tempo II Plus
Affinity Microsystems, Ltd.
1050 Walnut St., Ste. 425
Boulder, CO 80302
303-442-4840
800-367-6771

TypeReunion
Adobe Systems
1585 Charleston Road
P.O. Box 7900
Mountain View, CA 94039-7900
415-961-4400
800-833-6687

Virex
Microcom, Inc.
500 River Ridge Dr.
Norwood, MA 02062
617-551-1000
800-822-8224

Virtual
Connectix Corp.
125 Constitution Dr.
Menlo Park, CA 94025
415-324-0727
800-950-5880

Chapter 12
HyperCard

by Liza Weiman

In this chapter...

- ✔ Discovering what HyperCard is and how you can use it.
- ✔ A look at how HyperCard is organized.
- ✔ Using HyperCard stacks and creating your own.
- ✔ What is new in HyperCard 2.0.
- ✔ Finding the best HyperCard books, stacks, user groups, help sources, and development tools.

In every new Macintosh there's a disk called HyperCard. Although this disk can languish in the pile of reference materials that come in the box from Apple, it needn't. HyperCard was designed specifically to help nonprogrammers take full advantage of the power of the Macintosh. Without much training, you can use it to make the Macintosh do something for you, whether that means organizing information, teaching difficult concepts to others, or solving problems at work.

This chapter will introduce you to HyperCard's basic structure and tools. Once you've seen how powerful HyperCard is, you'll probably want to learn more, so the chapter concludes with a guide for beginning and intermediate HyperCard users to the best HyperCard books; good sources for shareware, public domain, and commercial stackware; the best places to go for help, advice, and really useful development tools.

The way people think — how HyperCard helps

Before you can tell a computer how to do something, you have to break a complex task down into simple, sequential instructions for the computer to follow in a step-by-step fashion. Unfortunately, people don't usually think in such a logical and highly organized way. Instead, we make extensive cross-references between disparate kinds of information — associating a movie we've seen with a conversation we once had, with a meal we once ate, with a date that we're sorry we went on. HyperCard was designed to allow people to organize information this way on a computer. Instead of forcing people to work with computers in a technical and mechanistic way, HyperCard helps people communicate with a computer on more human terms. HyperCard's designers want people to pay attention to what they *want* to accomplish, instead of on *how* to make a computer do their bidding.

The central organizing idea for HyperCard is that your information is located on a stack of individual index cards. Unlike paper index cards, though, Hyper-Card's cards can contain instructions that link them to other cards and analyze the information contained upon them. These cards can also play recorded music, control external devices such as videodisc players and CD-ROM players, display animations, and respond to user input.

Cards are organized into stacks. You can arrange the cards in your stack in any order. And once you've got the cards ordered in a way that makes sense to you, someone using your stack can travel through it in any order that *they'd* like. We are not used to this; most of what we

About the author

Liza Weiman is an Associate Editor for Features at *Macworld* magazine. She has covered HyperCard for *Macworld* for the last three years, coordinated the annual SuperStacks readers HyperCard contest, and produced *Macworld's* SuperStacks Winners Showcase CD-ROM.

read and see today is organized sequentially — to be read or viewed from beginning to end. But when you work with HyperCard you can create stacks that are nonsequential and they can be viewed in many different ways. Stacks can mirror the associative, interactive way that many people think.

At the Wilderness Tourism Council of British Columbia, for example, they needed a way to interest people in the diverse recreational possibilities of their province. Working with Motion Works, a group of HyperCard developers, they created the *Outdoor and Vacation Adventure Guide*, an encyclopedic guide to the wonders of northwestern Canada. If you are only interested, say, in guest ranches and trail riding, this stack makes it simple to immediately read about places to stay and locate them on a map of the territory. To help humanize this computer directory, they created Eddie, an animated tour guide who taps his feet if you take too long, tells you what to do in a goofy voice, and has misadventures throughout the stack to keep you amused (free, Tourism British Columbia).

> **Instead of forcing people to work with computers in a technical and mechanistic way, HyperCard helps people communicate with a computer on more human terms.**

In Baltimore, classrooms of elementary school students collaborated with each other to create a stack that covers eight major ecological problems facing planet Earth, discussing each problem and making concrete suggestions for what each of us can do to try and help solve them. Their drawings, essays, poems, animations, and narration were threaded together into one cohesive stack by two adults, who used HyperCard to unify and knit together the many pieces ($20, available through user groups).

If you've ever taken a music appreciation course, you'll remember that the combination of expert comment and guided listening to a work of music was like being let in on a great secret. Somehow the music became more understandable and more recognizable as you learned about its creation and history. HyperCard enabled music professor Robert Winter to construct an interactive tutorial on Beethoven's *Ninth Symphony*, merging expert commentary with guided listening, historical information, and even a challenging game ($99.95, The Voyager Company).

HyperCard's basic structure: stacks, cards, fields, buttons, and scripts

Creating a stack with HyperCard is like writing a letter with a word processor. Unlike a letter, though, your stack isn't just a record of the words you've typed — it actually contains instructions you've built in that tell it what to do and when to do it.

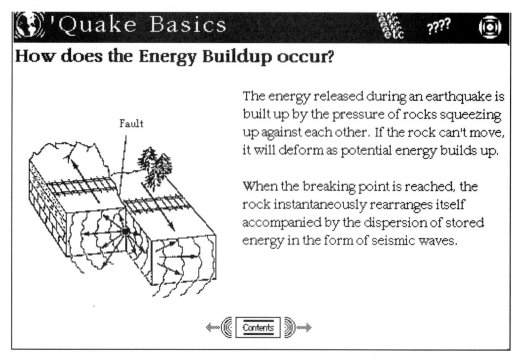

Figure 12-1: This card from Gaia Systems's Earthquake Preparedness Stack, makes extensive use of graphics and text to present complicated information in an interesting way.

If, for instance, you've left an instruction that tells HyperCard to flip to the card marked "glossary" whenever the cursor moves over the spot marked to the glossary, HyperCard will faithfully flip to the glossary card whenever the cursor moves over the correct spot on the card.

To build a stack, you create the individual cards that are contained within it. Cards can be virtually any size that you want, although all the cards in any one stack must be the same size. Figure 12-1 shows a card from the Earthquake Preparedness Stack (Gaia Systems, $35).

The graphics on this card do two things: they make the card look attractive and they convey valuable information about a complicated topic. You can import graphics created in other programs for your cards, but you are limited to bitmapped graphics, the kind that you create with MacPaint. You don't need to use other programs, though, because HyperCard provides MacPaint-like tools so that you can create graphics directly within the program. HyperCard's Tool palette is shown in Figure 12-2.

The Button tool

The
Browse
tool

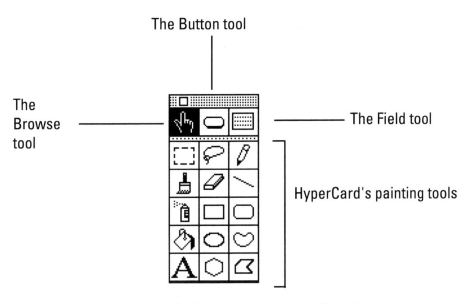

The Field tool

HyperCard's painting tools

Figure 12-2: HyperCard's Tool palette contains all of HyperCard's painting and authoring tools. With it, you can browse through stacks, paint on cards, create text fields, and create interactive buttons.

With these tools you can paint and fill objects using lines, fills, rectangles, ovals, squares, and other shapes. For finer control you've got an eraser, a pencil for free-hand drawing, a paintbrush, and a spray can. Using command keys on the keyboard gives you advanced control over these tools, allowing you to flip objects, invert them (change black pixels to white ones), lighten them, darken them, and even make them opaque or transparent.

You can also place text on your cards. You can use the Text tool in the Paint palette to write directly on your cards, but the minute you're finished that text becomes bitmapped text and you won't be able to change it. A better way to place text on your cards is to use the first of HyperCard's special features, *fields*.

A field is a rectangular area that you designate as a place to put text. Once you place a field on a card with the Field tool, the field acts like a container; you can place text typed from the keyboard inside the field, or you can invite your readers to type text there when they use your stack. You can mix type sizes and styles within a text field and style the text using any font that you've got installed in your system. Figure 12-3 shows HyperCard's Text Options box, which contains all of the text options open to you.

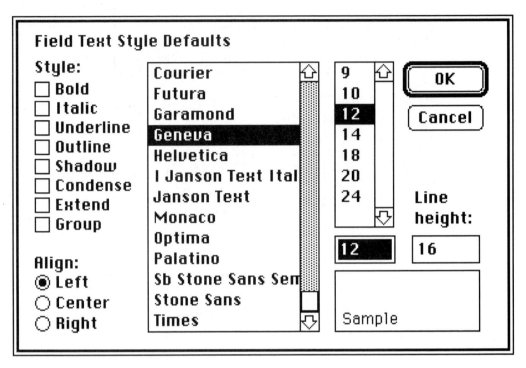

Figure 12-3: HyperCard's Text Options allows you to style text in any font that you've got installed in your system.

The real magic of HyperCard, and what differentiates it from most other Macintosh applications, are *buttons.* They cause something to happen when the user clicks on them. Buttons let you make your cards do things — say, flip to the next card in the stack, show an animation, or play a sound. Buttons make your stacks interactive.

To create a button, you select HyperCard's Button tool and place a new button on your card. Once you've created a new button, you can alter its shape and style, assign it a permanent graphic identity, link it to another card in the stack or to another stack altogether, or give it a more complicated assignment by writing it a script (see Figure 12-4).

The options in this dialog box enable you to create buttons that mimic familiar things in the Macintosh interface like check boxes and radio buttons, or that are transparent and invisible to the user. Invisible buttons can be placed over graphics or text, causing things to happen if the user clicks the mouse button on a particular word or picture.

```
Button Name: New Button
Card button number: 1
Card button ID: 1

☒ Show Name                Style:
☐ Auto Hilite              ○ Transparent
                           ○ Opaque
                           ○ Rectangle
                           ○ Shadow
   ┌─────────────┐         ◉ Round Rect
   │  Icon...    │         ○ Check Box
   └─────────────┘         ○ Radio Button
   ┌─────────────┐
   │  Effect...  │
   └─────────────┘
   ┌─────────────┐    ┌──────────┐  ┌──────────┐
   │  LinkTo...  │    │    OK    │  │  Cancel  │
   └─────────────┘    └──────────┘  └──────────┘
   ┌─────────────┐
   │  Script...  │
   └─────────────┘
```

Figure 12-4: HyperCard's Button Options are the interactive elements that differentiate HyperCard from most other Macintosh applications. With HyperCard's Button Options you can vary the size and style of a button, or assign them specific instructions, called scripts.

If you want to assign a permanent graphic to a button, so that a button that dials the phone always looks like a telephone, for instance, you assign an icon to the button. An icon is a small black-and-white graphic permanently identified with that button, allowing you to easily move buttons between cards or cut and paste buttons between stacks without losing their graphic identities. HyperCard comes with a whole collection of icons, and even provides a tool for capturing other graphics so that you can make your own. A selection of some of the icons that come with HyperCard is shown in Figure 12-5.

The way that HyperCard knows what to do when the user clicks on a button is by reading the instructions associated with them. These instructions are stored in a *script*. Buttons have scripts; what makes HyperCard really powerful is that fields, cards, and even entire stacks can also have scripts. You can leave instructions at every level of a stack, and the instructions can be simple or complex.

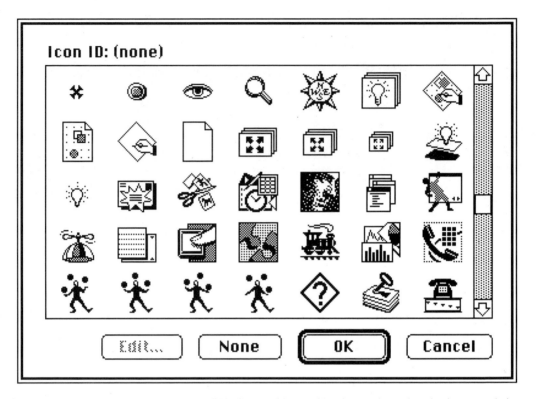

Icon ID: (none)

Figure 12-5: Icons are small black-and-white graphics that can be assigned to buttons to help the user understand what they do.

That's why HyperCard is used for everything from extremely simple educational purposes to communicating with mainframe computers over wide-area networks.

Scripts are made up of a series of simple statements written in HyperTalk, an English-like set of commands and functions. You don't have to be a computer programmer to write simple scripts. HyperCard helps even beginners write scripts that execute correctly by formatting scripts as you write them. If you accidentally misspell a word or put it in the wrong place, HyperCard will try its best to tell you what it can't understand.

Here is a simple script:

```
On mouseUp
   Go next card
End mouseUp
```

This script tells HyperCard that when a user clicks on the button it should flip to the next card in the stack.

Although writing more complex scripts certainly requires an understanding of computer logic, you don't have to write everything yourself. You can also copy cards, fields, and buttons from other people's stacks as long as they've given you permission to do so. And when you copy these parts of other people's stacks, the scripts associated with them will come along too, allowing you to share in the creativity and expertise of the HyperCard community. If you see a button that does something interesting or useful, for instance, you can (usually) copy it into your stack and gain the same functions for your project.

If HyperTalk doesn't offer the commands or functions necessary to solve a problem, it can be extended through the use of external commands (XCMDs) and external functions (XFCNs). These external extensions to HyperCard are really programs written in other programming languages that add capabilities to HyperCard that are not intrinsic to it. The ability to add these external capabilities makes HyperCard an adaptable system for solving diverse problems, even ones that the developers of HyperCard never anticipated. Again, you don't need to write XCMDs and XFCNs yourself; if someone else has already written one that solves your problem, you can (with permission) copy it into your own stacks. Many XCMDs and XFCNs are available in commercial packages, on on-line services, and at user groups (some of the best collections are listed in this chapter's "Resource guide — taking the next step"). If you've got a tough problem, someone else may have already solved it.

How do you use HyperCard?

The key to understanding how a stack works is to imagine using one. Unlike a book or magazine, there is no right order in most HyperCard stacks. Instead, the stack's creators try to offer you a coherent, logical set of cards with an under-standable system of navigation for traveling through the presented information. You can explore the stack in any order that you'd like to by using the Browse tool (the one that looks like a pointing hand on the Tool palette) and clicking on buttons. You might skip some sections entirely, read others in depth, and simply skim others for a few essential facts. Here, we'll explore the Earthquake Pre-paredness Stack again (see Figure 12-6). It is a good example of a highly informative stack with a clear organizational structure and an understandable user interface.

The Earthquake Preparedness Stack has the Contents card seen in Figure 12-6. There are six sections in the stack, similar to chapters in a book. Clicking on any of the buttons arranged down the center of the card will take you directly to the

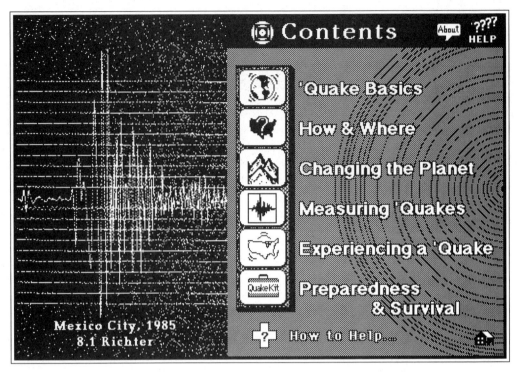

Figure 12-6: Most stacks are organized around a central table of contents that links all of the cards in a stack together in some logical way.

beginning of the section. A series of cards then follows, all offering related information about that specific topic. If you decide that the topic is not the one you are interested in, you can return at any time to the Contents card and begin a new topic.

Most stacks also contain a stack map, a schematic diagram that shows the relationship between cards in a stack and their overall organization (see Figure 12-7).

A stack map helps users understand where they are in a stack and gives them ideas about what they might want to explore next. You know at a glance how long a book is, and where you are in one as you read. But since you can't pick up (or even see) a stack, providing some indication of how things fit together and giving the user clues about how much is left to read is always a good design principle.

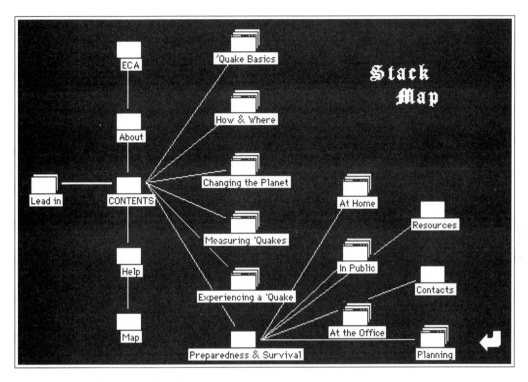

Figure 12-7: All stacks are not organized in exactly the same way, but all stacks have some kind of structure, or relationship, between their component cards. Here is a map showing the relationship between cards in the Earthquake Preparedness Stack.

In a well-designed stack, the cards, texts, graphics, and buttons all work together to provide an interesting and involving document (see Figure 12-8). In the Earthquake Preparedness Stack, the graphics along the left side of the cards illustrate key concepts, the text provides summarized information, and the buttons along the top menu bar and the bottom of the cards enable users to explore the stack in a non-sequential manner.

The words that are highlighted by black rectangles in this card are also buttons, when you click on them arrows appear in the graphic to show you what each word means; clicking on the words "sill plate," for instance, causes arrows to appear in front of the sill plates in the illustration at the upper left. When you click on the highlighted *i* in the upper right (which is also a button), more information about the featured topic will appear on the screen. The title bar along the top of the card

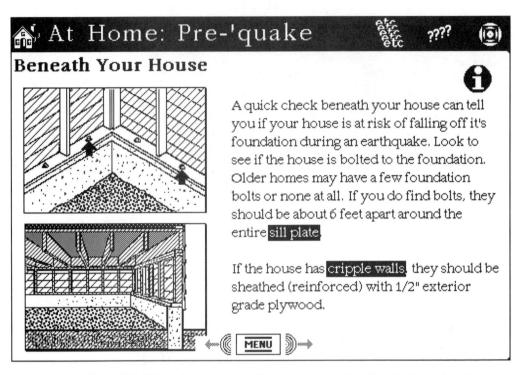

Figure 12-8: This card is an example of integrated navigation where the icons along the top of the menu bar (house, etc, ???, and circle) enable a user to quickly move to different sections of the stack. The arrows along the bottom allow you to move sequentially through the cards in this section.

contains buttons that take you to a glossary for all the vocabulary introduced in the stack (etc.), gives you help information on how to use the stack (?), and takes you back to the central table of contents (the icon in the upper-right corner). All these buttons provide you with the control necessary to explore the stack on your own terms. They let you see the amount of information that interests you and to view that information in the order that makes the most sense for you.

What comes in the box, what doesn't

There are thousands of wonderful stacks available, most at nominal cost. Exploring them is a great next step in learning about HyperCard. You can get them from user groups, on-line services, and stackware distributors (see "Resource guide — taking the next step"). The version of HyperCard that comes free with every Macintosh allows you to use and view all of these stacks. It includes HyperCard 2.0, an address stack, an appointment stack, and an audio help stack, along with a simple manual, *HyperCard Basics*. HyperCard has five user levels, each one providing access to more and more features of the program, and this version (although almost identical to the program available in the more expensive HyperCard packages) has been permanently set to a level that precludes creating stacks of your own.

If you'd like to create your own stacks and write HyperTalk scripts, you need to buy a version of HyperCard from Claris Corp. that allows access to the other user levels. For owners of an earlier version of HyperCard (shipped free with every Mac since 1987) the HyperCard 2.0 upgrade is available for $49. It includes 16 stacks full of examples, ready-made buttons, fields, scripts, and art, as well as on-line help and HyperTalk reference stacks. You'll also get two manuals, *New Features Guide* and the *Script Language Guide*. If you don't already own a version of HyperCard, the HyperCard 2.0 Development Kit, $199, offers all the stacks and manuals available in the upgrade, plus four more manuals: *Getting Started with HyperCard*, *HyperCard Reference Guide*, *HyperTalk: Beginner's Guide to Scripting*, and a *Quick Reference Guide*. The extra manuals will help beginners learn HyperCard and HyperTalk quickly. They are concise and well written, with plenty of hands-on examples and tips.

If you do own a previous version of HyperCard, but aren't sure whether or not to upgrade to version 2.0, several of the new features might entice you. Version 2.0 lets you vary the size of your cards (although all the cards in one stack must be the same size) and have up to 18 windows open at the same time. There are new visual effects and painting tools, improved printing features, an icon editor, and a shared text feature that makes it possible to enter common text on a background field (and prevent the Find command from finding it). In addition, many new HyperTalk features have been added including user-definable menus, improved dialog boxes, and group text (for more powerful hypertext capabilities). An extended XCMD interface allows support for color and gray-scale pictures, custom palettes, and a much improved script editor and debugger.

Resource guide — taking the next step

HyperCard is inexpensive and powerful, and it runs on every Macintosh. Without years of programming practice you can create custom applications, solve real-world problems, or just have a good time. If you are interested in learning more about it and in getting help, examples, and inspiration, a lot of excellent resources are available to you. The HyperCard community is a generous one, full of enthusiastic experts eager to help newcomers get hooked. Here is a highly selective listing of the best resources available to you.

Recommended books

A really good book can be worth its weight in gold. If it is well organized, accurate, and well written a book can save you time and money — even help keep your blood pressure down to a reasonable level.

When browsing the book stores, avoid HyperCard books that do any of the following: teach you how to use HyperCard to make an address book or database (there are already lots of programs out there that are much better for that purpose); don't offer any scripting examples that you can copy for your own use; don't have complete and accurate indexes; or don't make HyperCard sound like it might be fun to use.

Here are some of my favorite books:

Cooking with HyperTalk 2.0

Dan Winkler and Scott Knaster (Bantam Computer Books, 1990, $39.95)
You can't judge a book by its cover, but you can be pretty sure that this isn't just another bland book about HyperCard when you see the two grinning authors, in full chef regalia, on the cover of this book. It aims to provide you with all sorts of useful recipes (scripts) that you can use both for fun and for creating practical applications. The accompanying floppy disk contains all the stacks explained in the book, so you don't even need to do much typing. I recommend it for people who have a basic background in HyperCard and have written a few simple scripts, but want to learn more.

HyperCard 2.0 in a Hurry

George Beekman (Wadsworth, 1990, $20)
Aptly named, this book will get you up and running faster than virtually any other book I've seen. Arranged as a series of six chapters (roughly paralleling the user levels available in HyperCard itself), this book lets you learn about HyperCard by working through realistic problems. Each chapter begins with a clear outline of its main objectives and a brief summary of the real-world problem that you'll learn how to solve, making it easy to find the chapter that best meets your needs. It's generously illustrated with screen shots, patient in its explanations and instructions, and contains a table listing all of HyperCard's tools and their keyboard modifiers. I find this book to be extremely useful for beginners.

HyperCard Stack Design Guidelines
Apple Computer (Addison-Wesley, 1989, $16.95)
Many good stacks don't get used because they present a confusing or non-appealing interface to their users. Attractive graphics and clear navigational structure can make a good stack great, and a great stack terrific. But figuring out how to make your stack seem intuitive to use isn't easy. This book will help.

HyperTalk 2.0: The Book
Dan Winkler and Scot Kamins (Bantam Computer Books, 1990, $29.95)
Written in part by Dan Winkler, who designed and implemented HyperTalk, this book provides valuable insights and useful secrets on how to get the most out of your scripting efforts. For the casual user, *The Beginner's Guide to Scripting*, which comes with the $49 Claris upgrade kit, is a much better introduction, and Chapters 20 to 46 in *The Complete HyperCard 2.0 Handbook* are a good follow up for the intermediate user. But when you are ready to get serious, this book is ready for you.

The Complete HyperCard 2.0 Handbook
3rd Edition, Danny Goodman (Bantam Computer Books, 1990, 29.95)
This encyclopedic work is 928 pages long. If you can't find the answer to your question here, there probably isn't an answer available. In a step-by-step fashion, author Danny Goodman teaches you how to create stacks and scripts. It is full of practical examples and tips. My only complaint is that this book is almost too complete. For casual users and absolute beginners, it can be overwhelming at first. Used as a reference work, though, it is unbeatable.

The Waite Group's Tricks of the HyperTalk Masters
Edited by The Waite Group (Hayden Books, 1989, $24.95)
This collection of scripts will help turn you into a HyperTalk master if you are willing to read each chapter and study the many scripts used to illustrate each point. Although it was written before the release of HyperCard 2.0, there is still a lot of value in this book for people who would like to glean the kind of programming tips it usually takes years to gain.

Stack sources
Most stacks aren't commercial products. With few exceptions you won't see them at your local software store or in the Egghead catalog. Most stacks are available through companies that specialize in distributing stackware exclusively, or through user groups, who often make collections of stacks available for reasonable prices. There are, however, a few commercial publishers of high-quality HyperCard stacks, and virtually everything in their catalogs is innovative and imaginative.

Public domain and shareware stackware distributors

Educorp offers 11,000 public domain and shareware programs for $6.99 per disk. A special 5-disk sampler is available for $9.95 (plus $4 for shipping and handling) that offers fonts, games, utilities, DAs, and clip art.

Maxstax+ is a nationwide, mail-order publisher and developer of HyperCard software. They currently offer 65 different stacks.

Somak Software has over 300 stacks of public domain and shareware programs for $8.99 per disk.

Commercial stack publishers

ABC Interactive, a division of ABC News, has produced an excellent series of HyperCard products that work together with videodisc players to make the ABC archives (as well as original video shot specifically for these products) come alive. The titles in the series, which cover current events, health and science, and the U.S. government, use the power of video to teach and challenge students. The HyperCard stacks make the video interactive, allowing students to explore topics of interest, and then provides in-depth content that supplements the video clips. Students, for instance, can read the "I Have a Dream" speech after they've watched Dr. Martin Luther King Jr. deliver it. (Available through Optical Data Corp.)

Heizer Software offers over 300 stackware titles on diverse subjects, including recipes, education, and business in their Hyper Exchange. Stacks range in price from $6 to $99, and are all author-supported. They also offer The Heizer Select series, a collection of high-end developer tools (including Dialoger Professional, reviewed here).

The Voyager Company publishes excellent HyperCard-based titles, including interactive stories and games. The CD Companion Series uses HyperCard to control an audio CD to create interactive music education; titles include Beethoven's *Symphony No.9* and Stravinsky's *The Rite of Spring*. The Videodisc Companions Series combines HyperCard and videodisc players to create interactive videodisc titles on topics as diverse as the history of computer graphics, a tour through France's Louvre museum, and a study of Eadweard Muybridge's pioneering work in motion photography.

Warner New Media, a division of the Warner entertainment empire, is actively exploring the future of computer-based entertainment. Their titles include the Audio Notes series, which are HyperCard stacks and CD audio recordings that provide interactive music education, and Desert Storm, a stack-based CD-ROM that uses *Time* magazine's text and graphic archives to present the history of the U.S.'s involvement in Operation Desert Storm in the Persian Gulf during the winter of 1991.

User groups

User groups are another good place to start your search for stacks. Here are two of them that come to the national Macworld Expos. To find out about a user group near you, call Apple's user group hotline at 800-538-9696.

BMUG in Berkeley, California has more than 2,000 freeware stacks, organized by topic, available to members for $4 each (plus $3 shipping/handling). Their CD-ROM is full of HyperCard treasures for $100. They also have an on-line forum on America OnLine.

The Boston Computer Society, offers a monthly series of the best available stackware from all the major electronic bulletin boards and its own sources. Twice yearly they also offer compilations of the best of these monthly finds, the StackSet. All disks are $4 for members, $10 for nonmembers.

Finding good help

On-line services

A great source of information for HyperCard users are on-line information services. Here you'll connect up with hundreds of other people who are exploring the same issues that you are. If you can't get your questions answered on the bulletin boards, people can often direct you to other resources that will be able to help. And both of these services have extensive stackware libraries available for you to explore and download public domain and shareware stacks.

CompuServe is a text-based system at heart, which can be disorienting for Macintosh users. But it can be a rich resource for stacks, advice, and HyperCard gossip. $39.95 membership fee (includes 2 free hours of on-line time), $12.50/ hour for 1200 and 2400 baud connection, CompuServe Information service.

America OnLine's HyperCard forum has an extensive software library for downloading, as well as ongoing discussions on beginner's questions, commercial and public domain stacks, books and magazines, programming, XCMDs and XFCNs, and designing good interfaces. America OnLine has a graphical interface, and it makes working on-line similar to using standard Macintosh applications, although it doesn't yet have the kind of heavy user traffic that CompuServe has. $5.95/month includes one free non-prime time hour, $10/ hour prime time, from 6 a.m. to 6 p.m., $5/hour non-prime time, Quantum Computer Services.

Claris Corporation

Claris Corp. produces two free and useful guides: HyperCard Products, which lists shipping stack applications for business, stack development, education, and entertainment; and HyperCard Resources, a guide to user groups, stack sources, and books.

Recommended development tools

HyperCard already provides enough painting, scripting, and visual effects tools to keep most people busy for quite awhile. But there are some things that are fun to add to your stacks right away: color, animation, and sound. And as soon as you've created stacks that sing and dance, you'll probably start wondering how to make your stacks communicate with external devices like CD-ROM and videodisc players, or begin writing more complex scripts to customize HyperCard to your particular needs. Here are my favorite development tools for accomplishing those things.

Adding color, animation, and sound

AddMotion ($295, Motion Works, Inc.)
AddMotion enables you to create and edit color paint images and then animate them from within HyperCard 2.0. Without scripting you can create complex animations with up to 100 actors (animated images). The animations are path-based, and the Media Controller, a floating palette that controls each animation on a frame-by-frame basis, makes animation almost as easy as the flip-books we all created in elementary school.

MacRecorder ($249, Farallon Computing)
If you own a Macintosh LC or SI, you already have a built-in device for recording digital audio. But if you don't, you'll need a MacRecorder to make your stacks talk back. MacRecorder comes with HyperSound for recording within HyperCard, and SoundEdit, a stand-alone application for more extensive editing and special effects. You don't get high-fidelity recording here, but it is more than enough for playback on a Macintosh speaker, and it is lots of fun to use.

MIDIplay ($59.95, Opcode Systems, Inc.)
MIDI files are a compact, industry-standard way of representing music on computer systems. Rather than storing recorded notes, which require huge amounts of storage space, MIDI files describe which notes were played, their duration, and (depending on your equipment) their volume. The only catch to this elegant system is that you must have a MIDI instrument to play back the music. If you do have a MIDI instrument or sound module, however, MIDIplay allows you to play back MIDI files from within HyperCard.

Communicating with external devices

Four toolkits from Apple provide you with the XCMDs, XFCNs, source code, and HyperTalk tools necessary to run HyperCard over AppleTalk networks, control CD-ROM players and videodisc players, and communicate over the Mac's serial port:

HyperCard AppleTalk Toolkit v. 2.5 ($20, APDA)

CD Audio Toolkit 1.0 ($75, APDA)

Serial Communications Toolkit 2.5 ($75, APDA)

Videodisc Toolkit ($40, APDA)

Voyager CD AudioStack and The Voyager VideoStack ($99.95 each, The Voyager Co.) are two toolkits that offer all the tools you need to control CD-ROM or videodisc players from within HyperCard. A clear interface makes it easy to mark sections of audio or video information into named clips and assign the playback of these sections to buttons. The Audio stack comes with 25 ready-made buttons, the VideoStack with 35, and you can copy these buttons into your own stacks, instantly gaining the ability, for instance, to scan, pause, play, and skip sections of CDs or videodiscs. Each also comes with ideas and suggestions that help beginners understand how to make the best use of the available tools. Why reinvent the wheel when you don't have to?

Scripting aids

Bubble Help for HyperCard ($79.95, Randal Jones)
No matter how clear you might think your interface is, sometimes you need extra help to understand how to use a stack. You need bubble help — little pop notes that gently guide users whenever the cursor moves over an object on a card. Without doing any scripting, Bubble Help for HyperCard lets you add in such help.

Dialoger Professional 2.0.3 ($125, distributed by Heizer Software)
Adding custom dialog boxes to your stacks isn't easy, unless you have Dialoger Professional. By using HyperCard's buttons and fields and taking advantage of the extensive tutorial and help stack, you can install the dialogs you need into your stacks with a minimum of effort.

HyperRegister 2.1 ($10 for manual, stack is free, George Pytlik)
If you are looking for an external command or function, look here first. This directory stack has 438 current listings of external resources for HyperCard, including brief summaries of what they do and information on how and where to get them.

Dartmouth XCMD Volumes I-III v. 3.4.3 (free, Dartmouth College)
This collection of 36 XCMDs is an ongoing project at Dartmouth College. It is touted by members of the HyperCard development team as essential to anyone doing HyperTalk scripting, but that is not too surprising since a member of the Dartmouth alumni was the chief architect behind HyperCard version 2.0.

Wild Things ($150, Language Systems Corp.)
Wild Things comes on four disks containing 40 complete and ready-to-paste XCMDs and XFCNs, four animated stacks, and a stand-alone icon editor. You also get a 100-page manual that explains each XCMD in depth.

Summary

- HyperCard is a tool for organizing information. Without years of programming training you can create HyperCard programs, called stacks, that teach concepts, solve problems, or customize your Macintosh.

- HyperCard is organized around the metaphor of individual cards, each of which contain instructions that link them to other cards or analyze the information contained within them. Collections of cards are organized into stacks.

- Each card can contain text, graphics, fields, or buttons. Scripts can be written in simple, English-like language, HyperTalk, that allows HyperCard to react to user input and carry out instructions.

- HyperCard 2.0 adds many new features including variable-size cards, new visual effects and painting tools, improved printing features, an icon editor, and many new HyperTalk capabilities.

- HyperCard books are available that teach good programming technique and contain useful scripts ready for you to use. User groups, on-line services, and commercial stackware distributors are excellent sources of help, inspiration, and ready-made stacks. There are many development tools available that solve particularly thorny problems, provide easy ways to use HyperCard to control external devices, or make scripting easier. Look to all these sources as a way to get a head start on scripting without reinventing the wheel.

Where to buy

Addison-Wesley Publishing Co.
Jacob Way
Reading, MA 01867
617-944-3700

Apple Computer, Inc.
20525 Mariani Ave., MS 33G
Cupertino, CA 95014-6299
800-538-9696 (user group hotline)

Apple Computer, Inc. – APDA
20525 Mariani Ave., MS 33G
Cupertino, CA 95014-6299
408-562-3910 (Int'l.)
800-282-2732 (U.S.)
800-637-0029 (Canada)

Bantam Books
A Division of Bantam Doubleday
Dell Publishing Group, Inc.
666 Fifth Ave.
New York, NY 10103
212-765-6500

The Berkeley Macintosh User Group
1442A Walnut St., Ste. 62
Berkeley, CA 94709
415-849-9114 (taped message)
415-549-BMUG (gen'l info.)

The Boston Computer Society – Mac
48 Grove St.
Somerville, MA 02140
617-625-7080 (Mac office)
617- 252-0600 (BCS main office)

Bubble Help for HyperCard
Randal Jones
22307 65th Ave. West
Mountlake Terrace, WA 98043

Claris Corp.
5201 Patrick Henry Dr., Box 58168
Santa Clara, CA 95052-8168
408-727-8227

CompuServe Information Service
Customer Service Ordering Dept.
Box L-477
Columbus, OH 43260
614-457-8600
800-848-8990

EduCorp
7434 Trade St.
San Diego, CA 92121
619-536-9999
800-843-9497

Farallon Computing
2000 Powell St., Ste. 600
Emeryville, CA 94608
415-596-9100

Gaia Systems
3000 Alpine Road
Menlo Park, CA 94028
415-854-8288

Hayden Books
A Division of MacMillan
Computer Publishing
11711 N. College Ave.
Carmel, IN 46032
800-428-5331

Heizer Software
1941 Oak Park Blvd.
P.O. Box 232019
Pleasant Hill, CA 94523
415-943-7667
800-888-7667
415-943-6882 (FAX)

HyperRegister
George Pytlik
200 West Third St., Ste. 338
Sumas, WA 98295

Kids Can Save the Earth
Available through user groups

Language Systems Corp.
441 Carlisle Dr.
Herndon, VA 22070
703-478-0181

Maxstax+
4009 Everett Ave.
Oakland, CA 94602
415-530-1971

Motion Works Inc.
1334W. 6th Ave., Ste. 300
Vancouver, BC
Canada V6H 1A6
604-732-0289

Opcode Systems Inc.
3641 Haven Dr., Ste. A
Menlo Park, CA 94025-1010
415-369-8131

Optical Data
30 Technology Dr.
Warren, NJ 07059
800-524-2481

Quantum Computer Services
8619 Westwood Center Dr.
Vienna, VA 22182
703-448-8700
800-227-6364

Somak Software
535 Encinitas Blvd., Ste. 113
Encinitas, CA 92024
619-942-2556
800-842-5020

theResult Software, Inc.
1829 East Franklin St., Ste. 1020
Chapel Hill, NC 27514
919-968-4567

Tourism British Columbia
Ministry of Tourism, Parliament Bldg.
Victoria, BC
Canada V8V 1X4
800-663-6000

The Voyager Company
1351 Pacific Coast Hwy.
Santa Monica, CA 90401
213-451-1383
213-394-2156 (FAX)

Wadsworth, Inc.
7625 Empire Dr.
Florence, KY 41042
800-354-9706

Warner New Media
3500 Olive Ave.
Burbank, CA 91505
818-955-9999
818-955-6499 (FAX)

Chapter 13
Backup —
Defending Your Data

by Tom Negrino

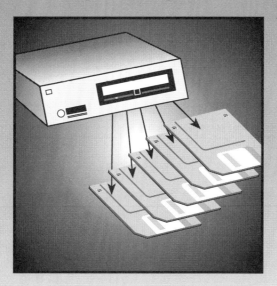

In this chapter...

- ✔ Understanding what backup is and why you should do it.
- ✔ Backing up to disk and removable-cartridge drives.
- ✔ Backing up to tape.
- ✔ Making the right backup buying decision.
- ✔ Picking the backup strategy that's right for you.
- ✔ A summary of tips for optimizing backup.

"Backup? No, I don't back up my hard drive. I know I should, but it takes too much time, and a disk crash isn't going to happen to *me*."

This sentiment seems to be shared by a large class of Mac users. But as soon as a crash or other data disaster happens to you, you'll get the backup religion. Better yet, see the light and start backing up before the disaster strikes.

What is backup, anyway? Quite simply, it's making a copy of all of the information on your hard disk, so that in the event of a problem, your data is safe. The biggest misconception about backup is that it takes too long. If you consider that it could take you weeks to recreate the documents on your hard drive if you were to lose them (and that's if you could recreate them at all), investing a few minutes a day in backing up your data makes a lot of sense. And if you're smart about the way that you back up, you can get your Mac to do most of the work; you can even have it back up while you're asleep.

What could go wrong?

About the author

Tom Negrino is a *Macworld* contributing editor, and a director of the Los Angeles Macintosh Group. He has worked as a Mac teacher and consultant since 1985, and is a cocreator of MacRag, an operations management program for garment manufacturers. Tom has been writing about Macintosh issues since 1987, beginning with the late *MacGuide* magazine. In 1988, he started writing for *Macworld*, and was named a contributing editor in early 1991. He has written the annual *Macworld* roundups of tape backup drives for the past three years. But like most people, it took a disk crash to get him to start backing up his hard drive regularly. Tom lives in Los Angeles with his wife, Betty, a talented singer and actress.

Our computers are pretty reliable. Most of the time you don't have any problems, aside from the occasional bomb, or the "Application has unexpectedly quit" message from MultiFinder. And if you always use a small, constant group of programs, a bomb may be rare indeed. But other things can go wrong, and in the worst way.

First and foremost, your hard drive could crash. The term *crash* is really a catch-all for a number of disk problems. In the general sense, it's any hardware or software problem with a disk that keeps you from using it normally. In the most specific hardware sense, it means that the read/write heads inside the hard drive, which normally skim less than a hair's breadth above the rapidly spinning disk platter, have contacted the platter. This can break the heads, damage the recording media on the platter, or both. Other possible hard drive problems: the hard drive's controller board can malfunction; the drive's spindle motor can fail; or the mechanism that moves the heads over the platter can break. If your hard drive has a hardware fault, the chances of recovering your data are slim.

Hardware failures, though, are less common than crashes caused by software. All hard drives have software, called the directory, that the Mac checks on start-up. The directory contains (among other things) data structures that specify the layout of the disk, which areas of the disk are in use, and where to find individual files. The Mac expects to find this information in a specific format, and if the information has been corrupted, the hard drive will refuse to boot. You'll see the disk icon with the blinking question mark, or you'll get the dreaded "This disk is damaged. Cancel or Initialize?" dialog box. Often, you'll be able to repair the disk or recover your data with a file utility such as the Norton Utilities (for more information on this, see Chapter 11), but some software crashes stump even the best utilities.

Aside from mechanical or software failure, the other culprits of data loss are the physical possibilities: fire, theft, flood, and (especially if you live in California like I do) earthquake. To protect yourself from these events, you'll need to have an offsite backup — a copy of all of your data that is stored off the premises. All these things may be low probability, but they do happen, and you want to have a safe copy of your work as a backup.

Archiving

A cousin of backup is archiving, a technique that backs up files, then usually removes them from the hard disk, freeing space for new files. You might want to archive projects that you have finished, but still keep them available for reference. You can use any of the media that you would use for backup, including floppy disks, removable cartridges, and tape.

The archiving software of choice is Dantz Development's Retrospect. It was originally designed for archiving, rather than backup, and it has superb tools for copying, moving, compression, cataloging, and retrieval of archived files. Retrospect keeps a catalog file of the archive on your hard disk, and updates the catalog whenever you add files to the archive. One interesting feature of Retrospect is that it never removes files from an archive. If you choose to not have Retrospect move files off of your hard drive after archiving, you'll have the current version of the file on the hard disk, yet all of the older versions will be available to you if you need them.

The medium is the message

Before you can start backing up, you have to choose from the possible backup options. The two basic choices for backup media are disks (floppy disks or removable-cartridge drives) and tape (many different varieties).

Removable disks

Floppy disks

The everyday floppy disk is an excellent backup choice, depending on how much data you need to protect. For most home and small-office users who have 40MB and smaller hard drives, floppies are the best choice. If your Mac can use them, the preferred choice is the HD (high density) floppy disks, since they hold more data (1.4MB) than the standard DD (double density, 800K) disks.

Removable cartridges

For a full description of removable-cartridge drives, see Chapter 7, "Hard Disks and Other Storage Devices." From the backup standpoint, any of these drives work well. I especially like the SyQuest and Bernoulli drives for backup, because they're fast and the cartridges are reasonably priced. The combination of a SyQuest or Bernoulli and either DiskFit or Redux backup software (see below) make for the speediest *incremental* backups (where only files that have changed get backed up).

Tape backup

Tape is a good backup solution (and sometimes the only reasonable solution) in a wide variety of circumstances. You can get tape drives in a large array of formats and capacities, one of which is very likely to fit your backup needs. Here's a rundown on the different types of tape units.

DC2000 — old reliable

Among the oldest tape formats, the DC2000 drives use small, rugged data cartridges, about the size of a credit card, containing $1/4$-inch-wide tape. A single DC2000 drive can have two different capacities, depending on whether you use standard- or extended-length tapes. And to confuse the issue further, manufacturers use two different models of DC2000 drives. The older model provides 40MB or (with an extended-length tape) 60MB of backup space, and the newer, faster 3M MCD II model gives you 86MB or 120MB to fill. No matter what size you get, you can count on two things: The drive will be reliable, and it will be slower than most other types of tape drive. As a group, the DC2000 units are the slowest tape backups on the market. In fact, Apple's Tape Backup 40SC has been at the bottom of the speed heap in the last three *Macworld* roundups of tape drives. Fortunately, Apple's drive isn't typical of the DC2000 group. Fifth Generation Systems' Fastback Tape uses the 3M MCD II mechanism, housed in a stylish case, and turns in respectable backup times. The cream of the DC2000 crop, however, is the Tecmar QT-Mac-80. Thanks to Tecmar's excellent backup software, this attractively designed drive is the fastest of all the DC2000 units.

As hard drive capacities increase, the DC2000 format is losing popularity. The 80MB to 120MB capacity of the units make them well suited for personal backup solutions, but the Teac 150MB data cassette drives (see below) hold more data, with faster performance, at a lower cost. Given this, the only reason to buy a DC2000 drive at this point is if you need to be able to exchange tapes with other users who are already using DC2000 units.

DC600

The DC600 format is a larger cousin to the DC2000. It uses data cartridges that are twice the size of DC2000 tapes, up to four times larger in capacity, and much faster. As with DC2000 drives, the capacity depends on whether you're using standard- or extended-length tapes. In the DC600 realm, however, there are three mechanisms from which to choose. The oldest model, now obsolete, held 120MB; the most common model holds 150MB and (with extended-length tape) 250MB; and the latest wrinkle is a 320MB/525MB unit.

Of the 150MB/250MB drives, high marks go to the Micronet MT-250, based on a Tandberg mechanism, and the Tecmar QT-150s, for excellent software, sleek design, and fine performance. The newer 320MB/525MB DC600 drive is a serious contender for high-speed backups of file servers, and for archiving large graphics files. Tecmar, FWB, Micronet, and Tandberg Data offer drives in this size, and their performance is very good. Tecmar and FWB write their own excellent backup software, and Micronet and Tandberg use the highly-regarded Retrospect, from Dantz Development.

Teac

Popular and reliable, the Teac drives are first-rate choices for a personal backup solution. At first, a Teac data cassette may look like a standard audio cassette, but a closer inspection reveals much better construction. Two varieties of the Teac mechanism are currently shipping: a 60MB version, and a faster 150MB version that can read, but not write, the 60MB format. The Teac drives are invariably good performers in *Macworld* Lab's speed tests. The 60MB units are speedier than all but the fastest DC2000 drives, and the 150MB units are faster still.

There are a lot of Teac drives to choose from, and there isn't too much difference between units from the various manufacturers. Price is a good guide here. At $995, Micronet's CPKT-155 drive breaks the $1,000 price barrier in a fast, sleek unit the size of an external floppy drive. Prices for Teac 150 drives from mail-order outlets, such as APS and Third Wave, are now as low as $559, and may be even lower by the time you read this.

The Teac 60MB format is rapidly losing popularity among manufacturers since the cost differential between the two types of drive is low. And the more aggressive manufacturers are passing this advantage on to the consumer, with their 150MB drives costing less than $100 more than their 60MB drives. Even if you don't yet need the extra capacity, it's worth spending the extra dollars to get the Teac 150 drive's superior performance.

Helical

For some systems, even the 525MB DC600 drives don't provide enough backup space. Hard drives with 600MB aren't unusual anymore, and the trends tell us that gigabyte amounts of hard drive storage will soon be commonplace. Fortunately, helical-scan tape drives are up to the challenge. By using technology borrowed from two consumer tape formats — 8mm video and Digital Audio Tape (DAT) — these drives provide immense amounts of storage. They're called helical-scan because they have four read/write heads, mounted on a spinning drum, that create diagonal tracks of data on the tape. The 8mm drives pack as much as 5 gigabytes (5 billion bytes) of data on the same kind of 8mm videocassette you'd use to tape the kids at Disneyland. Can't get a feel for a gigabyte? Well, 5 gigabytes is the equivalent of more than one hundred 40MB hard drives, or almost 6,000 floppies. DAT cassettes fit in the palm of your hand, yet can still hold up to 2.6 gigabytes of data.

> **❝ Hard drives with 600MB aren't unusual anymore, and the trends tell us that gigabyte amounts of hard drive storage will soon be commonplace. ❞**

All the 8mm drive mechanisms are made by one original equipment manufacturer (OEM), Exabyte. So the choice here is price and which manufacturer's software makes the mechanism perform best. PCPC's Netstream software has rated high in our speed tests, and also allows you to back up all of the hard drives on a network. Other notable 8mm units come from Tecmar and Optima. 8mm drives tend to be more expensive and slower than the DAT units. On the other hand, they have double the capacity of current DAT devices, and 8mm backup mechanisms are in regular use on other hardware platforms, such as Sun workstations and Digital Equipment Corporation's VAX minicomputers. There are conversion utilities that enable you to transfer Sun and VAX data to the Macintosh via 8mm backup tapes.

DAT drives have taken the backup world by storm, and there's a bewildering array to choose from. Most are based on one of a few basic OEM mechanisms, though. The Wangtek DAT mechanism has a data capacity of 1.3 gigabytes. The WangDAT 1300 drive also holds 1.3 gigabytes, while the WangDAT 2600 mechanism uses special hardware to compress data as it is backed up, allowing the unit to fit 2.6 gigabytes of data on the same size DAT cassette. Archive Corporation's Python mechanism, also called ARDAT, holds 1.3 gigabytes in the base configuration. Close to shipping as I write this are versions of the ARDAT unit that will use hardware data compression to fit as much as 5 gigabytes of data onto a DAT tape.

Performance among all of these mechanisms is very similar — these units are the fastest of all tape drives. The WangDAT 2600 mechanism wins the speed competition by a nose, but the others are close behind. The vast majority of manufacturers are bundling Retrospect backup software with their DAT drives, and several manufacturers, including APS, Micronet, and FWB, are offering units from both ARDAT and WangDAT.

> 66 *Choosing the right backup solution for your particular situation is important. Pick the wrong one, and chances are your data won't be adequately protected when the data disaster strikes.* 99

Since there are a limited number of mechanisms, and they are so similar, you should base your DAT buying decision first on capacity (do you need the 2.6 gigabytes capacity of a WangDAT 2600 unit?), and next on price. Naturally, you'll want to take warranty and service issues into consideration, too. You'll find that the ARDAT units are the lowest in price (APS and Relax are selling their ARDAT units via mail order for $1,499 as I write this).

Strategic defense

Choosing the right backup solution for your particular situation is important. Pick the wrong one, and chances are your data won't be adequately protected when the data disaster strikes. The driving factor in the choice of backup method is simple: How much data do you need to back up? Once you determine this, you should choose the combination of backup device and software that will cover your backup needs with the least effort on your part. Here's my breakdown, by backup size, of the best and most economical backup solutions.

Size of data to back up: 40MB and under

Preferred backup medium: Floppy disks

Products to use: DiskFit, Redux, Fastback II, Backmatic

If you've only got one hard drive to back up, and it holds no more than 40 megabytes, then backup onto floppy disks is the best solution. You can fit the entire contents of a 40MB hard disk onto 29 high-density disks, or about 50 800K floppies. That sounds like a lot of floppies, but when you consider that 50 floppies only cost about $75, it's easy to see that floppies are more economical than any other backup medium. But even though they're cheap, floppies are also the most labor-intensive. You have to be there to swap disks, and shuffling through more than about 40 or 50 disks requires great patience. The first time you back up the floppies will take you the most amount of time, because the entire contents of your hard disk must be copied. After that, you'll do incremental backups. When the data you need to back up is larger than about 40MB, it's time to look for another backup solution.

My first pick for a backup program for floppy disks is DiskFit from SuperMac Technology. It's remarkably easy to use. Start the program, hit the Return key, push in the first floppy, and press Return again. DiskFit scans your hard disk to see which files have been deleted, which are new, and which files have changed, then asks for only those disks that need changing in order to update the set. Files that have been erased from your hard disk get erased from the floppies; DiskFit then reuses the freed space. Incremental backups with DiskFit usually take less than ten minutes; your mileage may vary, depending on how much data changes on your hard disk.

Another good backup program is Redux, by Microseeds. For the novice user it is just as easy to use as DiskFit. The advantage of Redux over DiskFit is that it gives the power user more options for backup and restore (see Figure 13-1). Redux has a simple yet powerful scripting language (called, delightfully enough, BackTalk) that lets you select individual files or folders, or can select files by name, type, or date modified.

Fifth Generations System's Fastback II is a fine program that also works with several models of tape drive. Magic Software's Backmatic automatically prompts you to back up your hard disk when you shut down your Mac.

Size of data to back up:	40MB – 160MB
Preferred backup medium:	Removable cartridge drives, tape backup (Teac 150)
Products to use:	Retrospect, DiskFit, Redux

Removable-cartridge drives, especially the SyQuest units, are a great choice for backing up this amount of data. If you have an 80MB hard drive, you can use one 88MB SyQuest cartridge (or two 45MB cartridges) to back up, and incremental backups usually take less than five minutes. The other cartridge drives, by Bernoulli or Ricoh, work just as well, albeit more expensively. If you'll be using one of these three kinds of drives, I recommend that you use DiskFit or Redux as your backup software.

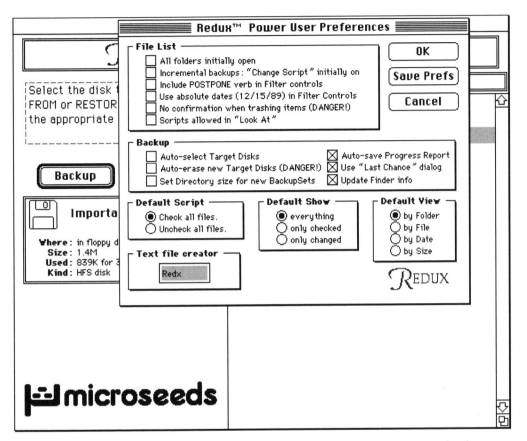

Figure 13-1: Redux gives the power user more options for backing up and restoring data.

In tape drives, this capacity is where the Teac 150MB mechanism shines. It's fast, the cassettes are inexpensive, and you can get a good drive for under $600. A Teac unit is the recommended solution for automatic, unattended backup (using Retrospect) in this size range.

Size of data to back up: 160MB – 300MB

Preferred backup medium: Tape backup (Teac 150, DC600, DAT)

Products to use: Retrospect, tape drive vendor's software

This amount of data is somewhat awkward to back up, because it falls within the range of possibilities of several different units. At the low end (160MB), you can use two of the 88MB SyQuest cartridges. But for convenience's sake, you'll probably want to use a tape drive. The Teac 150 is a candidate if you don't mind switching tapes once.

> **One of the most vexing problems for a network administrator is proper backup of all of the drives connected to the LocalTalk or Ethernet network.**

Unfortunately, the need to switch tapes eliminates one of the nicest advantages of using tape, automatic backup. A better choice is one of the 250MB DC600 units. And if you're using a 300MB drive, you'll probably want to consider a lower-priced DAT tape backup, such as an ARDAT-based drive. Prices on DAT drives keep falling, and they are becoming increasingly competitive with the DC600 units.

Most manufacturers are bundling Retrospect with their tape drives, but some, such as Relax and CMS, include other backup software. Performance with these other packages (SoftBackup, Express Tape, Total Recall, and ADMac Backup) is acceptable, but not as fast as Retrospect in *Macworld* Lab's testing.

Size of data to back up: 300MB and more

Preferred backup medium: DAT or 8mm tape backup

Products to use: Retrospect, tape drive vendor's software

Huge amounts of data need the highest-capacity storage solutions, and helical tape drives (DAT and 8mm) are just the ticket. These drives possess the capacity and speed to lick the toughest backup problem.

Your first choice should be a DAT unit. Virtually all the DAT drives on the market will suffice in terms of performance, so check for price, warranty, and availability of good service and technical support. Pick an 8mm drive if you have to back up more than the 2.6 gigabytes that you can fit on a DAT tape, or if you need to exchange data with other Mac 8mm sites, or with Sun or VAX computers.

Size of data to back up: Various, several drives backed up over a network

Preferred backup medium: Tape backup

Products to use: Retrospect Remote, Netstream Backup

One of the most vexing problems for a network administrator is proper backup of all of the drives connected to the LocalTalk or Ethernet network. Until recently, the best solution was to have the users back up their files to the central file server, and then use a tape drive to back up the server's hard drive. This isn't an optimal solution because of security problems (many users aren't willing to upload their private files to a shared disk) and because so many users simply forget to do the backup to the server. Another problem is that large portions of the server's hard drive must be devoted to backup. If you have 20 users, each with a 40MB hard drive, that's 800MB, and most administrators consider server hard drive space too precious to dedicate it to backup.

With the advent of tape drives with gigabyte capacities, network backup has become easy and feasible. First on the scene was PCPC, with a product called Netstream Backup. It works with the helical 8mm and DAT drives that PCPC sells. A newer entry, Retrospect Remote from Dantz, has done very well in the market. Retrospect Remote will work with any of the media that the single-user Retrospect does, which is to say virtually all media, so you can back your network up with any hardware from floppy disks to helical tape drives. And users of Retrospect can upgrade to Retrospect Remote by buying 10-paks of the Remote module.

Get Retrospect Remote and a tape drive with a capacity that can handle the total amount of data stored by all the hard drives on your network. This is usually going to be a helical tape drive like a DAT or 8mm unit, but you can get away with a smaller (and cheaper) drive if you have a relatively small amount of data to back up. But when buying the tape drive, don't forget to plan for expansion. As your network grows (and it almost always does), you'll have more data to back up, and you don't want to be caught without sufficient capacity.

How often should you back up?

It depends on how valuable your information is to you. As a rule of thumb, the more vital or irreplaceable the data is, the more often you should back up. If you're running your accounting system on your Mac, and you're entering data every day, then daily backup is mandatory. More casual users may choose to back up once a week. No matter how often you back up, it's a good idea to keep more than one set of backup media. That way, in the event of a failure of the backup media, you'll have an earlier version on which to fall back. For backup onto floppy disks or removable cartridges, use two complete sets of the media. Tape users can use one tape for each day of the week, with extras as weekly and monthly offsite backups.

> 66 *As a rule of thumb, the more vital or irreplaceable the data is, the more often you should back up.* 99

It's important to integrate backup into your standard work habits. It's much more likely to get done if you set a regular time for backup. Friday afternoons often seem to be a favorite time to back up. But no matter when you choose to back up, put the chore onto your schedule and make sure it gets done.

Backup regimens

For casual users: the once-a-week solution

You may want to protect your data against a crash, yet none of the files you keep would be especially difficult to recreate in the event of their loss. Backup once a week is for you. Pick a day and time every week for backup, and, in the words of a famous shoe manufacturer, Just Do It.

The middle ground: alternating daily backups

If your data changes daily, or if each document you create represents a substantial time investment, you'll want to have two backup sets, alternating between the two. Color coding your disks or tapes will help you keep the two sets straight. For the following example, I'm assuming that floppy disks are the backup medium, but you can follow the same procedure with removable cartridges or with tape.

Sample schedule for daily backup:

Monday: Do an initial full backup, and label your backup set in Red.

Tuesday: Using a new box of disks, do another full backup; label this set in Blue.

Wednesday: Using the Red set, back up the files that changed since Monday.

Thursday: You'll use the Blue set to back up the files that changed since Tuesday.

Friday: You're back to the Red set with another incremental backup.

Alternating between the two sets ensures that you'll always have a set of backup disks that are no more than 24 hours old, and having two sets ensures that if you back up a file that you later realize is corrupted, you'll still have a good version that you can go back to.

Mission critical: data defenders

If you're responsible for backup of vital data, such as manufacturing, personnel, or accounting information, you'll want multiple backups, with extra backups kept offsite.

One backup solution is to keep all your backup media (you can use either tape or removable cartridges; I'm assuming tape) in a fireproof safe. Remove the media from the safe only as needed, and return it promptly to the safe after use. You need seven tapes in your backup set. Five tapes, the daily backups, are labeled Monday through Friday. You back up to the daily tapes at the end of each weekday. The weekly offsite tape comes into the building once a week, backs up all data since the last weekly backup, then goes back offsite the same day, usually to a vault or safe deposit box. The seventh tape is also an offsite backup; it's the monthly backup. Again, it only comes into the building one day per month, backs up, and goes back to the vault until next month.

Sample backup schedule for vital data:

Monday — Wednesday:
>   Back up to daily tape at end of the workday.

Thursday: Bring weekly tape into the building. Back up daily tape. Do second backup to weekly tape. Leave with weekly tape; store at offsite location.

Friday: Back up to daily tape at end of the workday.

On the 1st or 15th of the month, add the monthly backup to the schedule.

By the way, I've chosen Thursday as the day to do the second (weekly) backup because it seems that people just don't want to do two backups on a Friday afternoon. It's one of those strange but true computer facts.

Data redundancy

Two backup techniques borrowed from the minicomputer and mainframe worlds are entering the Mac market. They promise to complement tape backup by providing continuous data protection (see Figure 13-2).

Disk mirroring is a technique, implemented in the hard disk driver software, that stores duplicate data on two hard drives connected to the same SCSI port. Usually the system will write the data to both drives, but will only read from one. If one of the drives fails, the user is notified and all operations switch to the good drive. Because each block of data is written twice in succession, write speed is cut in half, but the read time isn't affected. In fact, some manufacturers are designing their hard disk drivers so that the read time is improved on a mirrored system because the system reads from the drive whose heads are physically closer to the data. Mirroring systems are being sold by Storage Dimensions and Golden Triangle.

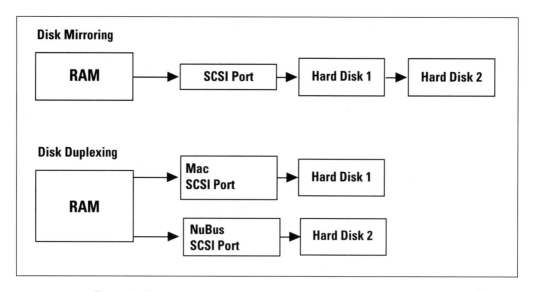

Figure 13-2: There are two backup techniques that provide continuous data protection: disk mirroring and disk duplexing. In disk mirroring (top) duplicate data is stored on two hard drives connected to the same SCSI port; disk duplexing (bottom) also uses two hard drives to store data, but each drive is connected to its own SCSI port.

Disk Duplexing also uses two hard drives, but instead of hooking both disks to the Mac's SCSI port, the technique adds a NuBus board that provides a second SCSI port to which the second hard disk is attached. Data is written to both drives simultaneously through the two SCSI ports. Write speeds on duplexed systems are not degraded, as they are with mirroring. Data is read from both hard disks and compared for error, ensuring the integrity of the data. On some systems, such as DiskTwin from Golden Triangle, when one disk fails it is automatically dropped off line, the user notified, and all operations are sent to the second disk, with no downtime. Duplexing systems are being offered by Golden Triangle, FWB, and Micronet.

There are trade-offs with the two approaches. Duplexing is faster than mirroring but costs more because it requires a NuBus board. Mirroring is software-based, so it is easier to update and improve in the future. The difference between these two schemes and other backup methods is transparency; as it is created, your data is being continuously duplicated. And because you have two identical disks, your downtime is minimized if one disk crashes. Just unplug the failed disk and continue operations with the remaining drive until the bad drive is

> **Being able to restore from a backup tape that was kept offsite could mean the difference between a temporary setback and a major calamity.**

repaired. However, a duplexed or mirrored system still needs to be backed up, usually to tape. Damage from viruses, corrupted disk directories, or even accidentally trashed files will be duplicated on both hard disks. And fire or other disaster could physically destroy both disks with your precious data. Being able to restore from a backup tape that was kept offsite could mean the difference between a temporary setback and a major calamity.

A complete data-protection system, which would include a mirrored or duplexed set of hard drives and a tape backup, requires a fairly large financial investment. For now, only users with large networked file servers or other installations where any data loss is unacceptable will be taking advantage of these backup options.

Backup tips

❖ Most backup programs have a Verify function that can be turned on or off. It adds an extra bit of protection by comparing the backup to the original and alerting you if the backup wasn't done correctly. Although verifying usually makes backing up take a bit longer, I strongly recommend that you use this function. To me, it's worth the extra time if I can be sure that I've got a good backup.

❖ If your backup program lets you set up an automated script for unattended backup, use it. My Mac, using Retrospect, backs up my two hard drives (about 100MB of data, as I write this) to my Teac 155MB tape drive at 3:30 a.m., three times a week. I'm asleep while the backup is happening. In the morning, I start up Retrospect and check the backup log, just to make sure that everything went as planned.

❖ Most backup media can wear out with constant use; this is especially true with floppy disks. Consider replacing your backup media once a year. I start a new set of backup tapes every January.

❖ If you can't do automated backups, because you're backing up to media that needs to be inserted, like floppy disks, use a calendar program like CE Software's Alarming Events or JAM Software's Smart Alarms to remind you when to back up. With either of these packages, you can set a recurring daily or weekly pop-up reminder.

❖ Don't forget to have a copy, on floppy disks, of your backup program close at hand. It won't do you any good to have an up-to-date backup if the only copy of the backup program is sitting on your crashed hard disk.

❖ If you think that your hard disk has gone south, *don't panic.* Sit down and calmly work out what you're going to do next. I once had a client who had a database file with all of his order entry data become partially corrupted. He had two good backups on two SyQuest cartridges; he could have restored the database file from the previous day's backup and been fine, losing only today's work. Instead he freaked out and, thinking he was protecting his remaining good data, backed up his hard disk twice onto the two SyQuest cartridges, overwriting the good backup files with the corrupted file. It took him weeks to rebuild his data from hard copies, and all that effort could have been avoided had he just taken a deep breath, sat down, and planned his next move.

Safe and sound

If you're a new Macintosh user, start out right by developing and using a backup strategy now. A little preparation can save you from a major problem down the line. And for those of you who've been flying blind, it's almost never too late to start backing up. The exception, of course, is when you decide you need to start backing up right after a data disaster. Keeping a regularly updated backup will turn a data loss from a calamity to a minor bump on the road.

Summary

✔ Archiving, disk duplexing, and disk mirroring are important adjuncts to backup. Archiving is the technique of backing up and removing files on a hard disk, freeing up space for other files; disk duplexing provides added security by using two hard drives to read data simultaneously which are connected to two SCSI ports; and disk mirroring, which also provides added security, uses two hard drives connected to the same SCSI port.

✔ Sooner or later, you're going to need a backup. It's better to plan a backup strategy now than to wait for disaster to strike.

✔ Backup isn't difficult; it just takes a little planning. One way to ensure backup gets done is to integrate it into your standard work habits.

✔ The driving factor in choosing a backup medium is simple: How much data do you need to protect?

✔ If you experience a problem with your hard disk, calmly work out what you're going to do next — panicking can make a minor problem a major one.

Where to buy

Apple Computer, Inc.
20525 Mariani Ave.
Cupertino, CA 95014
408-996-1010

APS
2900 S. 291 Hwy., Lower H
Independence, MO 64057
816-478-4596 (FAX)
800-233-7550

CE Software
1801 Industrial Circle
West Des Moines, IA 50265
515-224-1995

CMS Enhancements, Inc.
2722 Michelson Dr.
Irvine, CA 92715
714-222-6000

Dantz Development Corp.
1400 Shattuck Ave., Ste. 1
Berkeley, CA 94709
415-849-0293
415-849-1708 (FAX)

Fifth Generation Systems
10049 N. Reiger Road
Baton Rouge, LA 70809
800-765-8209

FWB, Inc.
2040 Polk St., Ste. 215
San Francisco, CA 94109
415-474-8055
415-775-2125 (FAX)

Golden Triangle
4829 Ronson Ct., #206
San Diego, CA 92111
619-279-2100
619-279-1069 (FAX)

JAM Software
P.O. Box 4036
Meriden, CT 06450
203-630-0055

Magic Software
2239 Franklin St.
Bellevue, NE 68005
402-291-0670

Micronet Technology
20 Mason
Irvine, CA 92718
714-837-6033

Microseeds Publishing, Inc.
5801 Benjamin Center Dr., Ste. 103
Tampa, FL 33634
813-882-8635

Optima Technology
17526 Von Karman
Irvine, CA 92714
714-476-0515

P.C.P.C.
4710 Eisenhower Blvd., Bldg. A-4
Tampa, FL 33634
813-884-3092
813-886-0520 (FAX)

Relax Technology
3101 Whipple Road
Union City, CA 94587
415-471-6112
415-471-6267 (FAX)

Storage Dimensions
2145 Hamilton Ave.
San Jose, CA 95125
408-879-0300

SuperMac Technology
485 Potrero Ave.
Sunnyvale, CA 94086
408-245-2202

SyQuest
47071 Bayside Pkwy.
Fremont, CA 94538
415-226-4150

Tandberg Data
2649 Townsgate Road, Ste. 600
Westlake Village, CA 91361
805-495 8384

Tecmar
6225 Cochran Road
Solan, OH 44139-3377
216-349-1009

Third Wave Computing
1826B Kramer Lane
Austin, TX 78758
512-832-8282
512-832-1533 (FAX)

Index

Product	Vendor	Location/Phone

Shopping Notes _____

Product	Vendor	Location/Phone

Product	Vendor	Location/Phone

Shopping Notes _____

Product	Vendor	Location/Phone

Product	Vendor	Location/Phone

Shopping Notes _____

Product	Vendor	Location/Phone

Product	Vendor	Location/Phone

Shopping Notes _____

Product	Vendor	Location/Phone

Product	Vendor	Location/Phone

Shopping Notes _____

Product	Vendor	Location/Phone

Product	Vendor	Location/Phone

Shopping Notes _____

Product	Vendor	Location/Phone

Master Your Macintosh with Macworld Books!

Macworld Guide to System 7

by *Macworld* Quick Tips columnist & bestselling author Lon Poole

This is the only System 7 book you need–filled with scores of undocumented secrets, expert tips & techniques, and advanced features. "Lon knows more about the Mac than any single person outside of the engineering group at Apple."   –Jerry Borrell, Editor-in-Chief, *Macworld*
$24.95, 402 pages, with FREE System 7 Reference Card

Macworld Complete Mac Handbook

by *Macworld* Getting Started columnist & bestselling author Jim Heid

This is the *ultimate* Mac reference! Your complete guide to getting started, mastering, and expanding your Macintosh. "The perfect guide for travelling anywhere in the Mac world."
–David Angell, Columnist, *Computer Currents*
$26.95, 548 pages, with FREE System 7 & 6 Reference Card

Macworld Music & Sound Bible

by music guru Christopher Yavelow

Due in December '91, this unique guide is the only book that covers music, sound, andmultimedia on the Mac. It looks at hundreds of products, and is filled with interviews with music superstars sharing their Mac problems and solutions.
$34.95, 1,024 pages

Call (800) 282-6657 to order now!

Fill this out—and hear about updates to this book and other IDG Books Worldwide products!

Name _____

Company/Title _____

Address _____

City/State/Zip _____

What is the single most important reason you bought this book? _____

Where did you buy this book?
- ❏ Bookstore (Name _____)
- ❏ Electronics/Software Store (Name _____)
- ❏ Advertisement (If magazine, which? _____)
- ❏ Mail Order (Name of catalog/mail order house _____)
- ❏ Other: _____

How did you hear about this book?
- ❏ Book review in: _____
- ❏ Advertisement in: _____
- ❏ Catalog
- ❏ Found in store
- ❏ Other: _____

How many computer books do you purchase a year?
- ❏ 1
- ❏ 2-5
- ❏ 6-10
- ❏ More than 10

How would you rate the overall content of this book?
- ❏ Very good
- ❏ Good
- ❏ Satisfactory
- ❏ Poor
- Why? _____

What chapters did you find most valuable/least valuable? _____

What kind of chapter or topic would you add to future editions of this book? _____

Please give us any additional comments. _____

Thank you for your help!

❏ I liked this book! By checking this box, I give you permission to use my name and quote me in future IDG Books Worldwide promotional materials.

- -

Fold Here

Place
stamp
here

IDG Books Worldwide, Inc.
155 Bovet Road
Suite 610
San Mateo, CA 94402

Attn: Reader Response